Algorithms, Automation, and News

This book examines the growing importance of algorithms and automation—including emerging forms of artificial intelligence—in the gathering, composition, and distribution of news. In it the authors connect a long line of research on journalism and computation with scholarly and professional terrain yet to be explored.

Taken as a whole, these chapters share some of the noble ambitions of the pioneering publications on 'reporting algorithms', such as a desire to see computing help journalists in their watchdog role by holding power to account. However, they also go further, firstly by addressing the fuller range of technologies that computational journalism now consists of: from chatbots and recommender systems to artificial intelligence and atomised journalism. Secondly, they advance the literature by demonstrating the increased variety of uses for these technologies, including engaging underserved audiences, selling subscriptions, and recombining and re-using content. Thirdly, they problematise computational journalism by, for example, pointing out some of the challenges inherent in applying artificial intelligence to investigative journalism and in trying to preserve public service values. Fourthly, they offer suggestions for future research and practice, including by presenting a framework for developing democratic news recommenders and another that may help us think about computational journalism in a more integrated, structured manner.

The chapters in this book were originally published as a special issue of *Digital Journalism*.

Neil Thurman is Professor of Communication in the Department of Media and Communication at LMU Munich, Germany, a Volkswagen Foundation Freigeist Fellow, and an Honorary Senior Research Fellow in the Department of Journalism at City, University of London, UK.

Seth C. Lewis is Professor and Shirley Papé Chair in Emerging Media in the School of Journalism and Communication at the University of Oregon, USA, Visiting Fellow with the Reuters Institute for the Study of Journalism at the University of Oxford, UK, and Chair of the Journalism Studies Division of the International Communication Association.

Jessica Kunert is Senior Research Associate in the Institute for Journalism and Communication Studies at the University of Hamburg, Germany.

Algorithms, Automation, and News

New Directions in the Study of
Computation and Journalism

Edited by
**Neil Thurman, Seth C. Lewis, and
Jessica Kunert**

Routledge
Taylor & Francis Group

LONDON AND NEW YORK

First published 2021
by Routledge
2 Park Square, Milton Park, Abingdon, Oxon OX14 4RN

and by Routledge
52 Vanderbilt Avenue, New York, NY 10017

Routledge is an imprint of the Taylor & Francis Group, an informa business

British Library Cataloguing in Publication Data
A catalogue record for this book is available from the British Library

ISBN: 978-0-367-56752-1 (hbk)
ISBN: 978-0-367-56754-5 (pbk)
ISBN: 978-1-003-09926-0 (ebk)

Typeset in Myriad Pro
by Newgen Publishing UK

Publisher's Note
The publisher accepts responsibility for any inconsistencies that may have arisen during the conversion of this book from journal articles to book chapters, namely the inclusion of journal terminology.

Disclaimer
Every effort has been made to contact copyright holders for their permission to reprint material in this book. The publishers would be grateful to hear from any copyright holder who is not here acknowledged and will undertake to rectify any errors or omissions in future editions of this book.

Contents

Citation Information

The chapters in this book were originally published in *Digital Journalism*, volume 7, issue 8 (2019). When citing this material, please use the original page numbering for each article, as follows:

Chapter 1
Algorithms, Automation, and News
Neil Thurman, Seth C. Lewis and Jessica Kunert
Digital Journalism, volume 7, issue 8 (2019), pp. 980–992

Chapter 2
On the Democratic Role of News Recommenders
Natali Helberger
Digital Journalism, volume 7, issue 8 (2019), pp. 993–1012

Chapter 3
Newsbots That Mediate Journalist and Audience Relationships
Heather Ford and Jonathon Hutchinson
Digital Journalism, volume 7, issue 8 (2019), pp. 1013–1031

Chapter 4
Public Service Chatbots: Automating Conversation with BBC News
Bronwyn Jones and Rhianne Jones
Digital Journalism, volume 7, issue 8 (2019), pp. 1032–1053

Chapter 5
Selling News to Audiences – A Qualitative Inquiry into the Emerging Logics of Algorithmic News Personalization in European Quality News Media
Balázs Bodó
Digital Journalism, volume 7, issue 8 (2019), pp. 1054–1075

Chapter 6
Making Artificial Intelligence Work for Investigative Journalism
Jonathan Stray
Digital Journalism, volume 7, issue 8 (2019), pp. 1076–1097

For any permission-related enquiries please visit:
www.tandfonline.com/page/help/permissions

Notes on Contributors

Balázs Bodó, Institute for Information Law, University of Amsterdam, the Netherlands.

Matt Carlson, Hubbard School of Journalism and Mass Communication, University of Minnesota, Minneapolis, Minnesota, USA.

David Caswell, BBC News Labs, British Broadcasting Corporation, London, UK.

Nicholas Diakopoulos, Department of Communication Studies, Northwestern University, Evanston, IL, USA.

Heather Ford, School of Communication, University of Technology Sydney, Australia.

Andrea L. Guzman, Northern Illinois University, Communication, DeKalb, USA.

Natali Helberger, Institute for Information Law, University of Amsterdam, the Netherlands.

Jonathon Hutchinson, Media and Communication, University of Sydney, Camperdown, NSW, Australia.

Bronwyn Jones, Institute of Design Informatics, University of Edinburgh, United Kingdom of Great Britain and Northern Ireland.

Rhianne Jones, BBC Research and Development, MediaCityUK, Salford, United Kingdom of Great Britain and Northern Ireland.

Jessica Kunert, Institute for Journalism and Communication Studies, University of Hamburg, Germany.

Seth C. Lewis is Professor and Shirley Papé Chair in Emerging Media in the School of Journalism and Communication at the University of Oregon, USA, a 2019–2020 Visiting Fellow with the Reuters Institute for the Study of Journalism at the University of Oxford, UK, and Chair of the Journalism Studies Division of the International Communication Association.

Marko Milosavljević, Faculty of Social Sciences, University of Ljubljana, Slovenia.

Jonathan Stray, Graduate School of Journalism, Columbia University, New York, NY, USA.

Neil Thurman, Department of Media and Communication, LMU Munich, Germany.

Igor Vobič, Faculty of Social Sciences, University of Ljubljana, Slovenia.

Algorithms, Automation, and News

Neil Thurman ⓘD, Seth C. Lewis ⓘD and Jessica Kunert ⓘD

ABSTRACT
This special issue examines the growing importance of algorithms and automation in the gathering, composition, and distribution of news. It connects a long line of research on journalism and computation with scholarly and professional terrain yet to be explored. Taken as a whole, these articles share some of the noble ambitions of the pioneering publications on 'reporting algorithms', such as a desire to see computing help journalists in their watchdog role by holding power to account. However, they also go further, firstly by addressing the fuller range of technologies that computational journalism now consists of: from chatbots and recommender systems, to artificial intelligence and atomised journalism. Secondly, they advance the literature by demonstrating the increased variety of uses for these technologies, including engaging underserved audiences, selling subscriptions, and recombining and re-using content. Thirdly, they problematize computational journalism by, for example, pointing out some of the challenges inherent in applying AI to investigative journalism and in trying to preserve public service values. Fourthly, they offer suggestions for future research and practice, including by presenting a framework for developing democratic news recommenders and another that may help us think about computational journalism in a more integrated, structured manner.

In recent times, algorithms and automation have become pervasive if not always fully understood facets of contemporary life. What we read and watch, how we meet people and develop relationships, and how decisions are made about jobs, loans, and insurance—these and many other features of the everyday are increasingly influenced by mathematical models and the data-driven systems behind them, each with varying degrees of opacity regarding how they operate, in whose interests, and with what implications. Algorithms and associated forms of computational automation can be defined technically or socially (Zamith 2019). Technical definitions, common in computer and information sciences, affirm that an algorithm follows a series of pre-designed steps or rules toward solving a problem (Latzer et al. 2016); social definitions, more common in communication and media studies, emphasize the human–machine dynamics, institutional arrangements, and environmental conditions (among other things) that give shape to algorithms as social, cultural, and material artefacts (e.g., Gillespie 2016; Napoli 2014). Despite their long history, algorithms and automation have never been so front-and-centre as shaping forces in public life (as described well in accounts such as Bucher 2018 and Diakopoulos 2019). Most strikingly, and perhaps controversially across many domains, the ubiquity of computing capabilities and auto- mated technologies has resulted in human decision-making being augmented, and even partially replaced, by software (Broussard 2018). Such augmentation and substitu- tion is already common, and even predominates in some industries, including through forms of "communicative AI," or artificial intelligence applied to contexts of human communication (Guzman and Lewis 2019). This trend is likewise rapidly accelerating in news media, leading one observer to conclude, "Algorithms today influence, to some extent, nearly every aspect of journalism, from the initial stages of news production to the latter stages of news consumption" (Zamith 2019: 1).

What exactly does such influence look like, and how are scholars and practitioners to make sense of it? That question animates this special issue of *Digital Journalism*. We began working on this project more than two years ago under the premise that, although the journalism studies literature had made great strides in assessing the digitization of news in the 2000s and the emergence, in the 2010s, of data, code, and software as key organizing components of contemporary journalism (see, e.g., Anderson, 2013; Ausserhofer et al. 2017; Lewis and Westlund 2015a; Usher 2016; Weber and Kosterich 2018), there was yet an opportunity to more fully capture and conceptualize the particular influence of algorithms and automation in newswork. By the mid-2010s, it had become clear that fully automated and semi-automated forms of gathering, filtering, composing, and sharing news had assumed a greater place in a growing number of newsrooms (Diakopoulos 2019; Dörr 2016), opening the possibility that there were places where shifts in the norms, patterns, and routines of news pro- duction were happening and even that, at a more fundamental level, taken-for- granted ideas about who (or what) does journalism were being challenged (Lewis, Guzman, and Schmidt 2019; Primo and Zago 2015). Some algorithms, for example, were being used to filter enormous quantities of content published on social media platforms, picking out what was potentially newsworthy and alerting journalists to its existence (Thurman et al. 2016; Fletcher et al. 2017). Other algorithms, meanwhile, were being used to produce automated journalism—thousands of stories at scale—by transforming structured data on sports results and financial earnings reports into nar- rative news texts with little or no human intervention (Carlson 2015). Moreover, by that point, automated processes were being used to test new forms of packaging and distributing news content, enabling consumers to request more of what they like and less of what they don't and also making decisions on consumers' behalf based on their behavioural traits, social networks, and personal characteristics (e.g., Thurman et al. 2019). And, in a larger sense, it was becoming apparent that algorithms, as part of a decades-long "quantitative turn" in journalism (Coddington 2015), needed to be understood as assemblages of human and machine—as configurations of social actors and technological actants (Lewis and Westlund 2015b) that require a more thorough- going investigation around issues such as algorithmic accountability (Diakopoulos

2015), the ethics of algorithms (Ananny 2016; Dörr and Hollnbuchner 2017), algorithmically organized information enclaves (Bruns 2019; Haim et al. 2018), and the symbolic value of machine-oriented journalistic work (Lewis and Zamith 2017; see also Bucher 2017).

Altogether, these developments have raised important questions about where algorithms and automation figure in relation to the social roles of journalism as a long-standing facilitator of public knowledge. In that spirit, this special issue represents a selection of papers that were originally presented at the 2018 Algorithms, Automation, and News Conference.[1] The articles in this special issue represent about a third of that conference programme and are introduced in more detail below. We have grouped the articles into four themes: 'Publics and public service', 'Personalization and politics', 'Professionals and practices', and 'Promise and possibilities'.

Publics and Public Service

Although chatbots, a form of conversational user-interface (CUI), are familiar in other contexts, such as customer service, their use as a news distribution medium has been less common. However, this is starting to change, and the development and deployment of chatbots by two public-service news organizations, the BBC and the Australian Broadcasting Corporation (ABC), is the subject of two articles in this special issue. The adoption of chatbots has, in part, been driven by changes in the use of social media platforms, as people have moved away from more public channels, such as Facebook's News Feed, to more private environments, such as WhatsApp and Facebook Messenger. Public service media (PSM), such as the BBC and ABC, often feel obligated to make their content, including news, available on the diverse media platforms that their audiences choose to use. Ford and Hutchinson's (2019) special issue article is a case study of the ABC's "newsbot," and uses ethnographically inspired methods to examine how this chatbot mediates the relationships between the ABC and its audience. They find that some of the public who use the chatbot are broadly positive about it and appreciate the informal, colloquial mode of address and the control the bot gives them about what information they receive, where, and when. Some of the journalists behind the bot are also broadly positive, seeing it as a way to reach underserved audiences. Despite these positive outcomes, Ford and Hutchinson also address the implications and possible consequences that flow from the ABC chatbot's reliance on the private infrastructure of Facebook and Chatfuel, including questions around who gets to own and use the public's data.

Jones and Jones' (2019a) special issue article is also a qualitative study of newsbots at a PSM organization, the BBC. As the authors show, the BBC has launched nearly a dozen newsbots across a mixture of third-party platforms—Twitter, Facebook, and Telegram—as well as on their own website, with some being conversational in nature. The article shows how, as with the ABC, the BBC's experiments with bots have been in part prompted by a desire to reach and engage with underserved audiences, particularly the young. Jones and Jones make the important point that robust empirical evidence about the success of such strategies is still very limited. These two articles will, we hope, both inform and inspire further research in this area. The issues raised by the involvement of third parties in the development and hosting of PSM newsbots, as discussed by Ford and Hutchinson, were also apparent at the BBC, which has begun to develop strategies to ensure public service values are preserved.

Personalization and Politics

As both Ford and Hutchinson's and Jones and Jones' articles make clear, chatbots can make news appear more personal, both in its tone and content. The personalization of news content has a history stretching back decades (Thurman 2019a). It is, however, an ever-evolving phenomenon necessitating ongoing oversight from the research community. The special issue article by Bodó (2019) does just this through a qualitative study of algorithmic news personalization at twelve European "quality" news outlets. Automated news content personalization is often discussed in negative terms because of its supposed promotion of so-called filter bubbles and echo chambers (see Bruns 2019; Nechushtai and Lewis 2019), and is often treated as if it were a single, homogeneous phenomenon. Bodó's article challenges this idea, making a crucial distinction between the personalization done by platforms and that done by publishers. For platforms such as Facebook, Bodó argues, personalization is driven by huge quantities of user data and content and enacted to maximize users' engagement so that their attention can be sold to advertisers, all without much, if any, editorial oversight of the content recommendations made. He argues that, in contrast, the news publishers that are the focus of his study personalize content in a very different way, with different outcomes in mind. They are more hands-on, driven by a desire to sell subscriptions or demonstrate the benefits of public subsidies, which often means using personalization to try to cultivate interest in quality information, including hard news, and to promote journalistic authority and reliability.

The different ways in which news content personalization can be enacted are at the heart of Helberger's (2019) special issue article, "On the Democratic Role of News Recommenders." In it she contributes to ongoing debates about the perils and promise of personalization by developing a conceptual framework based on what she sees as the three main democratic theories used in academic work on the media. Firstly, the *liberal* tradition, in which individuals' autonomy and rights to free expression and privacy are emphasized along with the decentralization of power. Secondly, the *participatory* model, which emphasizes a shared civic culture through the active participation of citizens. Thirdly, the *deliberative* theory of democracy, which shares much with the participatory model but has a greater focus on deliberation, with the media playing an important role as a sphere—open to all—in which many ideas are presented and debated.

Helberger then uses this democratic framework to examine the various roles that news recommenders have played, and may play, within society. She argues that the first wave of recommenders, including those on social media platforms, are broadly liberal in the priority they give to users' interests, although rather illiberal in their market concentration and lack of transparency, and in how they collect and share users' data. News recommenders that promote participatory democracy would, she suggests, put less priority on serving individual users' tastes and more on providing information that reflects the interests of society more broadly and on seeking to encourage citizens' involvement. Deliberative news recommenders are yet another step removed from liberal recommenders, placing the greatest level of importance on exposing users to a diversity of views and information and promoting discourse. With her article, Helberger casts fresh light on debates about news personalization, showing how judgements about its effects are very much dependent on one's democratic values and how, like most technologies, recommender systems are neither inherently good nor bad. Their outcomes for democracy are very much dependent on the values with which they are imbued.

Stray's (2019) article for this special issue also has the democratic role of the media at its heart but takes us to the other end of the news cycle, focusing on investigative news gathering rather than news distribution. He is interested in journalism's watchdog role—how it can reveal wrongdoing and discourage corruption—and the part that technology, and AI in particular, might play in that. While Helberger's article took political theory as its starting point, Stray's is grounded in his understanding of how AI works, his reflections on the nature of the data to which journalists have access, and the legal and commercial context in which news is published. Stray shows how, despite hopes that computational journalism would enhance journalism's watchdog role, the uses of AI in investigative journalism have, thus far, been modest. He suggests the reasons for this include the difficulties involved in acquiring data, the journalistic requirement for accuracy, the costs involved, the limitations of current technology, and the challenges involved in trying to codify news values. His article is a salutary lesson in how hopes that computation could be transformative for the way in which journalism is practiced have bumped up against the messy reality of the world as we find it. Nevertheless, Stray does see some near-term opportunities for AI in investigative journalism, particularly in the extraction of data from document caches and in how databases can be fused to reveal relationships that might otherwise remain hidden—for example, between offshore companies and their beneficial owners.

Professionals and Practices

An emphasis on news professionals and their practices has long been a central element of journalism studies in general and *digital* journalism studies in particular (e.g., see Eldridge et al. 2019; Robinson, Lewis, and Carlson 2019). This special issue is no exception. Following this tradition, Milosavljević and Vobič (2019) offer a comparative study of editors in the United Kingdom and Germany, seeking to understand how the core ideals of professional journalism are being rearticulated (or not) in relation to the "automation novelties" that increasingly are being deployed in legacy news institutions. They examine how automation—which ostensibly threatens to leave humans "out of the loop" as production techniques are progressively automated—is situated in tension with some longstanding ideals of journalism (such as public service, autonomy, and objectivity) while also potentially complementing others (such as timeliness). The editors they interviewed find journalism's professional ideology to be in a state of flux, with attitudes about automation that are neither euphoric nor dystopian, and which appear to tread something of a fine line between the civic-oriented normative aims of the newsroom and the profit-oriented financial aims of a business side that seeks to minimize costly human labour. Indeed, the central contribution of their study is to illustrate the extent to which humans remain "in the loop" in the strategic roll-out of newsroom automation, suggesting that "human journalists are still regarded as the dominant agents in news production and its continuous reinvention." This leads them to argue that the longer-term incorporation of automation hints at "a realistic promise of a 'hybrid state' in which both machine and human fingerprints will appear all over what is now understood as professional journalism—defining both its production and ideologisation."

Focusing particularly on the professional ideal of objectivity, Carlson (2019) in this special issue offers a creative exploration of "mechanical objectivity," or the belief that machine systems are capable of offering representations and outputs "that overcome the limits of human subjectivity." Carlson does this by comparing the history of photography and then photojournalism with the present introduction of news algorithms. In his conceptual essay, he shows how a historically grounded study of objectivity—particularly perceptions about what it constitutes, how it might be attained, and why human judgement matters (or not) in rendering an "objective" picture of reality—can open up a range of interesting questions about what technologies and associated techniques mean for news as a form of knowledge. Carlson adapts the idea of mechanical objectivity from Daston and Galison's (2007) study of photography's emerging role in scientific observation and recording in the nineteenth century—a period when scientists were initially fascinated by the potential of the "automatism of the photographic process," which appeared to promise "images free of human interpretation" (130–131). He then outlines the allure that photojournalism had as a means of mirroring the world through faithful reproduction at a time—the early twentieth century—when objectivity in journalism was coming to the fore, and relates that to the promise of algorithmic objectivity that has been a central claim (and point of contention) in our era. "What mechanical objectivity provides to journalism studies," he argues, "is a perspective for examining how algorithms are made to work as an epistemic actor within news"—one that raises essential questions about biases, judgements, representations, and the role of technologies in these issues.

Promise and Possibilities

The potential that is tantalizingly offered by mechanical forms of objectivity is indicative of a fourth and final dimension of these special issue articles: a hopeful vision of how journalism may develop when the full possibilities associated with algorithms and automation in news are understood. Nicely illustrating this is Caswell's (2019) piece, "Structured Journalism and the Semantic Units of News," which makes the case that computational journalism is a largely unfinished project. "Computational approaches to news have largely developed *ad hoc*, as opportunistic adoption of technical innovations originating in other fields," he writes, "and the academic study of computational journalism has similarly developed *ad hoc*, often as case-by-case responses to specific technologies applied to journalism" (cf. Thurman 2019b). The result, he suggests, is a space of practice and inquiry that is populated by intriguing tools, applications, and case studies, but one without "an integrated framework for understanding computational journalism," leaving the field "ill-equipped to proactively influence the adaption of journalism to a technologically mediated future." Caswell thus offers an analytical framework for organizing the many varieties of computational journalism. He illustrates how journalistic knowledge can be understood as "semantic units" that are smaller than the news article, and which can be expressed partially or in full as structured data. The representation of journalism as structured data—or "structured journalism"—is, he argues, more than a speculative conception and offers a compelling, semantic-unit paradigm for illustrating not merely a strand of computational journalism but indeed *all* of its forms. Such an approach, he suggests, points to a research agenda for computational journalism: e.g., for capturing (and structuring) repeating patterns in news events and storylines; for cataloguing "editorial micro-structures" in news articles; and for understanding the "semantic boundaries of computation" in journalism.

In a related vein, Jones and Jones (2019b)—in their second contribution to this special issue—analyse two of the BBC's recent initiatives in "atomising" the news. Atomization, in this case, refers to a news story being broken into "atoms" (or objects, units, or components) of discrete information, which algorithms and automation can then recombine into adaptable and scalable news products. "The atoms," they write, "live on within, and can continually build, databases of organised and structured information." Drawing on their own experience at the BBC, in combination with interviews and document analysis, Jones and Jones (2019b) illustrate how the BBC framed experimentation with news atomization (as seeking efficiency and personalization). They also identify three key characteristics of atomized approaches—recording, recombining, and re-use—that have implications for the way journalists produce news with machines and structure in mind. Importantly, they find "journalists are 'writing for machines' by converting unstructured information into structured data to enable automated recombination and future re-use of content." Beyond the technical shifts involved, these developments, Jones and Jones argue, call up the need for further research that accounts for, among other things, the "politics of structured or atomised journalism." This is particularly true, we would add, as algorithms, automation, and related dynamics come to play an ever-larger role in questions of power within journalism (cf. Robinson et al. 2019): Who has control, on what terms, in whose interests? There remains much for us to learn about what automatization means for journalism's roles and routines, norms and values, and authority and expertise, as these discursive debates and material struggles are negotiated in the coming years at the intersection of human and machine.

Looking Backward and Forward: Extending Research on Computational Journalism

In total, this special issue represents a significant step forward in digital journalism studies and in the field's approach to algorithms and automation and their implications for news. The issue and its contributions also represent a crucial bridging point, linking a long line of research on journalism and computation with scholarly terrain yet to be explored. This is particularly so as artificial intelligence—and the human–machine communication that it facilitates—becomes a more salient factor in the way people make sense of the world and create meaning, both with each other and in relation to machines (Guzman and Lewis 2019; Lewis et al. 2019).

The application of computing to news is not new. For at least half a century, investigative journalists have made use of computers in data analysis (Anderson and Caswell 2019). Harnessing software to select stories for, and present them to, individual audience members also has a decades-long history, with news publishers deploying recommender systems to personalize news since the 1980s, if not before (Thurman 2019a). After information is analyzed, but before the stories it informs can be distributed, those stories must, of course, be composed. Some of the pioneering publications on "reporting algorithms" (e.g., Hamilton and Turner 2009) underestimated the impact that automation would have on news composition. However, automated journalism—as it has become known—has now been adopted by a range of news organizations (Dörr 2016). So too has the use of computing in large-scale news gathering, with the high volumes of digital data, particularly on social networks, fueling this development (Thurman 2018).

Although some of these practices have been apparent for decades, it was not until 2006 that a term—'computational journalism'—was coined that encompassed them all and started to become widely adopted (Georgia Tech 2013).[2] The early computational journalism literature focused on how computing could help journalists act as watchdogs, monitoring the powerful and holding them to account (see, e.g., Hamilton and Turner 2009; Cohen et al. 2011) by facilitating better exploration and interpretation of data. Over time, the computational journalism literature has started to reflect the full range of uses that journalism is making of computation and has also started to problematize (see, e.g., Anderson 2011) the claims made on its behalf—for example, that it would increase "the public's ability to monitor power" (Cohen et al. 2011). Stray's (2019) article in this special issue is exemplary in this respect, sharing the noble ambitions of some of the early authors in the computational journalism field, but acutely aware of the challenges of applying AI to investigative journalism. Following Stray's lead, future research could better compare the hope and hype that develop around particular technologies with the stark realities that often emerge when such things initially prove underwhelming. Beyond merely critiquing such states of affairs, however, researchers can also take a cue from Stray by actually offering interventions and solutions.

While continuing to focus on news gathering, those researching computational journalism have begun to cast their gaze more widely, including toward the use of automation and algorithms to compose news texts (see, e.g., Graefe et al. 2016; Montal and Reich 2017; Thurman et al. 2017). Initially, the automation of traditional, static news texts was the primary object of study. However, as news chatbots have been developed and deployed, these novel, interactive interfaces have also come under academic scrutiny. Jones and Jones' (2019a) and Ford and Hutchinson's (2019) articles in this special issue are two ground-breaking examples of such work. Additionally, they set the stage for future research on human–machine communication in journalism studies (cf. Lewis et al. 2019), setting up a series of questions that deserve to be explored, such as: To what extent does the use of socialbots and other chat technologies alter the conditions for meaning-making around news, for journalists and audiences alike? What does it mean—socially, culturally, normatively, institutionally, and so forth—to organize news and information to suit automated forms of technology that are intended to mimic human communication and behaviour? And, to the degree that chatbots for news are perceived to have "failed" recently (Benton 2019), what might that suggest about audience interest in and engagement with automated forms of journalism—and with what broader meaning for human–machine forms of communication?

Meanwhile, news personalization goes back further than the automated composition of news texts, as do related discussions within and without the academy—back as far, one could argue, as 1889, when Jules Verne, and his son Michel, published their predictions for a personalized news service, with subscribers able to "give attention to one editor and refuse it to another" (Verne and Verne 1889). The Vernes' fantasy was set in the year 2889. In actual fact, forms of personalized news appeared considerably sooner, as early as 1989 (PR Newswire 1989). Their appearance has provoked a range of responses, often negative in tone. Sunstein (2001, 2007) suggested that cultural fragmentation and extremism could result from citizens being isolated in informational echo chambers, whether by their own choices or those of others. Pariser's (2011) *The Filter Bubble* also predicted dire consequences should pervasive information filtering centralize control over who sees what, thereby limiting the diversity of users' information diet. Recent analyses suggest that such fears are largely overblown (Bruns 2019), though the issue of how diverse the information environments created by algorithms and automation should be—or what sort of gatekeepers people would like machines to be (Nechushtai and Lewis 2019)—remains hotly debated. Helberger's (2019) and Bodó's (2019) articles in this special issue join what is now a considerable body of work on the personalization of news, but theirs are important and distinctive in reminding us that technology's effects are inexorably dependent on how publishers, platforms, and society at large decide to organize and implement such tools.

This recognition of the importance of the political and economic contexts in which computational journalism operates was not always apparent in the field's pioneering publications, which, some authors (see, e.g., Diakopoulos 2017) claim, concentrated on the applications that were being built, and failed to examine journalism's "larger … currents" (Anderson 2013: 1008). Anderson (2013) suggested adopting Schudson's (2005) political, economic, organizational, and cultural approaches to the sociology of news as a remedy. In many respects, scholarship on computational and algorithmic journalism has yet to realize that kind of multi-faceted sociological inquiry, though there have been some efforts to apply a Bourdieuan field perspective that Anderson also prescribed (see, e.g., Wu, Tandoc, and Salmon 2019). There has, it seems, been more of an emphasis on charting the latest trends and technologies at the intersection of computing and journalism than on interrogating the taken-for-granted assumptions underlying the news media industry's ceaseless chasing of "bright, shiny things" (Posetti 2018). However, Milosavljević and Vobič (2019) article in this special issue does help to address this imbalance, paying close attention to how journalists' and editors' attitudes about automation are influenced by the cultural and economic conditions that prevail in UK and German newsrooms.

That Anderson (2013) has placed importance on the study of the sociology of computational journalism has not prevented him from also inviting a closer evaluation of the "actual role played by materiality and technology in the processes of journalism" (p. 1016), a suggestion echoed by Primo and Zago (2015) and also by Lewis and Westlund (2015b), the latter of whom have written about the "distinct role of technology" and the "opportunity for developing a sociotechnical emphasis in journalism studies" (p. 21). The special issue articles by Caswell (2019) and Jones and Jones (2019a)—on 'structured' or 'atomised' journalism—can be seen as part of such a development. Their contributions offer a promising way forward for future research. They illustrate how to bring forward the material features, potentialities, and consequences of such technologies, and how to do so from both a conceptual (Caswell) and an empirical (Jones and Jones) point of view. Moreover, they point to a vast and largely unexplored domain of journalism studies: an entire rethinking of news that shifts away from "the news story" as the fundamental unit toward a more database-driven conception of news according to its semantic units, down to the smallest editorial micro-structures of events, actor names, dates, and so forth—all of it discrete pieces of information that, when captured and classified as structured data, can be reconstituted in a variety of forms and functions.

In conclusion, the study of the *computational* in journalism has matured over several decades, in connection with the digitalization of media and society and the concurrent rise of digital journalism (studies). This special issue both builds upon this research and extends it by examining a particularly prominent development in journalism today—the growing visibility and importance of algorithms and associated forms of automation in how news is organized, produced, and distributed. The articles in this issue offer an essential starting point for future research that will continue to evaluate the automatization of news and what it means for a range of concerns central to the field—from politics and personalization, to professional norms and practices, to the possibilities and pitfalls of remaking news in a way that prioritizes the logic of machines.

Notes

1. The conference took place on 22–23 May 2018 at the Center for Advanced Studies at Ludwig-Maximilians-Universität München, with support from The Volkswagen Foundation as well as additional support from the Shirley Papé Chair in Emerging Media and the School of Journalism and Communication at the University of Oregon. The meeting featured 29 papers from an international ensemble of speakers, presented across eight sessions, with a keynote address from Professor Philip Napoli of Duke University.
2. A search for "computational journalism" on Google Scholar on 24 September 2019 resulted in 1,360 results.

Funding

This work was supported by Volkswagen Foundation (A110823/88171).

ORCID

Neil Thurman ⓘ http://orcid.org/0000-0003-3909-9565
Seth C. Lewis ⓘ http://orcid.org/0000-0001-7498-0599
Jessica Kunert ⓘ http://orcid.org/0000-0001-6370-1558

References

Anderson, Christopher W. 2011. "Notes Towards an Analysis of Computational Journalism." HIIG Discussion Paper Series No. 2012–1. doi:10.2139/ssrn.2009292

Anderson, Christopher W. 2013. "Towards a Sociology of Computational and Algorithmic Journalism." *New Media & Society* 15 (7): 1005–1021.

Anderson, C. W., and David Caswell. 2019. "Computational Journalism." In *The International Encyclopedia of Journalism Studies*, edited by T. Vos & F. Hanusch. Hoboken, NJ: Wiley.

Ananny, Mike. 2016. "Toward an Ethics of Algorithms: Convening, Observation, Probability, and Timeliness." *Science, Technology & Human Values* 41 (1): 93–117.

Ausserhofer, Julian, Robert Gutounig, Michael Oppermann, Sarah Matiasek, and Eva Goldgruber. 2017. "The Datafication of Data Journalism Scholarship: Focal Points, Methods, and Research Propositions for the Investigation of Data-Intensive Newswork." *Journalism*. doi:10.1177/1464884917700667

Benton, J. 2019. R.I.P. Quartz Brief, The Innovative Mobile News App. Maybe "Chatting With the News" Isn't Something Most People Really Want to Do? *NiemanLab*. https://www.niemanlab.org/2019/06/r-i-p-quartz-brief-the-innovative-mobile-news-app-maybe-chatting-with-the-news-isnt-something-most-people-really-want-to-do/.

Bodó, Balázs. 2019. "Selling News to Audiences—A Qualitative Inquiry Into the Emerging Logics of Algorithmic News Personalization in European Quality News Media." *Digital Journalism*: 1–22. doi:10.1080/21670811.2019.1624185

Broussard, Meredith. 2018. *Artificial Unintelligence: How Computers Misunderstand the World*. Cambridge, MA: MIT Press.

Bruns, Axel. 2019. *Are Filter Bubbles Real?* Cambridge, UK: Polity.

Bucher, Taina. 2017. "Machines Don't Have Instincts': Articulating the Computational in Journalism." *New Media & Society* 19 (6): 918–933.

Bucher, Taina. 2018. *If… Then: Algorithmic Power and Politics*. Oxford, UK: Oxford University Press.

Carlson, Matt. 2015. "The Robotic Reporter: Automated Journalism and the Redefinition of Labor, Compositional Forms, and Journalistic Authority." *Digital Journalism* 3 (3): 416–431.

Carlson, Matt. 2019. "News Algorithms, Photojournalism and the Assumption of Mechanical Objectivity in Journalism." *Digital Journalism*: 1–17. doi:10.1080/21670811.2019.1601577

Caswell, David. 2019. "Structured Journalism and the Semantic Units of News." *Digital Journalism*: 1–23. doi:10.1080/21670811.2019.1651665

Coddington, Mark. 2015. "Clarifying Journalism's Quantitative Turn: A Typology for Evaluating Data Journalism." *Digital Journalism* 3 (3): 331–348.

Cohen, Sarah, James T. Hamilton, and Fred Turner. 2011. "Computational Journalism." *Communications of the ACM* 54 (10): 66–71.

Daston, Lorraine, and Peter Galison. 2007. *Objectivity*. New York: Zone Books.

Diakopoulos, Nicholas. 2015. "Algorithmic Accountability: Journalistic Investigation of Computational Power Structures." *Digital Journalism* 3 (3): 398–415.

Diakopoulos, Nicholas. 2017. "Computational Journalism and the Emergence of News Platforms." In *The Routledge Companion to Digital Journalism Studies*, edited by B. Franklin & S. Eldridge II, 176–184. Abingdon: Routledge.

Diakopoulos, Nicholas. 2019. *Automating the News: How Algorithms Are Rewriting the Media*. Cambridge, MA: Harvard University Press.

Dörr, Konstantin N. 2016. "Mapping the Field of Algorithmic Journalism." *Digital Journalism* 4 (6): 700–722.

Dörr, Konstantin N., and Katharina Hollnbuchner. 2017. "Ethical Challenges of Algorithmic Journalism." *Digital Journalism* 5 (4): 404–419.

Eldridge, Scott A., Kristy Hess, Edson C. Tandoc, and Oscar Westlund. 2019. "Navigating the Scholarly Terrain: Introducing the Digital Journalism Studies Compass." *Digital Journalism* 7 (3): 386–403.

Fletcher, Richard, Steve Schifferes, and Neil Thurman. 2017. "Building the 'Truthmeter': Training Algorithms to Help Journalists Assess the Credibility of Social Media Sources." *Convergence: The International Journal of Research Into New Media Technologies*. doi:10.1177/1354856517714955

Ford, Heather, and Jonathon Hutchinson. 2019. "Newsbots That Mediate Journalist and Audience Relationships." *Digital Journalism*: 1–19. doi:10.1080/21670811.2019.1626752

Georgia Tech. 2013. GVU Brown Bag Seminar: Computational Journalism. http://www.gatech.edu/hg/item/182791.

Gillespie, Tarleton. 2016. "Algorithm." In *Digital Keywords: A Vocabulary of Information Society and Culture*, edited by B. Peters, 18–30. Princeton, NJ: Princeton University Press.

Graefe, Andreas, Mario Haim, Bastian Haarmann, and Hans Bernd Brosius. 2016. "Readers' Perception of Computer-Generated News: Credibility, Expertise, and Readability." *Journalism* 19 (5): 595–610.

Guzman, Andrea L., and Seth C. Lewis. 2019. "Artificial Intelligence and Communication: A Human–Machine Communication Research Agenda." *New Media & Society*. doi:10.1177/1461444819858691

Haim, Mario, Andreas Graefe, and Hans-Bernd Brosius. 2018. "Burst of the Filter Bubble? Effects of Personalization on the Diversity of Google News." *Digital Journalism* 6 (3): 330–343.

Hamilton, James T., and Fred Turner. 2009. Accountability Through Algorithm: Developing the Field of Computational Journalism. http://web.stanford.edu/~fturner/Hamilton%20Turner%20Acc%20by%20Alg%20Final.pdf.

Helberger, Natali. 2019. "On the Democratic Role of News Recommenders." *Digital Journalism*: 1–20. doi:10.1080/21670811.2019.1623700

Jones, Bronwyn, and Rhianne Jones. 2019a. "Public Service Chatbots: Automating Conversation With BBC News." *Digital Journalism*: 1–22. doi:10.1080/21670811.2019.1609371

Jones, Rhianne, and Bronwyn Jones. 2019b. "Atomising the News: The (in)Flexibility of Structured Journalism." *Digital Journalism*: 1–23. doi:10.1080/21670811.2019.1609372

Latzer, Michael, Katharina Hollnbuchner, Natascha Just, and Florian Saurwein. 2016. "The Economics of Algorithmic Selection on the Internet." In *Handbook on the Economics of the Internet*, edited by J. M. Bauer & M. Latzer, 395–425. Northampton, MA: Edward Elgar.

Lewis, Seth C., and Oscar Westlund. 2015a. "Big Data and Journalism: Epistemology, Expertise, Economics, and Ethics." *Digital Journalism* 3 (3): 447–466.

Lewis, Seth C., and Oscar Westlund. 2015b. "Actors, Actants, Audiences, and Activities in Cross-Media News Work: A Matrix and a Research Agenda." *Digital Journalism* 3 (1): 19–37.

Lewis, Seth C., and Rodrigo Zamith. 2017. "On the Worlds of Journalism." In *Remaking the News: Essays on the Future of Journalism Scholarship in the Digital Age*, edited by Pablo J. Boczkowski and C. W. Anderson, 111–128. Cambridge, MA: MIT Press.

Lewis, Seth C., Andrea L. Guzman, and Thomas R. Schmidt. 2019. "Automation, Journalism, and Human–Machine Communication: Rethinking Roles and Relationships of Humans and Machines in News." *Digital Journalism* 7 (4): 409–427.

Milosavljević, Marko, and Igor Vobič. 2019. "Human Still in the Loop: Editors Reconsider the Ideals of Professional Journalism Through Automation." *Digital Journalism*: 1–19. doi:10.1080/21670811.2019.1601576

Montal, Tal, and Zvi Reich. 2017. "I, Robot. You, Journalist. Who Is the Author?" *Digital Journalism* 5 (7): 829–849.

Napoli, Philip M. 2014. "Automated Media: An Institutional Theory Perspective on Algorithmic Media Production and Consumption." *Communication Theory* 24 (3): 340–360.

Nechushtai, Efrat, and Seth C. Lewis. 2019. "What Kind of News Gatekeepers Do We Want Machines to Be? Filter Bubbles, Fragmentation, and the Normative Dimensions of Algorithmic Recommendations." *Computers in Human Behavior* 90 : 298–307.

Newswire, P. R. 1989. "USA Today Launches Sports Center Information Service." Retrieved from the Nexis database.

Pariser, Eli. 2011. *The Filter Bubble*. London: Penguin Books.

Posetti, Julie. 2018. *Time to Step Away From the "Bright, Shiny Things"? Towards a Sustainable Model of Journalism Innovation in an Era of Perpetual Change.* Retrieved from Reuters Institute for the Study of Journalism, University of Oxford website: https://reutersinstitute.politics.ox.ac. uk/sites/default/files/2018-11/Posetti_Towards_a_Sustainable_model_of_Journalism_FINAL.pdf.

Primo, Alex, and Gabriela Zago. 2015. "Who and What Do Journalism? An Actor-Network Perspective." *Digital Journalism* 3 (1): 38–52.

Robinson, Sue, Seth C. Lewis, and Matt Carlson. 2019. "Locating the 'Digital' in Digital Journalism Studies: Transformations in Research." *Digital Journalism* 7 (3): 368–377.

Schudson, Michael. 2005. "Four approaches to the sociology of news." In *Mass Media and Society.* 4th ed., edited by J. Curran & M. Gurevitch, 172–197. London: Hodder Arnold.

Stray, Jonathan. 2019. "Making Artificial Intelligence Work for Investigative Journalism." *Digital Journalism*: 1–22. doi:10.1080/21670811.2019.1630289

Sunstein, Cass R. 2001. *Republic.com.* Princeton, NJ: Princeton University Press.

Sunstein, Cass R. 2007. *Republic.com 2.0.* Princeton, NJ: Princeton University Press.

Thurman, Neil, Konstantin Dörr, and Jessica Kunert. 2017. "When Reporters Get Hands-on With Robo-Writing: Professionals Consider Automated Journalism's Capabilities and Consequences." *Digital Journalism* 5 (10): 1240–1259.

Thurman, Neil, Steve Schifferes, Richard Fletcher, Nic Newman, Stephen Hunt, and Aljosha Karim Schapals. 2016. "Giving Computers a Nose for News: Exploring the Limits of Story Detection and Verification." *Digital Journalism* 4 (7): 838–848.

Thurman, Neil, Judith Moeller, Natali Helberger, and Damian Trilling. 2019. "My Friends, Editors, Algorithms, and I: Examining Audience Attitudes to News Selection." *Digital Journalism* 7 (4): 447–469.

Thurman, Neil. 2018. "Social Media, Surveillance, and News Work: On the Apps Promising Journalists a "Crystal Ball." *Digital Journalism* 6 (1): 76–97.

Thurman, Neil. 2019a. "Personalization of News" in *The International Encyclopedia of Journalism Studies*, edited by Tim Vos and Folker Hanusch. Hoboken, NJ: Wiley.

Thurman, Neil. 2019b. "Computational Journalism" in *The Handbook of Journalism Studies.* 2nd ed., Karin Wahl-Jorgensen and Thomas Hanitzsch. New York: Routledge.

Usher, Nikki. 2016. *Interactive Journalism: Hackers, Data, and Code.* Urbana-Champaign, IL: University of Illinois Press.

Verne, J., & Verne, M. (1889). In the Year 2889. *The Forum.* http://www.gutenberg.org/files/19362/19362-h/19362-h.htm.

Weber, Matthew S., and Allie Kosterich. 2018. "Coding the News: The Role of Computer Code in Filtering and Distributing News." *Digital Journalism* 6 (3): 310–329.

Wu, Shangyuan, Edson C. Tandoc, and Charles T. Salmon. 2019. "A Field Analysis of Journalism in the Automation Age: Understanding Journalistic Transformations and Struggles Through Structure and Agency." *Digital Journalism* 7 (4): 428–446.

Zamith, Rodrigo. 2019. "Algorithms and Journalism." In *Oxford Encyclopedia of Journalism Studies*, edited by H. Örnebring, Y.Y. Chan, M. Carlson, S. Craft, M. Karlsson, H. Sjøvaag & H. Wasserman. Oxford: Oxford University Press.

On the Democratic Role of News Recommenders

Natali Helberger

ABSTRACT
Are algorithmic news recommenders a threat to the democratic role of the media? Or are they an opportunity, and, if so, how would news recommenders need to be designed to advance values and goals that we consider essential in a democratic society? These are central questions in the ongoing academic and policy debate about the likely implications of data analytics and machine learning for the democratic role of the media and the shift from traditional mass-media modes of distribution towards more personalised news and platforms Building on democratic theory and the growing body of literature about the digital turn in journalism, this article offers a conceptual framework for assessing the threats and opportunities around the democratic role of news recommenders, and develops a typology of different 'democratic recommenders'.

Introduction

Are AI and algorithms a threat to, or an opportunity for, the democratic role of the media? Although it is clear that algorithmic news recommendations will have an important role in shaping the democratic contribution of the press, it is still subject to debate whether this development is for the better or the worse. There are those who warn about the potentially negative implications for democracy – filter bubbles, sphericules, polarisation, fragmentation and the general demise of the public sphere (Pariser 2011; Sunstein 2001). Others are concerned about the "black box" character of recommenders and the difficulty of holding algorithms accountable for their public value implications (Diakopoulos and Koliska 2017). Yet others emphasise the opportunities that arise for the news media – opportunities to rejuvenate the media, allow more responsiveness to the interests of readers, deploy exciting new business models and find smarter, data-driven ways to engage with their audiences.

In the 2018 Reuters Report, almost three quarters of the editors, CEOs and digital leaders interviewed indicated that they were already experimenting with AI or were planning to do so (or were planning to do more experimenting), and that the particular focus of their initiatives would be, in addition to robo-journalism, algorithmic news recommendations (Newman, 2018, 29). The task of algorithmic news recommenders is to filter the growing abundance of online information. Generally, four types of news recommender algorithms can be distinguished, namely algorithms that make personalised recommendations on the basis of metadata (content based), insights into what other users like to read (collaborative filtering), data on their users (knowledge based), or a combination thereof (Karimi, Jannach, Jugovac, 2018). Another important distinction is that between self-selected recommendations (users determine the selection criteria and feed the system with their own preferences) and preselected recommendations (media determine the selection, based on volunteered or inferred data; Thurman and Schifferes 2012). Depending on the media outlet and the metrics that recommendation algorithms are being optimised for, news recommendations can be used to increase time spent, advertising revenues and user satisfaction, but also to actively guide readers and match individual readers with the news it is apt for them to receive. The focus of this article is on the latter, and it will be argued that the power to actively guide and shape individuals' news exposure also brings with it new responsibilities and new very fundamental questions about the role of news recommenders in accomplishing the media's democratic mission. How diverse or not diverse, and how personally relevant and inclusive should recommendations be? How far should the media go in engaging with the audience, and what is the role of other values, such as participation, transparency, deliberation and privacy? What are the longer term societal implications of personalised information exposure? And more generally, what are the objectives and values that recommendations should be optimised for?

In order to be able to answer these questions, we need more insights into the different values at stake and how personalised recommendations can positively or negatively affect the realisation of these values (Helberger, Karppinen, and D'acunto 2018; Helberger 2011). The objective of this article is therefore to explore how democratic theory can offer a useful frame for assessing the threats posed by news recommenders to the democratic role of the media, and the opportunities they present. In so doing, the article hopes to prepare the ground for a more nuanced discussion of algorithmic recommenders, AI and filter bubbles, and help to explore how news recommenders can contribute to democratic goals and editorial missions.

News Recommenders and Democracy – Hopes and Concerns

The media are a central institution in any democratic society (Balkin 2018) and they have at least two important roles to play. One is to inform citizens, to provide them with the information they need to make meaningful political choices and help to hold their democratically elected representatives accountable. Part of this information function is to critically investigate and report about important societal and political matters, and warn citizens about misconduct and problematic situations that require the attention of voters (the "watchdog function" of the media). The other is to create a diverse public forum where the different ideas and opinions in a democratic society can be articulated, encountered, debated and weighed. As we will see, the relative weight that the different theories of democracy attach to these two roles varies, and in the case of news recommenders the roles can even conflict, which is an important source of concerns about the democratic role of recommenders.

Better Informed Citizens versus Concerns about the Demise of the Public Sphere

Many citizens consider recommenders a good way to get the news and to navigate their way through the growing abundance of information, and in some circumstances they even consider them preferable to journalistically curated choices (Thurman et al. 2018). The ability to filter and customise the information offer enables the media to be more responsive to the concrete information needs of users, and brings journalists one step closer to truly engaging with their audience. In so doing, algorithmic recommendations respond to an old criticism of liberal authors about the media patronising the user (Wentzel 2002) and the lack of media responsiveness, which some have even described as "one of the most difficult problems for media regulation" (Gibbons 1998). Usher (2010) predicts that audience tracking will "turn[…] journalism from elitism of writing for itself and back to writing what people are actually looking for." Hindman goes one step further, arguing it is an obligation for journalists to use audience analytics, for exactly this reason (Hindman 2017). What is more, personalised news recommendations allow the media not only to help users find relevant information, but also to inform them better and more effectively. 'The audience' is not homogenous but consists of a diversity of audiences, each with its own preferences, interests and information needs, as well as different levels of education and ways of processing information. By using AI and algorithms, news recommenders can better accommodate these differences.

The ability to serve individual users better and more effectively is also the source of some of the most prominent concerns about the impact of recommenders on democracy. In an environment in which each user gets the news she needs, will there still be a public forum where diverse ideas and opinions can meet? Not only academics but also regulators warn that there is at least "a risk that recommendations are used in a manner that narrows citizens' exposure to different points of view, by reinforcing their past habits or those of their friends" (OFCOM 2012). Lively debates about the extent to which news recommenders enclose users in filter bubbles (Pariser 2011) and echo chambers (Sunstein 2001) and about a public sphere that gradually dissolves into sphericules (Gitlin 1998) are essentially concerns about the tension between a media environment in which algorithms sort people into information profiles and interest bubbles, and the public forum function of the media. Concerns about a fragmentation of the media landscape with the effect that people no longer encounter counter-attitudinal or unexpected information and therefore become less tolerant, more polarised or even radical existed before the arrival of news recommenders (Helberger, 2006). What distinguishes the filter bubble scenario from more general concerns about the ongoing media fragmentation is the relative lack of user agency, particularly in instances of preselected recommendations, and the opacity of the process. Furthermore, with recommenders, stereotypes and prejudices can be reinforced through perpetual algorithmic feedback loops. As a consequence, the fault lines between the different groups or fragments in society deepen, and in the worst case become impossible to bridge.

Hopes for, and Concerns about, the Future of the Media as a Democratic Institution

At a more structural level, scholars increasingly worry about the implications of AI and algorithms for the sustainable future of the media as an institution. Will the media still be able to independently observe and report what is worth reporting when it is no longer the editor who decides what is newsworthy, having been replaced by algorithms and the quantified interests and preferences of the audience? (Anderson 2011). Ferrer-Conill and Tandoc (2018, 13) are among those who warn that "[a]vailable metrics then become proxies to … journalistic ideals, especially for overworked journalists." An important factor in this context is the degree of internal and external commercial pressure (Coddington 2015) from advertisers (Turow 2005), and from other sources of "commercial optimalisation" such as search engines, social media platforms and web analytics companies (Newman 2018, 31; Belair-Gagnon and Holton 2018, 15; see also Lewis and Usher 2016). The alleged opacity of algorithms (Diakopoulos and Koliska 2017) adds to these concerns, as this opacity can make it more difficult to identify external influences on the media, as well as to hold the media accountable for the way they carry out their democratic task and journalistic mission. Finally, in the digital environment the traditional media find themselves in fierce competition with truly digital natives, such as social media platforms and search engines, some of which have far more data than the traditional media, and far more expertise and experience in the competition for the attention of users (Moore 2016).

At the same time, data and data analytics offer the news media economic and strategic advantages, and could thus very well be a means for them to regain (and hold) both territory and the attention of their readers. Societal concerns about the lack of transparency and diversity and the danger of filter bubbles in the online environment also provide an opportunity for the traditional media to create a profile for themselves distinct from that of social media platforms that optimise for commercial goals that are very different from the goal of promoting better informed citizens and the public sphere. In addition, the ability to optimise for advertising (Newman 2018), paying readers and more efficient internal routines (Zamith 2018, 423) can help newsrooms both to make more sense of the media economy in which they operate and to survive in the "battle for audience attention" (Cherubini and Nielsen 2016, 9).

Concerns about Surveillance, Manipulation and the Erosion of Intellectual Privacy

If the task of the media is to inform citizens and provide a public forum, how much distance between the media and their audiences is actually needed to ensure that the media can fulfill this task? In other words, what is the role of data and privacy, and what are the potential dangers of the media knowing too much about their audience? Because many (though not all) news recommenders will use personal data to optimise their results and better match results with individual users, new concerns about this constant tracking and monitoring accompany the media's quantitative turn. As Richards (2008, 392) explains, a certain measure of intellectual privacy is "critical to the most basic operations of expression, because it gives new ideas the room they need to grow". The constant surveillance can also affect more directly the democratic role of the media, for example where there may be chilling repercussions for users' exercise of their free speech rights, or where digital technology is used to manipulate opinions. Put differently, protecting the privacy of their users can be a way of protecting the very activity we expect media users, as citizens, to engage in, namely critical and diverse thinking.

As this brief overview shows, the debate about the role of news recommenders in a democratic media landscape has been characterised by varied hopes and concerns, assumptions and anecdotal evidence. Some of these hopes and concerns contradict, others seem unconnected. What is missing is a conceptual framework for assessing the threats and opportunities of news recommenders that helps to critically question some of the assumptions made and, more generally, to understand news recommenders in the broader context of the democratic role of the media. This is why the next section takes a step back and, building on theories of democratic media, sets out to develop such a framework.

A Conceptual Framework for Assessing the Democratic Role of News Recommenders

Many excellent scholars have developed theories of democracy and the media – work that has contributed greatly to informing our expectations about the role that the media and informed citizens should play in a democracy (Christians 2009; Strömbäck 2005; Dahlberg 2011; Ferree et al. 2002; Curran 2015). Their work forms the point of departure for the current investigation. Given the central role that the media play in a democratic society, democratic theories form a logical normative framework to concretise the societal role of the media, as well as to evaluate their performance. This article argues that, by extension, the same must be true for news recommenders, to the extent that news recommenders are a tool for the media to fulfill their roles. Since it would be impossible to recount all democratic theories within one article, this article focus on what are arguably the three main and most commonly used theories in academic work on the media (Karppinen 2013b): liberal, participatory and deliberative theories. Carving out the different theoretical approaches behind these theories will allow the development of three different perspectives on the democratic role of recommenders. Although it would undoubtedly be extremely interesting to discuss news recommenders against the background of a far richer and more differentiated approach to democratic theory (such as critical democratic theory, which this article only briefly touches upon), space is limited and the main point that this article wishes to make is that there are multiple ways in which recommenders can contribute to the democratic role of the media, provided they are developed out of a vision of the values that recommenders are used to serve. Different democratic theories foreground different values and expectations for news recommenders.

Liberal Models of Democracy

Within the liberal tradition, further distinctions are made, such as Christians' pluralist model (Christians 2009), which corresponds largely with Strömbäck's (2005) competitive model of democracy, or Curran's (2015) rational choice model. Common to all these perspectives is the idea of a decentralised model of political power, where different groups and ideas compete for influence and ultimately political power in the "market place of ideas" (Napoli 1999; see also the critical analysis by Karppinen 2013a), and do so unhampered by the state or other institutions. Central shared values are individual freedom – including fundamental rights such as the right to privacy and freedom of expression – dispersion of power, personal development and autonomy.

The challenge for liberal democracy is to eventually aggregate all these different views and ideas into political will in a process that Christians (2009, 97) describes as "constant negotiation". Accordingly, elections are a central democratic moment. It is at election time that citizens can express their political will, by voting for the party that best represents their interests. In the liberal model, democratic participation and being a good citizen therefore largely revolve around the act of voting, as opposed to more participatory or deliberative models where citizens' active participation in the public discourse is far more central. As Ferree et al. (2002, 290) put it: "Citizens need policy makers who are ultimately accountable to them but they do not need to participate in public discourse on policy issues. Not only do they not need to, but public life is actually better off if they don't."

With respect to the information needs of citizens, this means that there is little reason why citizens should not read and watch what they like, as long as in the run-up to elections, they are sufficiently informed to cast their votes (Ferree et al. 2002, 291). There is a strong focus on personal autonomy – the freedom to choose the information one is interested in. What does that mean for the information role of the media? If one follows Christians (2009, 100), "[r]ather than trying to inform citizens about issues over which they have no direct and immediate control, journalism serves an administrative democracy by alerting the community to crises ... [and providing] detailed accounts of campaign promises and platforms, especially during the months preceding a contested election" (in a similar vein, Strömbäck 2005, 335). This is Zaller's "burglar alarm" standard, where rather than aspiring to an ideal (and unrealistic) situation in which citizens are broadly informed on all matters relevant to public affairs, the media instead must make them aware of acute problems that merit their immediate attention (Zaller 2003).

Implications for a Liberal Recommender

From the perspective of liberal democratic traditions, recommenders, then, could potentially have quite literally laiberating role, to the extent that they put the interests and information preferences of users centre stage. True, the orientation towards the user, and the possible resulting hyper-responsiveness of the press, might result in a situation in which newsrooms select content based on users' preferences, and not on what the audience 'ought to know'. But how worrisome are these concerns under a more liberal perspective on democracy? From the liberal perspective, it is essentially a prerogative of citizens to decide which information they need so they can make well-informed decisions, and they should be able to do so free from external influences. And if citizens primarily choose to look at cat videos and celebrity news? Under more liberal conceptions of democracy, that could be perfectly fine as long as doing so is a result of the way they exercise their autonomy and freedom of expression. Or to quote Strömbäck (2005,334): "How people choose to spend their time and their mental energy is up to themselves, as long as they do not violate the basic democratic freedoms and rights. To demand that people in general spend their lives keeping up with the news, getting informed, and participating in public life, is to demand too much."

It may be that people have already gathered from other sources the information they need to make informed decisions, for example from non-personalised parts of the website or conversations with friends. It may be that the citizen can actually be trusted to demand the information that she needs to cast an informed vote. It may also be that newsrooms are not the perfect and uncontested arbiters of what citizens "need to know" (Boczkowski 2013). The point is: user-driven content choices do not necessarily have to be undemocratic, and the same is true for news recommenders that provide users with user-driven recommendations. There is arguably some minimal information that the population should receive, for example information about democratic, economic and social crises. This information, however, does not necessarily need to be provided in the form of recommendations; it could be offered as part of the general website, with the recommender being nothing more than an added service. One could also argue that recommendations could differ during and outside election times, and that the balance between what people want to know and what they need to know to take informed election decisions could vary. What is important is that no opinion should intentionally be excluded (Ferree et al. 2002, 293). Whether or not it is prominently presented, or even ranked high enough to be noticed, will depend on its popularity and the size of the audience that wants to hear that view. In other words, there is no obligation to provide equal representation; nor is there a right to an audience (Christians 2009; Napoli 2011, 108). It would be perfectly logical for a recommender to give more prominence to those ideas that have the greatest popularity or dominance within society.

A necessary precondition is, of course, that a recommendation does realise users' autonomy and right to receive information (Eskens, Helberger, and Möller 2017). While it is true that recommenders can potentially make the media more responsive to the information needs of, and demands from, citizens, recommendation technologies can also ignore or misinterpret signals from users (Ekstrand and Willemsen 2016). Much will depend on the quality and the sophistication of the analytics and metrics, and the extent to which they are truly able to uncover people's news needs and interests (Hindman 2017, 189). If algorithms are used to nudge or influence citizens against their will (Calo 2014) or in an attempt to manipulate their political choices, then they pose a danger to liberal democracies. From a liberal perspective, then, perhaps the more important point of attention regarding the potential democratic role of recommenders is their editorial independence from external parties, such as advertisers, political parties or marketing divisions. Another important point of attention under the liberal model would be the extent to which the control over algorithmic recommenders and, perhaps even more importantly, the datasets needed to fuel them, could lead to the creation of new concentrations of market or opinion power, for example in the form of social media platforms. From the perspective of liberal democracy, and its strong focus on the dispersion of power (compare (Karppinen 2013a, 31: dispersion of power as "the basis of liberal democracy"; Edwin Baker 1998), this is a serious threat to democracy. From the perspective of public policy, herein lie two tasks, namely to prevent data-driven concentrations of opinion power and to ensure that recommenders do indeed reflect the free and autonomous choices of citizens, rather than becoming tools for manipulating public opinion and tinkering with citizens' minds.

A more liberal perspective on democracy would also suggest a more organic and more "interest-driven" approach to diversity. So far, diversity has mostly been discussed in terms of what the audience 'needs to know'. With a more liberal recommender, it would be perfectly acceptable to speak of information that the heterogeneous citizenry "wants to know." Therefore, a well-designed, diverse recommender would also incorporate a certain element of flexibility, allowing citizens to customise the recommendations to better reflect their interests and preferences, even if not all users will make use of that opportunity, a decision that would be fine as long as it constituted an expression of their autonomy (Harambam et al. 2018). In fact, preselected choices, particularly when they do not allow citizens to understand why they have received particular recommendations, or do not provide them with the means to influence the settings, are suspicious from a liberal theory point of view. One could even go a step further and argue that a liberal recommender would do more than just inform people. It would also allow people to have a say regarding the proper balance between their right to information and personal development, and other rights, such as the right to privacy. Seeing that algorithmic news recommendations operate through the collection of large amounts of data, offering users a choice between receiving relevant information and reading anonymously, or perhaps using recommenders that personalise on the basis of meta-data rather than on the basis of users' inferred interests, would fit perfectly well in the liberal tradition of putting individual rights and freedoms centre stage. This is not to say that the rights to privacy and data protection are less relevant under the other democratic perspectives, but it is under the liberal perspective that a strong argument can be made that the right to privacy, personal autonomy and freedom of expression can outweigh other interests, such as displaying particular "public interest content" more prominently, or nudging users to consume more diverse or more "valuable" information and engage more with the perspectives of others.

How about concerns over filter bubbles? Interestingly, from a more liberal perspective one could argue that a situation in which users are recommended exactly the information that they request or find interesting could help them to deepen their knowledge and expertise, and thereby enable them to play their role in the democratic process even better and more efficiently. Much depends on the conception of what an 'ideal' citizen is – an information omnivore, an "expert citizen" or an "everyday maker?" (compare Li and Marsh 2008). Particularly interesting here is the role of experts in more liberal models of democracy. As Ferree et al. (2002, 292) explain, the relatively low normative expectations of what it means to be a good citizen are counterbalanced by a prominent role for experts "in defining the issues before they reach the stage at which decisions need to be reached." In other words, under more liberal democratic models recommenders that feed the focused information needs of expert citizens could fulfill an important role in a democratic society. In such a situation, filter bubbles become "expertise bubbles" and have an important role in helping expert citizens to become even more expert. We could possibly also see the development of two, or even more, types of recommenders: "general interest recommenders" – which serve people's diverse information needs and preferences – and more "expert" recommenders, which help to make the experts more expert. Indeed, from the perspective of dispersion of power, pluralism in the future could extend not only to a diversity of media sources and content, but also to a diversity of recommenders for a diversity of user needs.

Participatory Models of Democracy

In contrast to the libertarian focus on autonomy, user agency and dispersion of power, the central focus of more civic (Christians 2009, 101), respectively participatory (Strömbäck 2005) or republican models of democracy is on a shared civic culture and commitment to citizenship (Christians 2009, 102). And unlike in the more liberal model discussed in the previous section, in the more participatory understanding of democracy, the active participation of citizens is key and the central mechanism for political will formation. Only if all citizens are (at least in theory, and ideally in practice) able to actively participate, have their say or even exercise political functions, can we speak of a true participatory democracy. Accordingly, the values that proponents of more participatory models of democracy bring to the fore are very different from those emphasised by proponents of the liberal model: inclusiveness instead of representativeness; equality and tolerance instead of proportionality; and community, active participation and civic virtue instead of self-development, autonomy and ultimate freedom.

In the discussion about the democratic role of recommenders, two ideas are particularly relevant: one is that societal interest trumps individual self-interest, and the other, which is closely related, is that there are high normative expectations of what it means to be a good citizen. Central to advancing welfare is not the sum of individual actions (or preferences), but active collaboration, engagement and subordination to the common good (Etzioni 1996). This ideal of more or less direct self-government cannot be achieved without a certain moral attitude of the citizen or "homo politicus" (Held 2006, 29). This is a citizen who cannot afford to be uninterested in politics and who understands that political participation is "a necessary aspect of the good life" (Held 2006, 35) or at least absolutely necessary to secure one's own liberty and that of the community.

It is clear that with the more active political role of the citizen, the information needs of the citizen change. Instead of having a basic knowledge of political institutions and political alternatives, the active, informed citizen needs to have a far deeper knowledge of not only the political system, but also the different issues on the political agenda – even more so to the extent that she is interested in playing an active part in the making of politics. Accordingly, the media have an important task in satisfying citizens' demands for in-depth information - documentaries about social issues, background information and more general information about the political climate (compare Strömbäck 2005, 339). Arguably, and in stark contrast to the liberal model, the role of the media, and here in particular the public service media, shifts from merely informing to actively educating and coaching the active citizen. Tandoc and Thomas (2015, 244) characterise this position well: "If journalism is to help bring about the common good, it must provide the public with more than just what the public wants."

Here, also, the expectations with regard to diversity are greater; there is a different and potentially more demanding idea of what constitutes a diverse information offer. Diversity is less about presenting alternatives and accommodating the heterogeneous interests of a heterogeneous citizenry. Diversity must represent "all significant interests in society" (Curran 2015), including political parties, political, economic and civil society interest groups, religious groups, professional organisations, and so on. A diverse media offer speaks to the different groups in society and inspires them to take an active part in society. Inclusiveness is critical (Edwin Baker 1998, 334; Balkin 2018), as is visibility. Only when citizens are aware of the different perspectives, interests and concerns in a society and are able to tolerate and even further them, is political participation deserving of the name. For the media in the digital environment, this creates an extra challenge: to order and present content in such a way that it reflects the diversity of ideas and opinions. This necessitates not only a process of inclusion but also a process of exclusion. In other words, the information task of the media includes making responsible selections, and also making conscious decisions about what not to show because the attention span of people is limited and screen space is scarce. Or, in the words of Meiklejohn (Meiklejohn 1948), 19): "What is essential is not that everyone shall speak. But that everything worth saying shall be said." It becomes clear that news recommenders, as ultimate selection tools, can have a very important democratic role to play in a participatory democracy.

Please note that, so far, participation has been discussed primarily with reference to the public as a whole. Participation as a democratic value can also require consideration of those who are typically excluded from participation, such as marginalised groups or minorities. This is particularly the case under more critical theories of democracy that require citizens to discover and experience the many marginalised voices in public and private life. Arguably, this could even mean privileging marginalised voices so they "can offer the 'double vision' of those who are 'outsiders within' the system" (Ferree et al, 2002, 307).

Implications for a Participatory Diverse Recommender

The particular challenge and opportunity for the participatory recommender will be to make a selection that gives a fair and inclusive representation of different ideas and opinions in society, while also helping a user to gain a deeper understanding and to feel engaged, rather than confused, by the abundance of information out there.

Instead of simply giving people what they want (at this particular moment), a participatory recommender will be committed to a far more principled understanding of "participatory diversity." It must proactively address the fear of missing out on important information and depth, as well as concerns about being left out. The participatory recommender is not simply a smarter means to increase user satisfaction and better serve readers: it becomes an important element of active curation of the digital news offer.

Arguably, even though the main thematic focus of the participatory recommendations will be on political content/news, non-political content must also be fairly represented, so as to enable ordinary people to reflect on daily-life challenges and issues and how they can be approached. For the same reason, in-depth discussions, background content and commentary will also become more important. Alternatively, a news medium might decide to leave the task of presenting a diverse selection of content to the front pages, and instead use recommendation technology to recommend further reading, in-depth information on similar topics and historical items about the same topic from the archive. Overall, the performance of a diverse recommender that seeks to promote active involvement in politics will be measured by its success in addressing and mobilising all groups in society.

More attention is also required concerning the form in which the news is delivered. Because the ultimate goal is participation, recommendations should seek to galvanize. The media "should frame politics in a way that mobilizes people's interests and participation in politics" (Strömbäck 2005, 340). To be truly empowering, media content therefore needs to be presented in a diversity of formats and communication styles (Ferree et al. 2002, 298; Christians 2009, 102; Zaller 2003, 122). Where the mission is to stimulate active participation, more engaging, emphatic, emotional, critical and even activist tones should be used. And where the objective is fostering tolerance, the general tone may be more reconciliatory, non-threatening, non-sensationalist, rational, and compassionate.

But the participatory recommender is potentially more than a tool to inform. Taking seriously the idea of the role of the news media in engaging and galvanizing the readership, participatory recommenders can have an important role in actively coaching and engaging users. If a user spends a large amount of screen time on celebrity news or sports, a recommender could nudge her to also try some political news. If a user prefers to sit in her own left/right/centrist bubble, a responsible participatory recommender could recommend content from a different perspective. Preselected recommenders, in particular, offer clear opportunities in that context. And seen from the perspective of more critical democratic theories, recommenders could be turned into even more powerful instruments to draw our scarce attention to the marginalised, invisible or less powerful ideas and opinions in societies with the objective of escaping the muffling standard of civility and the language of the stereotypical "middle-aged, educated, blank white man" (Young 1996, 123–124).

Clearly, actively nudging users also invokes tricky ethical questions about the fine line between information, education, and manipulation (Spahn 2012), as well as the media's responsibility to "pop" filter bubbles. Filter bubbles, in the sense of filtering decisions that include like-minded and exclude different-minded content, can be a real concern for a participatory democracy. A worrisome outcome from the participatory democracy perspective is a situation in which certain people will never become aware of particular ideas and opinions in society, with the filters "ghettoizing citizens into bundles based on narrow preferences and predilections rather than drawing them into a community" (Tandoc and Thomas 2015, 247). Having said that, in certain circumstances filter bubbles can also be conductive to the values of a participatory democracy (and even more so under certain critical theories of democracy). Filter bubbles could be a very good thing to the extent that they act as incubators of constructive speech, allowing the more marginalised voices in society to join forces and pluck up the courage to speak out (compare Ferree et al. 2002, 309). This involves a challenge for the media, academics and policymakers to establish clear guidance on how a diverse recommender design can actually help to promote a vibrant, inclusive and diverse media landscape, as well as include and galvanize disengaged or uninterested segments of the population. The combination of news recommendations and social media functions could offer interesting perspectives, as long as the media, platforms and policymakers succeed in controlling undesirable side effects, such as hate speech, the spread of misinformation and the abuse of digital technology to polarise and radicalize.

In a situation where algorithmic selection decisions are driven more by editorial logic than by individual citizens' information needs, and the societal function of the media comes more to the fore, the ability of society to hold the media accountable for algorithmic selection decisions becomes more important. Much of the criticism levelled at algorithmic news recommendations is centred on their opacity and 'black box' character (Diakopoulos and Koliska 2017). This lack of transparency and the consequent inability of the community to hold the media accountable can be particularly problematic from the participatory democracy perspective, where "freedom of the press exists to serve the interests of the community, not the interests of journalists and their manager. The community, rather than market forces or even the newsroom itself, needs to be the final arbiter of journalism's quality and value" (Christians 2009, 104). Transparency about the editorial logic behind recommendations and why citizens are being shown certain content and not other content becomes not only a matter of compliance with data protection laws' requirement of explainability, or a way to enhance personal agency, but also a matter of central democratic interest: transparency in this sense makes it possible for the community to hold the media accountable and to judge the value of recommendations.

Deliberative (or Discursive) Models of Democracy

The participative and the deliberative models of democracy share a focus on community, the placing of societal interest above individual self-interest, and the importance of active, interested citizens. One of the major differences, however, is that the deliberative model operates on the premise that ideas and preferences are not a given, and that we must focus more on the process of identifying, negotiating and, ultimately, agreeing on different values and issues (Ferree et al. 2002, 300; Held 2006, 233). This involves a process of actively comparing ideas, and engaging with ideas that may be contrary to our own (Manin 1987). Or as Timothy Garton Ash (Garton Ash 2016,

212) has put it so succinctly: "I cannot fully express myself – that is, my self – unless I identify my differences with others." Doing so requires a sphere of mutual shared values and equality: "The dynamics of deliberative democracy are characterised by the norms of equality and symmetry; everyone is to have an equal chance of participation" (Dahlgren 2006). With regard to the role of the media, the deliberative conception of democracy thus places particular emphasis on the media's public forum function. In addition to fostering critical values such as deliberation, critical and rational reflection, equal chances to participate, tolerance and open-mindedness, creating a public forum and optimal conditions for engagement becomes a value in itself.

Under a deliberative perspective, it is thus not enough to "simply" inform people. The media should provide "an arena for everyone with strong arguments and direct its attention to those who can contribute to a furthering of the discussion" (Strömbäck 2005, 341). Not only is this an invitation for the media to actively guide users' attention; it suggests the media also have a duty to proactively confront the audience with different and challenging viewpoints that they have not considered before, or not in this way: "Deliberation requires not only multiple but conflicting points of view because conflict of some sort is the essence of politics" (Manin 1987, 352). Here, diversity becomes instrumental in challenging users to compare and modify their opinions and broaden their horizons. What is more, exposure to diverse information is essential as a means of fostering a certain open mindedness and tolerance, or what Ferree et al. (2002, 303) call "readiness for dialogue." Only if people are actually interested in, and curious about, the positions of others, or are motivated to research different perspectives on a particular subject, are they ready to engage in critical reflections with themselves and deliberations with others. Interestingly, diversity in this reading acquires an almost personalised component: in the deliberative tradition the recommendation that is truly diverse is that which can challenge a particular individual; that is, recommendations that exposes her to ideas and opinions she has not previously been exposed to and challenges her established beliefs. But as users cannot deliberate upon all ideas and opinions (Manin 1987, 356), some element of purposeful filtering is necessary, particularly under the deliberative perspective.

Implications for a Deliberative Recommender

It is under the deliberative conception of democracy that algorithmic recommendations can present the greatest opportunities to the democratic process, as well as the most profound threats. Not surprisingly, the main critics of algorithmic filtering come from this tradition and warn about polarisation, fragmentation and filter bubbles. This is because under the deliberative tradition in particular, the ability to inform people in a more targeted, personally effective way clearly clashes with the second, public forum function of the media. Using recommendations to limit people to information that they find agreeable and that appeals to their own interests, excluding voices that challenge, and depriving them of a comprehensive overview of the different ideas and opinions that exist in a society, is in direct conflict with the deliberative ideal.

But recommendations could also be used in a completely different way: precisely because they are data-driven, recommenders can also take each individual's different ideas, beliefs and opinions and use them as points of departure, suggesting alternative viewpoints that the individual has not yet thought of. Interestingly, personalisation could become a critical feature of a deliberative recommender, as it allows particular individuals to be challenged and exposed to ideas and opinions that they would not have come across on their own. Thus, news recommenders' democratic role may be not only to inform users but to educate them and nudge them to broaden their horizons and make them practised in tolerance. Recommenders could expose the reader to extra, in-depth background material. They could present different perspectives alongside each other, and also make the user aware of what her current place is in the ideological spectrum. They could become an important instrument for fostering critical reflection and open-mindedness.

This means that the path to realising the opportunities offered by algorithmic recommendations and the path to countering the threats they pose are actually one and the same: diversity-sensitive design. Recommenders can be designed using relatively simple metrics such as clicks and likes, or what content friends liked, but there is no reason why recommendations cannot employ more sophisticated metrics. The real challenge for academics, policymakers, editors, journalists and the developers of recommender algorithms is to jointly conceptualise diversity in terms of metrics that deliberative algorithms can be optimised for. The overall goal must be to ensure that citizens remain exposed to a diversity of information, and to counter the undemocratic effects of recommendation that make a significant impact on public opinion formation in a way that is counter-productive to a general "readiness for dialogue" in parts of the population.

Specifically, in recommendations where the focus is more on fostering tolerance and open-mindedness, the ratio of content featuring different cultures and different ethnic, national and linguistic groups, or representatives thereof, will be more relevant, as will presenting content in different languages and giving prominence to content that describes shared experiences ("challenging diversity"). And while under the representative liberal model it would probably be acceptable if the recommender presented a proportionally larger share of content that conforms to the ideas and opinions of political majorities, what is key under the deliberative model is not proportionality, but equality.

A deliberative recommender will be successful if it can contribute to mutual understanding, foster open-mindedness and help people to look beyond their own narrow-minded horizons. One can also imagine that a deliberative recommender will strive to present a greater amount of balanced content, commentary, discussion formats and background information, as well as articles that present various perspectives and a diversity of emotions, from a range of different sources and tailored to the background, level of expertise and interests of the user. Such a deliberative recommender could give particular visibility to public service media content, at least to the extent that the public service media in a particular country has the function of fuelling and facilitating the public discourse. It could also offer additional social features for users to comment, engage, agree/disagree and debate.[1] Finally, serendipity could play a far larger role here as well, to the extent that serendipitous encounters can promote open-mindedness and mental flexibility (Schoenbach 2007).

To stimulate reflection and informed debate, not only the content but also the tone and style of the information provided must promote active discourse, as tone and style are "at the heart of the discursive tradition" (Ferree et al. 2002, 301). The focus will be on styles of communication that are impartial rather than polarising, and rational rather than emotional, and informative styles will be favoured over provocative ones that grab the user's attention and force her to focus on one particular viewpoint.

Finally, transparency about the logic behind including or excluding views and opinions plays an almost fundamental role in this type of recommender. More than in any other democratic conception of recommendations, it is important that people are aware of the "editorial analytical" choices (compare Cherubini and Nielsen 2016, 21) so that they do not assume they are receiving a comprehensive overview of the relevant ideas and opinions when they are not.

Four Types of Democratic Recommenders

So far three distinct types of algorithmic recommenders have been identified, and a fourth hinted at: the liberal, participatory, critical and deliberative recommender. Their main characteristics are summarized in the Table 1.

It can be argued that the first wave of recommenders corresponded with the liberal model of democracy. Liberal recommenders can be found on social media platforms or in early news personalization projects. Liberal recommenders offer users personally relevant information. Often criticized for supposedly narrowing users' views, from the perspective of liberal democracy, liberal recommenders serve perfectly legitimate goals. A necessary pre-condition is that users still have the choice to gather information about politics from alternative sources and that their privacy and personal autonomy are respected.

The strong focus on user-driven recommendations may not sit easily with the editorial ambitions of some of the quality media that envision a more active role in society. These news outlets may prefer a more engaging, participatory recommender. Participatory recommenders will strive to map the diversity of ideas and opinions in society, and use the affordances of digital technology to respond to differences in information needs, styles and communication preferences.

Conforming to more deliberative conceptions of democracy, deliberative recommenders would need to do more – they would also need to find ways to re-create common spaces in an increasingly fragmented media environment. Exposing users to information that they may not have looked for, deliberative recommenders are tools for educating users to remain open to new or different voices in society. It is unlikely that the deliberative recommender can be found on social media platforms or in some of the commercial media, but this type of recommender could be a viable option for public service media.

Finally, the article has briefly touched upon more critical recommender types, recommenders that nudge people to encounter and acknowledge minority opinions, push readers out of the comfort zone of established opinions and engage the more marginalized voices in society. As unlikely as it is that such a type of recommender

Table 1. Four types of democratic recommenders.

Recommender	Liberal	Participatory	Deliberative	Critical
Values to optimize for	Autonomy, self-development, dispersion of power	Inclusiveness, participation, active citizenship	Deliberation, tolerance, open-mindedness, public sphere	Including marginalized voices, defy prejudices
Characteristics	More prominence for more prominent topics Main political issues, particularly during election time For the rest: little distance from personal preferences Choice between different formats, topics, genres, sources Choice of recommendation logics Expert recommenders	Tool of active editorial curation, drawing attention to items that citizens "should know" Activating Inclusive and proportional representation of main political/ideological viewpoints in society Focus on political content/news, but also: non-news content that speaks to broader public Background information Political advertising	Higher share of articles presenting various perspectives, diversity of emotions, range of different sources Equal representation, including content dedicated to different ethnic, linguistic, national groups Balanced content, commentary, discussion formats, background information Prominence public service media content Personalised nudging to consume news content this citizen should know	Prominence for less popular content, minority and marginalized voices Actively nudging Critical tone Content that is purposefully provocative, opposes, challenges
Form and presentation	Possibilities for active user curation, autonomy enhancing, no nudging, privacy friendly design, data portability	Accessible, multi-platform, heterogeneity of styles and tones, can be emotional, empathic, galvanizing, reconciliatory, transparency and accountability	Preference for rational tone, consensus seeking, inviting commentary and reflection, social media elements	Heterogenous, narratives, preference for contents that are affective, emotional, provocative, figurative

would develop under normal market conditions, critical recommenders could turn into interesting tools for NGOs, civil rights groups but also the public service media.

Concluding Remarks

News recommenders can both pose threats to, and offer real opportunities for the democratic role of the media. This is why it is so important to implement the technology with a profound understanding of the democratic values algorithmic recommendations can serve. Too often news recommenders are developed as part of an R&D project, or with purely commercial objectives in mind. Inspired by democratic theories of the media, this article has developed a framework for theorizing about the democratic potential of algorithmic recommenders, and identified three types of democratic recommenders (and hinted at a fourth one). Different democratic theories place different values on, and have different expectations concerning, the role of the media and making citizens central. Sometimes these expectations can conflict. Whereas under more liberal perspectives that emphasise privacy, autonomy and self-development, recommenders that make recommendations based on users' interests function well and have a clear democratic role, the same recommender would be assessed very poorly under more participatory conceptions that place societal interest above individual self-interest Similarly, a participatory recommender that succeeds in informing and galvanizing different users through personalised information could still be a concern under a more deliberative model that prefers a reconciliatory, balanced tone to contributions that inspire and engage. In other words, there is no gold standard when it comes to democratic recommenders and the offering of diverse recommendations. This is why there is a typology of recommenders and different avenues the media can take to use the technology in the pursuit of their democratic mission.

Another important insight derived from this analysis is that the potential anti-democratic effects, such as filter bubbles and restricted diversity, cannot be studied in isolation, but need to be considered in relation to the values at stake. So instead of simply asking whether, as a result of algorithmic filtering, users are exposed to a limited media diet, we need to look at the context and the values one cares about. Depending on the values and the surrounding conditions, selective exposure may even be instrumental in the better functioning of the media and citizens. Also, as this article has shown depending on the democratic theory one follows, diversity in recommendations can take very different forms, from more "interest-driven" liberal conceptions of diversity, to more galvanizing forms of "participatory diversity," to more inclusive forms of "challenging diversity."

The more a democratic theory focuses on furthering societal goals rather than individual self-development, the stronger the arguments are to move away from simple, short-term metrics such as clicks towards more sophisticated metrics and responsible, editorial mission-driven design. Clearly, there is a challenge here for the media as well as for policymakers to engage in more active consideration of how recommenders could further the editorial mission. In addition, the stronger the societal interest in well-informed citizens, the less responsiveness to the interests of users alone is considered a good thing, and the more recommenders could become an indispensable tool for the media to alert, inform or even educate readers and push them out of their intellectual comfort zones. Alternatively, the more focus there is on individual free-doms and self-development, the more recommenders become a tool in the hands of the user, and should, first and foremost, offer the user agency with regard to her choices.

The analysis also has interesting implications for the role of users: theories that expect less active citizenship in political matters can still have high expectations regarding citizens' management of their own information diet, and recommendations can be an important tool in that. Self-selection recommenders are the preferred option in more liberal models, as opposed to more participatory or deliberative models where preselected recommenders offer more opportunities to present readers with informa-tion they "ought to read" (and where nudging them to read such information is actu-ally a good thing). Where societal interest in well-informed, active and open-minded citizens is the dominant interest, individual interests such as privacy, autonomy and accuracy must be balanced against the opportunities that data and AI offer for better informing and even educating citizens. Algorithmic news recommendations in themselves are neither good nor bad for democracy. It is the way the media use the technology that creates threats, or opportunities.

Note

1. The author is indebted to one of the autonomous reviewers for making this point.

Acknowledgments

The author would like to thank Dr. Judith Moeller, Sarah Eskens, Max van Drunen, Mariella Bastian, Mykola Makhortykh, Jaron Harambam, Balazs Bodo, three anonymous reviewers, the (guest) editors of this special journal and the participants of the Algorithms, Automation and News Conference, Munich 2018 for valuable feedback and insights.

Disclosure statement

No potential conflict of interest was reported by the authors.

Funding

The research was funded by the European Research Council (grant no. 638514), and was con-ducted under the PERSONEWS ERC-STG project.

References

Anderson, Chris W. 2011. "Deliberative, Agonistic, and Algorithmic Audiences: Journalism's Vision of its Public in an Age of Audience Transparency." *International Journal of Communication* 5: 529–547.

Balkin, Jack M. 2018. "Free Speech in the Algorithmic Society: Big Data, Private Governance, and New School Speech Regulation." *UC Davis Law Review* 51:1149–1210.

Belair-Gagnon, Valerie, Holton, Averie E. 2018. "Boundary Work, Interloper Media, And Analytics in Newsrooms: An Analysis of the Roles of Web Analytics Companies in News Production." *Digital Journalism* 6 (4): 492–508.

Boczkowski, Pablo J. 2013. *The News Gap: When the Information Preferences of the Media and the Public Diverge*, edited by Eugenia Mitchelstein and (Organization) JSTOR. Cambridge, MA: The MIT Press.

Calo, R. 2014. "Digital Market Manipulation." *George Washington Law Review* 82 (4): 995–1051.

Cherubini, F., Nielsen, R.K. 2016. *Editorial Analytics: How News Media are Developing and Using Audience Data and Metrics*. Oxford: Reuters Institute for the Study of Journalism.

Christians, Clifford. 2009. *Normative Theories of the Media: Journalism in Democratic Societies*. Urbana, IL: University of Illinois Press.

Curran, James. 2015. "Reinterpreting the Democratic Roles of the Media." *Brazilian Journalism Research* 10 (2): 28–53.

Dahlberg, L. 2011. "Re-Constructing Digital Democracy: An Outline of Four 'Positions'." *New Media and Society* 13 (6): 855–872.

Dahlgren, Peter. 2006. "Doing Citizenship." *European Journal of Cultural Studies* 9 (3): 267–286.

Diakopoulos, Nicholas and Michael Koliska. 2017. "Algorithmic Transparency in the News Media." *Digital Journalism* 5 (7): 809–828.

Ekstrand, M. D. and M. C. Willemsen. 2016. RecSys 2016. Proceedings of the 10th ACM Conference on Recommender Systems.

Eskens, Sarah, Helberger, Natali, Moeller, Judith 2017. "Challenged by News Personalisation: Five Perspectives on the Right to Receive Information." *Journal of Media Law* 9 (2): 1–26.

Etzioni, Amitai 1996. "The Responsive Community: A Communitarian Perspective Presidential Address, American Sociological Association." *American Sociological Review* 61 (1): 1–11.

Edwin Baker, C. 1998. *Media Concentration and Democracy: Why Ownership Matters*. New York: Cambridge University Press.

Ferree, Myra, Gamson, Wiliam, Jürgen, Gerhards, and Rucht, Dieter. 2002. "Four Models of the Public Sphere in Modern Democracies." *Theory and Society; Renewal and Critique in Social Theory* 31 (3): 289–324.

Ferrer-Conill, Raul, Tandoc, Edison C. 2018. "The Audience-Oriented Editor: Making Sense of the Audience in the Newsroom." *Digital Journalism*, 21(6): 436–453.

Garton Ash, Timothy. 2016. *Free Speech: Ten Principles for a Connected World*. New Haven, London: Yale University Press.

Gibbons, Tom 1998. *Regulating the Media*. 2nd ed. London: Sweet & Maxwell.

Gitlin, Todd. 1998. "Public Sphere or Public Sphericules?" In *Media, Ritual and Identity* edited by T. Liebes and J. Curran, 168–174. London: Routledge.

Harambam, Jaron, Helberger, Natali & van Hoboken, Joris. 2018. "Democratizing algorithmic news recommenders: how to materialize voice in a technologically saturated media ecosystem". Philosophical Transactions of the Royal Society A: Mathematical, Physical and Engineering Sciences 376 (2133).

Helberger, Natali, Karppinen, Kari and D'acunto, Lucia. 2018. "Exposure Diversity as a Design Principle for Recommender Systems." *Information, Communication & Society* 21 (2): 191–207.

Held, David. 2006. *Models of Democracy*. Stanford: Stanford University Press.

Karppinen, Kari. 2013a. *Rethinking Media Pluralism*. 1st ed. New York: NY: Fordham University Press.

Karppinen, Kari. 2013b. "Uses of Democratic Theory in Media and Communication Studies." *Observatorio (OBS*)* 7: 1–17.

Lewis, Seth and Usher, Nikkie. 2016. "Trading Zones, Boundary Objects, and the Pursuit of News Innovation: A Case Study of Journalists and Programmers" *Convergence: The International Journal of Research into New Media Technologies* 22 (5): 543–560.

Li, Yaojun & Marsh, David. 2008. New Forms of Political Participation: Searching for Expert Citizens and Everyday Makers. British Journal of Political Science 38 (2): 247–272.

Manin, Bernard. 1987. "On Legitimacy and Deliberation. Political Theory." *Political Theory* 15 (3): 338–368.

Meiklejohn, Alexander. 1948. *Free Speech and its Relation to Self-Government.* New York: Harper and Brothers.

Moore, Martin. 2016. *Tech Giants and Civic Power.* London: Centre for the study of Media, Communication & Power.

Napoli, Philip. 1999. "The Marketplace of Ideas Metaphor In Communications Regulation". Journal of Communication 49 (4): 151–169.

Napoli, Philip M. 2011. *Audience Evolution: New Technologies and the Transformation of Media Audiences.* New York: Columbia University Press.

Helberger, Natali. 2011. "Diversity by Design." *Journal of Information Policy* 1: 441–469.

Newman, Nic. 2018. *Journalism, Media, and Technology Trends and Predictions.* Oxford: Reuters Institute.

OFCOM. 2012. *Measuring Media Plurality. Ofcom's Advice to the Secretary of State for Culture, Olympics, Media and Sport.* London: OFCOM.

Pariser, Eli. 2011. *The Filter Bubble: What the Internet is Hiding from You.* New York: Penguin.

Richards, Neil. 2008. "Intellectual Privacy." *Texas Law Review* 87(2): 387–445.

Schoenbach, Klaus. 2007. 'The Own in the Foreign': Reliable Surprise – An Important Function of the Media?" *Media, Culture & Society* 29(2): 344–353.

Spahn, Andreas. 2012. "And Lead Us (Not) into Persuasion … ? Persuasive Technology and the Ethics of Communication." *Science and Engineering Ethics* 18 (4): 633–650.

Strömbäck, Jesper. 2005. "In Search of a Standard: Four Models of Democracy and their Normative Implications for Journalism." *Journalism Studies* 6 (3): 331–345.

Sunstein, Cass. 2001. *Republic.Com.* Princeton, NJ: Princeton University Press.

Tandoc, Edson C. and Thomas, Ryan J. 2015. "The Ethics of Web Analytics: Implications of Using Audience Metrics in News Construction." *Digital Journalism* 3 (2): 1–16.

Turow, Joseph. 2005. "Audience Construction Culture Production: Marketing Surveillance in the Digital Age". *Annals of the American Academy of Political and Social Science* 597 (1): 103–121.

Thurman, Neil, Schifferes, Steve. 2012. "The Future of Personalisation at News Websites: Lessons from a longitudinal study." Journalism Studies 13 (5): 775–709.

Thurman, Neil, Moeller, Judith, Helberger, Natali & Trilling, Damian. 2018. "My Friends, Editors, Algorithms, and I". Digital Journalism, online first.

Wentzel, Dirk. 2002. *Medien Im Systemvergleich: Eine Ordnungsökonomische Analyse Des Deutschen Und Amerikanischen Fernsehmarktes.* Stuttgart: Lucius & Lucius.

Young, Iris Manon. 1996. "Communication and the Other: Beyond Deliberative Democracy." In *Democracy and Difference. Contesting the Boundaries of the Political*, edited by Seyla Benhabib, 120–136. Princeton: Princeton University Press.

Zaller, John. 2003. "A New Standard of News Quality: Burglar Alarms for the Monitorial Citizen." *Political Communication* 20 (2): 109–130.

Zamith, Rodrigo. 2018. "Quantified Audiences in News Production: A Synthesis and Research Agenda." *Digital Journalism* 6 (4): 418–435.

Newsbots That Mediate Journalist and Audience Relationships

Heather Ford (iD) and Jonathon Hutchinson (iD)

ABSTRACT
News media organisations are experimenting with a new generation of newsbots that move beyond automated headline delivery
to the delivery of news according to a conversational format
within the context of private messaging services. To build the
newsbot, journalists craft statements and answers to users' questions that mimic a natural conversation between a journalist and
user. In so doing, journalists are experimenting with styles of
communication that reflect very particular journalistic personas.
We investigate the persona of the news chatbot created by the
Australian Broadcasting Corporation (ABC), the better to understand how the public broadcaster's forays into social media service delivery and automation are shaping new relationships
between public service broadcasters and their audiences. We find
that, for a section of the audience that uses it, the friendly newsbot contrasts favourably with their previous experience with news
and the journalists who produce it. The public service journalists
who operate the bot are, in turn, using the bot to try to reach
new audiences by experimenting with a more informal, intimate
relationship with citizen users. The supposedly "intelligent" (but in
actual fact very much human-crafted) newsbot is the vehicle
through which this new relationship is being forged.

Introduction

Bots are software applications that perform automated tasks over the internet.
Journalists have used bots for tasks relating to both the production and dissemination
of news, with the term "newsbots" typically applied to applications that help journalists (and sometimes their followers or readers) keep track of particular topics or stories
by extracting news headlines automatically from other news sources (Lokot and
Diakopoulos 2015). When newsbots have interacted with readers on social media platforms such as Twitter and Facebook, they have tended to function predominantly as
rebroadcasters of traditional news content to social media (Lokot and Diakopoulos
2015, 694): to alert, aggregate and monitor content for its users, as Bradshaw
(2016) argues.

A more recent development, however, has seen the migration of newsbots from public social media platforms to private messaging services such as Facebook Messenger. This development results in newsbots incorporating features of chatbots in addition to functioning as disseminators of news. Chatbots are computer programs that respond to user input by simulating how a human would behave as a partner in a conversation.

Technological advancements in bot conversation capacities have also been propelled by changes in user practices, both by the move to private messaging channels (and away from the public channels of social media platforms) and an increasing acceptance by users of conversational interfaces. Since 2015 users of messaging apps (including WhatsApp, Facebook Messenger, WeChat and Viber) have outstripped active users of the most popular social networks (BI Intelligence, quoted in Newman et al. 2017, 15). According to Newman et al. (2017, 17), this is because "people increasingly prefer to share content not on big open networks … but within apps like WhatsApp, Snapchat and Facebook Messenger where they can have more control".

The 2018 Reuters Digital News Report announces an increase in news consumption via mobile and the growing use of voice-activated speakers (such as Amazon Echo and Google Home) to access news (Newman et al. 2018). Asking your smart speaker for the latest news may therefore become a significant way of receiving news in the future.

In this paper, we investigate the changing relations between media organisations and audiences enabled by this new generation of newsbot by considering the newsbot of the Australian Broadcasting Corporation (ABC), which was launched in 2016. The ABC is Australia's national public broadcaster. Founded in 1932, it is principally funded by the Australian government, but maintains a set of principles that ensures its independence from government. These principles include public service commitments to universality, excellence, diversity, accountability and innovation (Tracey 1998).

Each of the public media principles is subject to reconfiguration with the shift from public service broadcasting (PSB) towards public service media (PSM) in the context of an increasingly networked environment. The role of PSB now includes not only producing and procuring content for its traditional television and radio offerings, but also designing and developing digital information and distribution services that align with an ever-splintering public that has specific and niche demands (McClean 2011). This shift to PSM, alongside the legislated requirement to innovate, situates public media not only at the coal-face of technological development, but also as an ideal institution to experiment with and integrate a number of human–machine communication approaches.

Such developments inevitably impact on the principles underlying public service media organisations. Van de Bulck and Moe (2017, 16) demonstrate how the majority of such organisations in Europe are moving towards algorithmic personalisation which they see "as a tool to realise universality in new ways". Van Dijck and Poell (2015, 148), looking at PSMs and their integration into social media, note that when "the boundaries between public and corporate online space are becoming progressively porous, the meaning of 'publicness' is contested and reshaped".

There are diverging opinions about whether these changes are positive or negative. Some contend that increasing pressures to adopt personalisation technologies or to work with third-party (commercial) social media players to deliver services have a negative effect on issues such as universality, diversity and accountability (see, e.g., Born 2005). Others (including Flew 2011; Debrett 2010; Jakubowicz 2007) are optimistic about the changes, arguing that public media organisations are innovating with new modes of delivery that enable them to reach diverse publics across multiple platforms, thereby complementing, rather than undermining, the principle of universality.

Beyond these scholarly debates, an alternative path towards understanding how new technologies influence the values and principles underlying public service media involves investigating how those technologies mediate new relationships between the PSM organisation and the citizens they serve. In doing so, we move from framing newsbots as a medium with which we have a relationship towards framing them as a medium that *mediates* existing social relationships (in this case between audiences and PSM organisations).

By investigating the case of the ABC news chatbot, we offer insights into the opportunities and challenges that such technologies create for media organisations, particularly public service media organisations. After situating our research questions in the context of relevant theory and empirical research and describing our methods, we introduce the ABC's newsbot, beginning with a description of what the bot does, situating this within the context of the ABC and highlighting the ways in which its designers talk about it. We then move on to the newsbot's reception, outlining three key aspects of the newsbot's personality as identified by a selection of its audience. The article concludes with an analysis of what the bot's personality (as designed by journalists and received by users) tells us about the relationship between public service media organisations and the publics they serve.

We argue that the move from using newsbots on public social media channels such as Twitter to using them on private messaging channels such as Facebook Messenger has resulted in key changes that demand a redefinition of newsbots for Journalism Studies. The changes are twofold. First, the emphasis in providing news by newsbot is not on an area of coverage (a topic, beat or location of interest) but on the *method* of coverage, in this case according to temporal conditions (at a time specified by the user) and applying a conversational form of news delivery. Changes to the method of coverage result in key changes to journalistic practice.

More importantly, however, the move also represents an important shift in the relationship between journalists and citizens as the journalistic organisation moves into the private, conversational realm of messaging services. This shift requires a redefinition of the role, function and possibilities of newsbots.

Literature review

Research investigating the ways in which automated processes influence the news and news media organisations is preceded by a long history in the field of human–computer interaction, where research has investigated how humans receive information delivered via automated processes or sources. In their experimental research on computer personality, for example, Moon and Nass (1996) found that it was possible to operationalise a computer's personality using "a rudimentary, text-based system with scripted responses" (668) and that their research participants recognised computer personalities as "psychologically real" (651). Finding that people preferred different types of personality that corresponded with their own, they concluded that "attempts to design a single computer personality that appeals to all users are (therefore) misguided" (668).

If people recognise the personality traits programmed into a technology and act towards that technology as if it were a human, the relevant question for journalists is what types of characteristic are deemed most credible? Sundar and Nass (2001) asked research participants to rate the credibility, likeability, quality and representativeness of online news stories as a function of different types of communication sources. They found that when either the computer terminal or other audience members were perceived to be the source of news, the stories were rated higher in quality than when news editors were perceived to be the source (65).

Recent studies have reinforced this earlier work, pointing towards trustworthiness that users ascribe to third-party, computerised actors and algorithmic processes used for selecting and curating the news. Thurman et al. (2018), for example, demonstrate a link between respondents' trust in news organisations and their assessment of the utility of algorithmic and editorial news selection. They found that as trust in news organisations falls, people are less likely to recognise news selection by editors and journalists as a good way to get news. By contrast, agreement that automated personalisation is a good way to receive news is less affected by distrust in the media. They concluded that users do not recognise the link between automated news personalisation and the operation of news organisations, "believing the technology has a degree of immunity from contamination by a politically compromised or untrustworthy news media" (17).

Despite these trends, there are still major gaps in our understanding of trustworthiness and credibility in relation to automation. The Reuters Digital News Report (Newman et al. 2018), for example, reports that 65% of people surveyed from 40 countries said they prefer to get news via search engines, social media or news aggregators (this figure goes up to 73% for under 35s) rather than native news websites. But when asked what sources of news they trust, only 34% trust search engines and 23% trust news from social media most of the time.

In order to understand the consequences for trustworthiness in the case of newsbots, we extend the research in this area by focusing on a particular case. We frame the study not in terms of newsbots as a medium with which we have a relationship, but in terms of newsbots as a medium that *mediates* existing social relationships (in this case between audiences and media organisations). Here, we follow Höflich (2013) who proposes a triadic model of human–robot interaction rather than the traditional dyadic model and suggests that robots can be either a connective or divisive element in the inter-group relationships that they mediate.

Writing about the role of social robots in the context of interpersonal relations, Höflich (2013) explores the idea of social robots as media. Instead of seeing a social robot as a machine with which humans interact, Höflich argues that robots need to be recognised both as a medium with which humans interact and also as a medium that mediates. This triadic analysis of media-oriented behaviour recognises the robot as a third (person) in interpersonal relations that affects how we see ourselves and how we relate to others. Höflich explains that the robot as third (person) can either connect or separate the persons whose relationship it mediates.

We apply Höflich's framework to the case of newsbots within a larger mass communication context. The newsbot, in this case, is recognised as a third entity that presents the frame of communication between audiences and PSM organisations, and is also framed (or recognised) on its own (43). This relational perspective enables us a glimpse into the meaning of the newsbot in context, i.e., as a third party that can either connect or separate. The question in this case, then, becomes whether the newsbot connects audiences to their public service broadcaster, or separates them from it, and what role automation plays in this relationship.

Method

Our method employed several ethnographically inspired techniques and practices (Pink et al. 2015). The goal of the project was to explore not just what the newsbot did, but who the bot was for readers and journalists, and for the PSM organisation that constructed it, and then explore the connections between them. We adopted Nagy and Neff's (2015, 1) framing of human–computer relations that include "users' perceptions, attitudes, and expectations; the materiality and functionality of technologies; and the intentions and perceptions of designers" (themes that we have used to structure our findings). Following Guzman (2017, 76), our tracing of relations focused on "both what others say about (the bot) and what it says about itself (verbally and nonverbally), keeping in mind the cultural contexts that surround these elements".

We implemented a mixed methodology that draws on what Seaver (2017) calls the "scavenger" approach, which was particularly helpful in gleaning information from diverse sources. As Seaver notes, "The scavenger replicates the partiality of ordinary conditions of knowing – everyone is figuring out their world by piecing together heterogeneous clues – but expands on them by tracing cultural practices across multiple locations and through loosely connected networks" (6). In implementing this method, we combined data from interviews, surveys, field diaries, policy documents and our own experience of using the newsbot to expose the triadic relationship between the three key stakeholders.

We interviewed via phone and email the managers and designers behind the ABC newsbot. The team is located in Brisbane, Queensland, and is responsible for the technological development of the News Division around the country.

Those same ABC employees provided access to user survey data and user responses to the bot including the results from an August 2017 survey of 3404 newsbot users, a selection of 120 substantive anonymous user responses about the bot (from 8000 pieces of feedback that included topic suggestions, technical issues and emojis) and 101 responses from users about why they uninstalled the bot, as well as internal presentations of user feedback and survey responses. We qualitatively coded the substantive responses in order to look for themes emerging from the data. The policy documents we examined were a mix of ABC public and internal strategy documents, including the ABC Annual Reports, legislated Acts and external-facing advertising material.

We also recorded our own field notes when we installed and used the bot for a period of over six months (Light, Burgess, and Duguay 2018). During this time, we took screenshots and then annotated them according to surprises, reflections and iterative interpretations. Tracing a divergent set of data points that had been scavenged from a number of sources helped us to identify and understand the media assemblage surrounding the newsbot: a media assemblage of corporate technology providers, the public service media institution, journalists, technologists and the public, along with non-human actors including the newsbot and the technologies that are summoned in justifying the new service.

In the following three sections, we analyse the ABC's newsbot according to its materiality and functionality, the intentions and perceptions of its designers and newsbot users' attitudes towards, and expectations of, the bot.

The materiality and functionality of the bot

G'day Jono, welcome to ABC News on Facebook Messenger, your Australian news assistant. We're here to get you up-to-speed ASAP whenever you need us, with morning and evening news summaries, breaking news alerts and more.

We can also tell you when major news breaks, so you can finally conquer your FOMO.

Don't worry, this will only be for the really big stuff. And the best bit is we won't just tell you WHAT has happened, we'll tell you WHY it's important.

Are you in?

This was the response that greeted us after we searched for ABC News on Facebook and clicked on the "Message" button to start a conversation with the ABC newsbot. We selected "I'm in" and then moved through the news topics that we wanted to follow (including politics, world politics, entertainment, business, sport, announcements and quiz). The newsbot asked whether we wanted to subscribe to breaking news in addition to daily summaries of the topics, and we were able to select a time to receive the news summaries.

Interacting with the newsbot, we saw that daily news summaries include three stories of interest: an article of high public interest, an article of local significance and a "feel good" story. At each point, the user is presented with a list of options for responding to the bot, such as "tell me more", "why did this happen?" and "what does this mean?". While this is the standard approach of the ABC newsbot, the user is also presented with the option to delve deeper into surrounding news items through the "more like this" option.

In terms of newsbot functionality, then, the newsbot delivers automated news alerts at a time specified by the user, is also able to deliver targeted news according to topics that the user is interested in, to register responses from the user to individual message elements (using Facebook's "reactions" including thumbs up, thumbs down, etc.) and to answer questions composed by the user.

For example, we asked the bot:

What's your name?

To which it answered:

My name is ABC newsbot. Because I'm a newsbot … from the ABC.

That's a clever name, right?

During important national events, the bot might be taken over by a special reporter who gives a personal take on what is happening, why it is important and what readers should know about it. During the May 2017 federal budget announcement, the chatbot was operated by ABC journalist Peter Marsh who used his personal experience "as a political nerd heading into a budget lockup for the first time" to give readers "an inside look at how it all happens" (Marsh 2017). The bot introduced Marsh to audiences and provided updates throughout the night's proceedings. According to the journalist,

> There was a mix of actual news from the budget and lighter personal commentary from me and we weren't afraid to get playful with the tone, considering the audience. (Craig McCosker, personal communication, 9 October, 2018)

As previously stated, the chatbot typically delivers three headlines to the user in a daily news summary delivered via Facebook Messenger (see Figure 1 below).

The bot is structured around a question and answer format. Newsbot users can receive headlines and choose to "tap through for more" information based on these headlines. Each snippet contains an image followed by two or three sentences highlighting the key points of the story. Users can then ask for more information about the story when delivered a prompt such as "tell me more" or they can "move onto the next story". Alternatively, prompts may be more specific to the context of the story reflecting questions that might pique the user's curiosity.

The example below from 12 September 2017 demonstrates how a story might unfold on the newsbot:

> The United Nations Security Council has imposed new sanctions on North Korea in response to last week's nuclear test.

> But they're not as tough as the US wanted.

Users are then prompted with the question "How so?" When this option is clicked, the story evolves:

> America wanted an oil embargo, but instead crude oil exports to North Korea will be capped at current levels.

> The new sanctions also ban textile exports from North Korea and prohibit all countries from authorising new work permits for North Koreans.

> US envoy to the UN Nikki Haley said North Korea had 'not yet passed the point of no return'."

Users can then either "read the story" on the ABC's website or move on to the "next story".

In addition to daily news and news alerts being delivered in this interactive format, users are also able to ask a question or send a message to the bot.

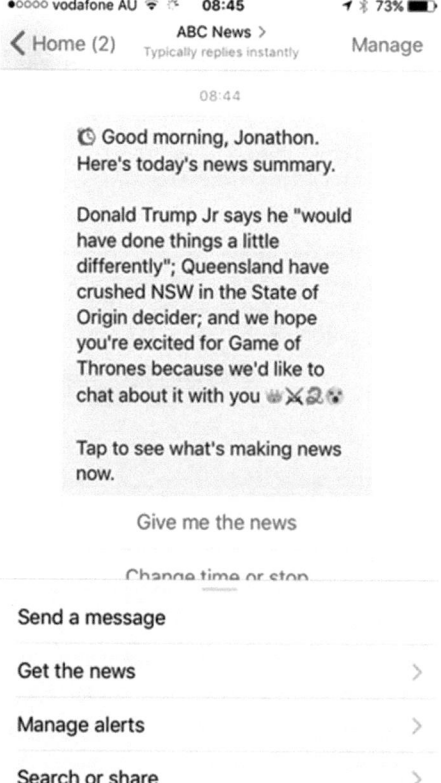

Figure 1. An example of an ABC News chatbot morning news alert. Screenshots are from the mobile version of the newsbot built using ChatFuel from within Facebook's Messenger environment.

Testing the functionality of free text questions to the bot, we realised that its ability to respond to questions is limited. For example, when we asked the bot "Who is Justin Timberlake?" after a message delivering a headline about Timberlake at the Super Bowl, the bot responded with "I can do a search of the news for you if you like?" (a typical answer to queries of this type).

When we provided the bot with its requested keywords (in this case: "Justin Timberlake"), it returned a story about Timberlake from that morning's news, rather than an answer to our question. Although the newsbot will respond to questions about what the latest news is, it was not able to answer our question about what was trending on social media (see Figure 2 below).

Although the bot simulates a human conversation in terms of the placement of its modular story segments, the user response options within each story are decided by the news creators. If users have questions other than "And then what happened?" for example, the conversation will reach a dead end, unless they choose to ask the bot-free text questions. Users can respond to the bot's statements with Facebook's "reactions", but cannot comment on the news in the way that they might be able to with news articles on a news site.

It is unlikely that users, when choosing from different options, will believe they are engaging with a human rather than a bot, as the responses to user input are

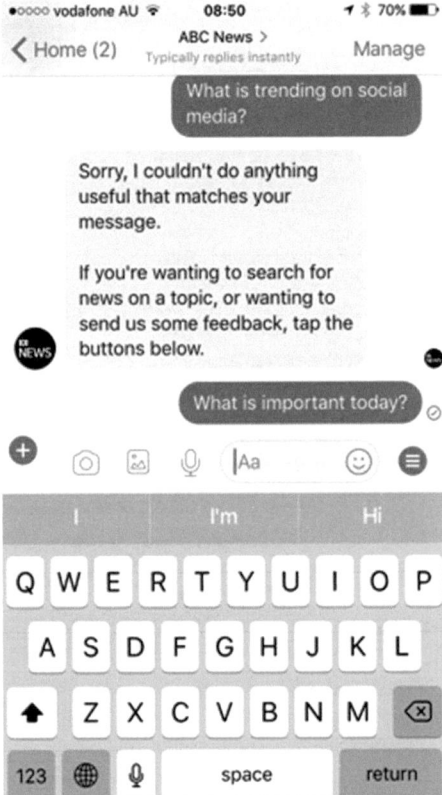

Figure 2. The ABC newsbot's response to our question: "What is trending on social media?".

instantaneous and free text questions to the bot are so limited. Users may, however, question whether their responses to specific requests for feedback or to individual story elements using Facebook's carousel of reactions are being read and listened to by journalists at the ABC.

The intentions and perceptions of designers

The content for the bot (including daily news summaries, breaking news and answers to free text user queries) is developed by the ABC News Mobile team, located in the News Technology Division in Brisbane. The team is also responsible for developing content for the ABC's other mobile news products. While the majority of the news broadcast comes out of the Sydney studios, a significant amount of the news technology is developed and deployed from the Brisbane location.

The newsbot was built using ChatFuel, a Web-based platform. Founded in 2015 by Russian entrepreneurs Dmitrii Dumik and Artem Ptashnik and based in Silicon Valley, ChatFuel is primarily focused on enabling non-developers to build bots within Facebook's Messenger service. The company offers free services and also subscription services that remove ChatFuel branding and provide access to more fine-tuned data about the audience. While the ABC started with the free version, they have since moved to the premium version to enable greater personalisation.

Craig McCosker, product manager for ABC News Mobile team, led the development of the newsbot. When we asked about the development process for the bot, McCosker talked about the team's experimentation with the available technology, with topic selection, news story explanations and the personality characteristics of the bot. According to McCosker, the conversational, guided, interactive approach to designing newsbots in the messaging context requires much more effort than the automatic delivery of stories with standard headlines and descriptions.

One of the greatest challenges for news producers developing newsbots in the conversational format is the personality of the bot. A chatbot's personality is developed by its creators through the tone and character of the answers provided to users' questions (Verma 2018). Enabling the bot to respond to a wide variety of free text responses from users through artificial intelligence applications (at the level of the application) and delivery (at the level of content production) is a key challenge. The challenges are not only technical, however. Newsbot designers developing the chat facilities in messaging environments must also develop a style of conversation that is both authoritative and personable.

The question that bot designers and developers are asking is: "What kind of human will the bot be?" This applies not only to the ways in which the bot "reads the news" – or, in this case, delivers and frames the news – but to the tone with which the bot responds to user queries. Making the bot sound "human" is a challenge for journalists, as is the fact that the colloquial nature of conversation is often at odds with the goals of authority and credibility that may result in news products of a very different tone.

According to the ABC team, newsbot messages need to feel personal (rather than "robotic"), but they were initially uncertain about "how far to go regarding the creepiness of personalisation" by addressing users by name. However:

> [W]e tested it and overall people found it more engaging and/or got used to it after a short time. (Craig McCosker, personal communication, 9 October, 2018)

The style and tone of the ABC newsbot has been the target of continuous readjustment. The team imagines the newsbot as "a smart, newsy friend in your pocket". This phrase highlights both the personality characteristics of the newsbot and the relationship the team is working towards in the development of conversations with users.

In relation to personality characteristics, the team initially tried signalling the automated nature of the newsbot using icons, but abandoned the "friendly robot icon" and the "news robot style personality", because they felt that this was "constraining and unnecessary" (McCosker interview, 9 October, 2018). The style of conversation has been more difficult to refine, as the ABC news team continuously tries to achieve a balance that makes the newsbot acceptable to a wide range of audiences. McCosker reported that while some liked the conversational style that involves being guided through the news in dialogue form, others wanted the more traditional approach that enabled them to immediately view all the headlines from which they could select individual stories.

> [While] many people [were] keen to engage in a conversational style of news … others found it too slow and [an] unnecessary overhead compared to … scanning lots of headlines on [a] website or app homepages. The conversational, emoji, background and shared experiences-rich style that resonated with many young people was a turn off for

older people who wanted to use the bot but found the style used to talk about each story trivial, condescending and not serious enough – just the facts please. The style used is now more middle of the road and is accessible for more people but it's an open question for research [whether we] have we lost an edge with a younger audience. (Craig McCosker, personal communication, 9 October, 2018)

The prospect of attracting this younger audience (along with other previous "non-users" of ABC news products) is what most excited the news team about the newsbot's development. Since its launch in 2016, the user base has grown to about 600,000. That audience, according to the chatbot news team, is younger (66% of users surveyed in the latest poll were under 45) and more likely to be female (55%) than the typical ABC News audience, reflecting general trends in social media demographics (Tolliday 2017). This is an audience that the chatbot team recognises is traditionally underserved by ABC News. One of the core aims of the newsbot, for the team, has been making news more accessible to these previous non-users.

It's about lowering barriers around background knowledge and [increasing] motivation to [engage] with the news … making it accessible to people with lower levels of education and interest in current affairs. (Craig McCosker, personal communication, 23 March, 2018)

Another aspect of the relationship with users that the ABC newsbot team is aiming for is reflected in their conception of the newsbot as a "smart friend in your pocket". The intimacy of the term "friend" reflects the personal, conversational design of the service and also the particularly trusted role that the ABC sees for itself. According to McCosker, "The ABC is very trusted. We see ourselves as a guide or companion via a mobile that is with you all day … [and is] trusted to reach out to you and push-alert you with news". In McCosker's view, the ABC newsbot provides an "essential, informative, concise and approachable" take on news media, inviting the audience to participate in a personalised news experience.

The team regularly receives information about their users' responses and feedback to individual stories and the service as a whole. McCosker views this constant feedback as a means of cultivating a closer relationship between the ABC and their audiences than is provided by other services on offer.

We have also been increasingly doing calls out to the Messenger audience to share their experiences and perspectives to build out our newsgathering and make storytelling richer. I see all of this as an attempt to make a news service distinctive through having a closer relationship with audiences in contrast to the commodification of news content we see broadly on the mobile web. (Craig McCosker, personal communication, 9 October, 2018)

The ABC may see themselves as trusted providers of news, but what do users think of the newsbot? Is it as credible and trustworthy as the ABC claims? In the next section, we highlight three traits of the newsbot's personality as experienced by some of its users.

Newsbot users' attitudes and expectations

One theme that emerged through the qualitative analysis of the more substantive responses generated from the 2017 survey (see "Method" above for more detail) was the experience of a group of users who characterised themselves as non-users of traditional news products. These users wrote about their experience with the newsbot as distinct from their previous experiences with the news and the journalists who author it. They indicated that they were "by no means a lover of politics" (A2[1]) or that they "don't watch the news or read the paper" (A1) or that they often "don't have the time to watch the news" (A7) – sometimes because of work, at other times because they were full-time carers. These users appreciated "having someone sending little updates" (A1) or "keeping [them] updated" (A2) or "having small bites of information [they] could access at any time" (A18). Access to the newsbot made them feel more empowered and more knowledgeable: they "love[d] knowing what is going on in the world so quickly and easily" (A5).

These users appreciated the personal nature of the communications. One user remarked:

I like the tone of all the ABC news messages. They feel professional yet personal. (A12)

Many of the positive comments mentioned the tone of the bot. Tone refers to the style in which the bot delivers the news, the attitude towards the subject expressed by the speaker, and the personality of the bot as shaped by the bot's creators. It is the result of writing style, the mix of textual and graphical elements, the ways in which the bot addresses the reader and the algorithms and data processes employed by the bot team to deliver news to the user.

In addition to asking what the bot does, it is important to understand the persona of the bot, how that persona is shaped by the bot's creators and how users respond to the bot. Who is the bot to the user? Many of the comments about the bot referred to characteristics normally understood as human traits. In the next section, we highlight three traits of the ABC newsbot as experienced by a selection of the newsbot's users. The bot is perceived by this group to be unpretentious, optimistic and helpful.

Unpretentious

Users expressed appreciation for the non-intimidating, non-threatening tone of the bot. User A1 remarked that the "news is presented in a fun, non-intimidating way and emojis and other quirky little additions just make the news that much more user friendly". Another wrote that the bot makes "reading the news a lot of fun" (A7).

News stories are fashioned using informal vocabulary native to social media. An emoticon waves at the user when they have finished reading the news, users can respond to stories with the same emoticons that Facebook enables in responses to posts on the site, and stories are almost always accompanied by some kind of graphic – either a photograph or animated gif with references to popular (internet) culture and internet memes. Accompanying a story from 7 February 2018 about the UK banning the purchase of bitcoins by credit card, for example, is an animated gif of a character from the Futurama animated comedy series with the words "Shut up and take my bitcoin" based on a popular internet meme[2] from Reddit.

The style of writing, too, is irreverent and frames the news in original ways. A news alert from 8 February 2018, for example, covering Nancy Pelosi's eight-hour speech to the US Congress about the "Dreamers" – the immigrants brought to the US as children who now face deportation after President Trump threatened to remove their protection – begins with:

> Someone please get Nancy Pelosi a drink of water!

This is followed by:

> The Democratic leader just finished making an EPIC speech in the US House that went for a record-breaking 8 hours straight.
>
> And it argued against a deal that would keep the government open …

The satirical opening to this story reflects ABC journalists' wish to use an informal style associated with conversations between friends. If users click through the introductory snippet, they are able to navigate to the ABC website where the story is presented in full. These introductory snippets frame the story in ways that pique the user's curiosity by focusing on personalities and individuals' behaviours, before moving on to the policy issues. This accessible tone assures newsbot users that they too could find the news useful and interesting.

Optimistic

The bot is also perceived as being optimistic by a number of users surveyed, particularly because of the focus on good news. Users can sign up for a special news alert for "good news". The interface for selecting this option is framed as follows:

> Tap 'I'm in' if you'd like us to send you a wrap-up of good news at noon each Wednesday. We think it'll give you that little bump of positivity you need to get through the day."

The bot typically starts the daily news message with two hard news stories (usually covering politics, major global or Australian headlines) and one feel-good story relating to entertainment, celebrity or technology. At the end of 2017, there was a special feature with a "list of 12 good news stories you might have missed while you were worrying about a nuclear war". One user responded to the good news angle:

> Just love the ability to get the news that is current and is apt to my interests AND the good news stories not just the sad or terrible stories! (A64)

The creators have timed the delivery of the good news wrap-up for the mid-point of the week, when they think users might be most in need of a boost, and their general openness to the idea of positivity reflects a more intimate engagement with the needs of the bot users.

Helpful

In addition to the bot being perceived as optimistic and non-intimidating, it is also perceived as useful. Many users commented positively on the "informative" nature of the bot. When the bot delivered a special feature on the Australian budget, one user stated:

I love these bots … and the budget, it is explained in a way that I understand. All the fluff taken out and simple to understand. (A22)

Two distinct categories of content are integrated in the bot's daily headlines. A news element focuses on telling the reader what has happened, whereas an information element directly assists the reader in decision-making. A story about the Australian Bureau of Statistics' (ABS) release of its latest Household Expenditure Survey, for example, indicated that "it isn't looking good for the average consumer" because "[w]e're spending more on the basics … than six years ago". If users chose the option of finding out how to cut down on household expenses, they were taken to a series of suggestions from experts about how to spend less.

A further example of the informative aspect can be found in the "News Explained" section of the newsbot. After running through the standard headlines, users are given the option of having the key news items of the day explained to them and are taken to a broader "explainer" article that breaks the story into smaller descriptive texts (see Figure 3 below). This includes information on *why* the news item has emerged, what the *key aspects* of the news item are and what the *implications* of the news item are. The audience is not only being exposed to the issues, but is having them explained in an accessible way.

What the bot is not

The remarks by some users about what the newsbot is *not* are perhaps as interesting as what they say it *is*. These users seemed to be saying that the bot, unlike journalists, is not pretentious, does not talk down at them and is not always the bearer of bad news. Prior to their experience of news via the newsbot, the news for these users was depressing, intimidating and/or irrelevant. The bot, however, made one user "feel less overwhelmed when the morning/evening news arrives" (A15). It framed the news in ways that left some users feeling empowered, because they now knew what was going on in the world "quickly and easily" and in a way that avoided the negative effects of daily news that they had previously experienced and/or perceived. This enabled the bot to promise that the service would "conquer [the user's] FOMO" (fear of missing out), a message delivered when we first activated the bot, directly engaging with what the bot creators recognise as users' emotional needs.

These users respond to the bot because it frames the news for them in ways that are warm, welcoming and personal. One user noted that news items "feel professional yet personal" (A12). By the term "personal" they meant that the bot speaks to their personal/emotional needs, not that they think the bot is speaking to them personally in a way that will enable them to conduct a conversation with the bot.

For the publics that make up the bot's audience, then, the bot signals a new relationship with journalists and journalism. As one user commented:

(I) feel like I can see some curly haired guy called Sid sitting in the ABC offices typing them out. (A12)

It is the personal tone of the bot, crafted by the journalists, that they appreciate and connect with.

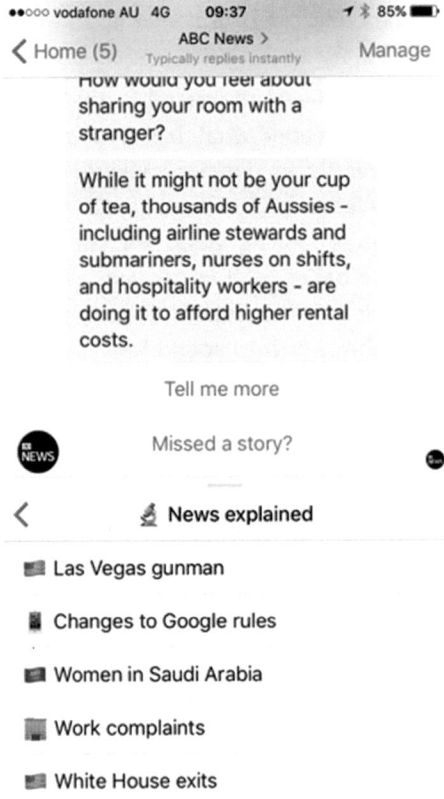

Figure 3. Users are provided with an "Explainer" for the news headlines.

A very human newsbot

In this study, we examined how an ostensibly automated product (the newsbot) is actually constructed through the careful work of humans – in this case journalists who carefully craft entry points into the news in ways that are experienced by at least some of its
users as unpretentious, optimistic and helpful. The delivery of news appears to these
users as just one part of a two-way conversation between themselves and the news
organisation. Users of the bot respond in ways that reflect a new relationship with a
media organisation that they might previously have rejected. The bot's utterances reflect
a change in the tone of the news and in the persona of the journalist. This acceptance of
the news chatbot (and the consequent credibility of its utterances) is achieved through
the use of familiar, informal, colloquial language crafted as part of a conversation with
individual users, rather than through formal announcements or proclamations.

Previous research on Twitter newsbots has defined newsbots as "automated
accounts that participate in news and information dissemination on social networking
platforms" (Lokot and Diakopoulos 2015, 683). However, the new generation of newsbots, as exemplified by the ABC newsbot, introduces fundamental changes to what
newsbots might *do* and *enable* in the relationship between journalists and their audiences. Hoflich argues that robots should be seen in the context of a relationship with
a medium but also as a medium that "mediates". In this case, newsbots are introduced
in the context of social media messaging platforms using a conversational format.

When the newsbot moves into the private, conversational and intimate space of social media messaging platforms (as opposed to the public spaces on these platforms) and adopts a particular persona, it becomes a significant third (person) mediating the relationship between audiences and their public service media organisation.

Changes are not only to the format of news produced for this audience; they are to the tone of the news and the authorial persona presenting it. The newsbots enable an intimate relationship between journalists and at least some of their audiences. For the journalists involved, the bot offers a way to experiment with a new kind of informal, irreverent, conversational style of news and information sharing that represents an evolution of their relationship with their audiences. Journalists, in other words, are practicing a kind of ventriloquism with the bot, and some of the public participates in the ruse because it is entertaining and amusing, and because news is told in a kind of style that they can relate to.

If the ABC newsbot works to connect the public service media organisation and this particular audience, how is this achieved? In the case of the ABC newsbot, we find that new connections are enabled by replacing the journalist with what this section of the audience experiences as an unpretentious, optimistic and helpful journalistic persona that speaks their language and understands their needs. For the audience that uses it, the friendly newsbot often contrasts with their understanding of what they previously thought journalists to be. The public service journalists who operate the bot are, in turn, using the bot to try to reach new audiences by experimenting with a more informal, intimate relationship with ABC users. The supposedly "intelligent" (but in actual fact very much human-crafted) newsbot is the vehicle through which this new relationship is being forged.

In other words, the change to newsbots is the result of the newsbot's design, its method of delivering news via modular dialogic elements that simulate a human conversation, and the ways in which the bot is perceived in terms of personality characteristics by its niche audience. No longer is the newsbot characterised by its ability to disseminate news to a single, monolithic audience. In the ABC newsbot, we see the particular personality of the newsbot forging a trusted relationship with a niche audience who have indicated that they previously did not engage with the news, via changes to the tone and authorial voice of the journalistic persona delivering it.

The ABC newsbot team recognised early on that this audience was dissatisfied with news that they perceived as depressing and that they were intimidated by what the news expected from users. The newsbot team crafted a personality for a bot that is able to achieve what journalists may not be able to achieve as individual professionals. The bot is able to fill in gaps in basic knowledge, provide explainers and insert colloquialisms through the use of humour and satire, while imagining what the audience might say about the news when they share it among friends.

For the ABC, the news chatbot enables them to perform their public information function that both experiments with innovative digital information distribution and targets an audience that did not previously consume news, pushing messages about important public issues and events (about the national budget, about the same sex marriage referendum, about natural disasters in the area) in a way that provides an opportunity to be more readily viewed and talked about. The ABC newsbot, then, fulfils important universality goals for the organisation, potentially bringing new audiences to the public domain. It forges new connections with audiences by re-charting public space. Instead of multiple ways of broadcasting the same news to an audience that gathers in the PSM sphere, these newsbots are comprised of a collection of intimate conversations conducted within the more personal space of the messaging environment. In this way, automation and personalisation features serve to enhance trust in the ABC – at least among those who use (and appreciate) the newsbot.

It is important to recognise, however, that the positive consequences for universality and trust that we currently see in this newsbot are subject to complex relations embedded in the delivery of the newsbot service. Although the ABC focuses a significant amount of attention on its journalistic efforts on third-party platforms such as Facebook, Twitter and YouTube (Levy 2017; Mason 2016; ABC 2017) and sees their connection with third-party providers as a way of advancing universality, this undoubtedly has consequences for the PSM accountability principles. In this case, the ABC is dependent on the private infrastructure of Facebook and ChatFuel. This raises issues relating to data ownership, the tracking and privacy of citizens and audiences' perceptions about the trustworthiness of the companies operating private messaging environments (Lokot and Diakopoulos 2015; Guzman 2017). Such matters will only become more relevant as news is delivered increasingly via smart speakers and controlled by the few global corporations with the expertise, data and resources necessary for leading such developments.

Understanding how public service media organisations are engaging with automation through partnerships with private companies and the effects of such engagement on the relationship between citizens and their public service media organisation is critical in order to ensure that innovations by public service bodies remain closely aligned with the values and goals that they aspire to. Our study has demonstrated the importance of the public's response to novel news formats – particularly in relation to conversational journalism and personalised news. Recognising and respecting the attitudes of citizens who have previously been left out of news consumption is critical in evaluating the democratic value of such developments. But further research is necessary in order to understand the significance of newsbots in terms of the developing relationship between the public and their public service media, particularly as the realm of smart speaker technology expands.

Notes

1. Letters and numbers refer to our numbering scheme for coding anonymised responses.
2. See http://knowyourmeme.com/memes/shut-up-and-take-my-money

Acknowledgements

The authors would like to thank the School of Media and Communication at the University of Leeds and the School of Literature, Arts and Media at the University of Sydney for supporting the Visiting Research Fellow Scheme that enabled this pilot research project. The authors would also like to acknowledge the input of Craig McCosker and Lincoln Archer from ABC News Digital. Finally, thanks to our reviewers for their constructive feedback that proved extremely helpful for improving the article.

Disclosure Statement

There is no potential conflict of interest as part of this research.

ORCID

Heather Ford (iD) http://orcid.org/0000-0002-3500-9772
Jonathon Hutchinson (iD) http://orcid.org/0000-0001-7349-1662

References

ABC. 2016. "ABC Annual Report, 2016." *ABC*, February 21. http://about.abc.net.au/wp-content/uploads/2016/11/ABCAnnualReport2016.pdf

ABC. 2017. "The ABC on Third Party Sites." ABC, December 2. http://about.abc.net.au/wp-content/uploads/2016/07/ABCThirdPartySitesGDE.pdf.

Born, Georgina. 2005. *Uncertain Vision: Birt, Dyke and the Reinvention of the BBC*. London: Random House.

Bradshaw, Paul. 2016. "2016 Was the Year of the Bot — Here's a Brief History of How They Have Been Used in Journalism." *Online Journalism Blog*, December 21. https://onlinejournalismblog.com/2016/12/21/how-bots-came-to-play-a-role-in-journalism-a-brief-history/.

Debrett, Mary. 2010. *Reinventing Public Service Television for the Digital Future*. Bristol: Intellect.

Edelman. 2018. "2018 Edelman Trust Barometer." https://www.edelman.com/trust-barometer.

Flew, Terry. 2011. "Rethinking Public Service Media and Citizenship: Digital strategies for news and current affairs at Australia's Special Broadcasting Service (SBS)." *International Journal of Communication* 5 (2011): 215–232.

Guzman, Andrea L. 2017. "Making AI safe for humans: A conversation with Siri." In Robert W. Gehl & Maria Bakardjieva (Eds.), *Socialbots and their friends: Digital media and the automation of sociality*. London: Routledge.

Höflich, Joachim R. 2013. "Relationships to Social Robots: Towards a Triadic Analysis of Media-oriented Behavior." *Intervalla: Platform for Intellectual Exchange* 1 (1):35–35.

Jakubowicz, Karol. 2007. "Public Service Broadcasting: A Pawn on an Ideological Chessboard." In *Media Between Culture and Commerce*, edited by Els de Bens, 115–150. Chicago: Intellect.

Levy, David. 2017. "The ABC: A Case Study in Updating PSB in Politically Polarised and Cash-Strapped Times." White Paper. Oxford: Reuters Institute for the Study of Journalism. http://reutersinstitute.politics.ox.ac.uk/sites/default/files/2017-07/Levy%20-%20The%20ABC.pdf

Light, Ben, Jean Burgess, and Stefanie Duguay. 2018. "The Walkthrough Method: An Approach to the Study of Apps." *New Media & Society* 20 (3): 881–900. doi: 0.1177/1461444816675438.

Lokot, Tetyana, and Nicholas Diakopoulos. 2015. "News Bots: Automating News and Information Dissemination on Twitter." *Digital Journalism* 4 (6): 682–699.

Marsh, Peter. 2017. "Backstory: Getting Personal on Facebook Messenger." *ABC News Online*, October 7. http://www.abc.net.au/news/about/backstory/digital/2017-10-07/abc-news-getting-personal-in-messenger/8987354

Mason, Max. 2016. "ABC's Michelle Guthrie says Netflix deal allows for quality programming." *Financial Review*, November 16. https://www.afr.com/business/media-and-marketing/tv/abc-md-michelle-guthrie-says-netflix-deal-allows-for-quality-programming-20161116-gsqoe4

McClean, Georgia. 2011. "Multicultural Sociability, Imperfect Forums and Online Participation." *International Journal of Communication* 5: 1649–1668.

Moon, Youngme, and Nass, Clifford. 1996. "How "Real" Are Computer Personalities?: Psychological Responses to Personality Types in Human-Computer Interaction." *Communication Research* 23 (6), 651–674.

Nagy, Peter, and Gina Neff. 2015. "Imagined Affordances: Reconstructing a Keyword for Communication Theory." *Social Media + Society* 1 (2), 1–9.

Newman, Nic, Richard Fletcher, Antonis Kalogeropoulos, David AL Levy, and Rasmus Kleis Nielsen. 2017. *Reuters Institute Digital News Report 2018*. Paris: Reuters Institute for the Study of Journalism.

Newman, Nic, Richard Fletcher, Antonis Kalogeropoulos, David AL Levy, and Rasmus Kleis Nielsen. 2018. *Reuters Institute Digital News Report 2018*. Paris: Reuters Institute for the Study of Journalism.

Pink, Sarah, Heather Horst, John Postill, Larissa Hjorth, Tania Lewis, and Jo Tacchi. 2015. *Digital Ethnography: Principles and Practice*. New York: SAGE.

Seaver, Nick. 2017. "Algorithms as Culture: Some Tactics for the Ethnography of Algorithmic Systems." *Big Data & Society Advance online publication* 1–12.

Sundar, S. Shyam, and Clifford Nass. 2001. "Conceptualizing Sources in Online News." *Journal of Communication* 51 (1), 52–72.

Thurman, Neil, Judith Moeller, Natali Helberger, and Damian Trilling. 2018. "My Friends, Editors, Algorithms, and I." *Digital Journalism, Advance online publication* 1–23.

Tolliday, Rob. 2017. "Sensis Social Media Report 2017." *Sydney Sensis*, October 28 2018. https://www.sensis.com.au/about/our-reports/sensis-social-media-report

Tracey, Michael. 1998. "Principles of Public Service Broadcasting." Chap. 3 in *Decline and Fall of Public Service Broadcasting*. London: Oxford University Press.

Van de Bulck, Hilde, and Halvard Moe. 2017. "Public Service Media, Universality and Personalisation Through Algorithms: Mapping strategies and exploring dilemmas." *Media, Culture & Society* 40 (6): 875–892.

Van Dijck, Jose, & Thomas Poell. 2015. "Making Public Television Social? Public Service Broadcasting and the Challenges of Social Media." *Television and New Media* 16 (2): 148–164.

Verma, Vaibhav. 2018. "This 50-Time Chatbot Designer Shares the Basics of Creating Engaging Chatbots." *Tech in Asia*, February 9, 2018. https://www.techinasia.com/talk/50-time-chatbot-designer-basics-engaging-chatbots.

Public Service Chatbots: Automating Conversation with BBC News

Bronwyn Jones ⓘ and Rhianne Jones ⓘ

ABSTRACT
Automation of journalistic tasks is growing with the development of increasingly sophisticated software for newsgathering, production, and distribution. Bots are one form of algorithmic technology that has found a place in the modern newsroom, with chatbots leading the way as news organisations seek to attract new audiences using conversational forms of journalism. Recent advances in artificial intelligence (AI) and machine learning (ML) have fuelled increasing experimentation with machine autonomy and there has been much hyperbole in the press about the extent and impact of this on journalism. Looking at on-the-ground trials in audience-facing bots at the UK's largest public broadcaster, we find a significantly more restricted picture. News bots at The BBC to-date have been basic, do not use ML, and have rarely been integrated into news production. The organisation is laying groundwork for development of more interactive news formats with an increasingly conversational tone and individual mode of address as part of a strategy for increased personalisation, which is likely to involve growing levels of ML. In the process, bots are reconfiguring working practices and infrastructure, posing new editorial and technical challenges, and redefining relationships with audiences. We discuss the implications of this for public service media.

What's a Chatbot? Let's Talk

Following a rapid growth in the development of automated software agents known as bots since 2016, the news industry is increasingly exploring how they can be put to use for news production and distribution. Bots are just one of the many examples of automated software in journalism that are opening up opportunities for creating content at scale, at previously unattainable speed, and in a customised or individually personalised manner. They form part of what has been termed "robot," "automated" and "algorithmic journalism" (Carlson 2015; Caswell and Dörr 2017; Dörr 2015; Montal and Reich 2017) alongside other computational approaches such as fact-checking (Graves 2018), which build on the foundations of computer-assisted reporting (Flew et al. 2012). Chatbots – a subset of bots that have caught the imagination of news publishers – are software programmes designed to converse with a human through natural language (Gorwa and Guilbeault 2018). To-date, most have been text-based, messenger-type interfaces, although innovation in voice interaction has grown recently (Barot 2017; Newman 2018, 34). This study illuminates the state of play in news bot innovation at the end of 2017 in the UK's largest public service broadcaster, the BBC. It analyses how the research and development arm of the BBC has developed and employed bots, including chatbots, for news and the implications of this for public service journalism.

Chatbots are part of a wider group of Conversational User Interfaces (CUIs), which mimic everyday human dialogue in the form of a conversation, usually by employing informal and friendly language. They range from very basic and rule-based to more intelligent or "smart" bots driven by artificial intelligence (AI) and machine learning (ML) technologies[1] (e.g., Jones 2018). The most basic chatbots are automated (or semi-automated) but not autonomous – they play out only the functions that are inscribed into them by a programmer, using pre-scripted and pre-organised inputs. They reply to humans by traversing pre-coded decision trees using rules, thus simulating interaction but never actually deviating from pre-scripted narrative structures. A familiar sight in customer service, they are also now common in news and information distribution (Lokot and Diakopoulos 2015). ML-driven chatbots are, however, becoming more widespread. Most use systems that convert unstructured human input (speech, text, or gestures) into machine-readable form, apply Natural Language Processing (NLP), and translate the output using Natural Language Generation (NLG) to mimic human speech/text. An oft-cited example of an ML-powered chatbot is Microsoft's Tay, a Twitter bot which learnt from users' interactions and became notable as much for going awry as for its innovative technology – after it was shut down because of obscene and inflammatory tweets (Neff and Nagy 2016). Chatbots are, however, just one example of a much wider set of automated software agents known as bots, a term derived from "robots." Fundamentally, a bot is a software programme that completes an automated task. The term has become a buzzword in the news industry (Barot 2015), and AI- and ML-driven bots are only now beginning to play a part in news gathering, production, and distribution (Lokot and Diakopoulos 2015; Thurman, Dörr, and Kunert 2017). They are part of a broader growth in computational journalism (Flew et al. 2012) using digital and networked technology in the newsroom and fit within a recent turn to data (Coddington 2015).

As powerful mediators of social interaction online, social media platforms such as Twitter, Facebook and Instagram have become hubs of activity for people developing and deploying bots for various purposes. Scholars have looked at the implications for sociality of the relationship between humans and these "software processes that are programmed to appear to be human-generated within the context of social networking sites" (Gehl and Bakardjieva 2016, 2). They have explored use of such bots for news and information dissemination (Lokot and Diakopoulos 2015) but also for public opinion manipulation and computational propaganda (Woolley and Howard 2017), including spamming, harassment, and falsifying trends and consensus. Lokot and Diakopoulos argue that in paying attention to the more nefarious uses of bots, critics have overlooked the "potentially positive and beneficial utility of automated news and information sharing," including how bots may "contribute to positive effects in the public media sphere if employed ethically and conscientiously" (2015: 3).

It is clear that bot development has been uneven across the news industry, and unhelpful hyperbole about not only the risks and dangers but also the benefits of bots has been characteristic of the media attention they garner. Nuanced analysis of how news production is being reshaped by the shift toward computational and algorithmic journalism is therefore vital (Anderson 2012), and any such analysis must recognise the co-construction of technology and society and approach technologies as complex, socio-material phenomena (Gillespie, Boczkowski, and Foot 2014). What this requires is a recognition that technologies are not neutral and that they exert influence through materiality but are also enacted in material-discursive practices (Bucher 2018) – a process of mutual shaping in situated practice. In the case of developing new technology for journalism, the shaping of what is desirable for the technology, and of the conditions that determine what is possible for the technology, is being done by engineers and developers alongside journalists and managers, who all bring values and priorities from their specific organisational and cultural backgrounds. As Lewis and Westlund argue, a socio-technical emphasis in the study of institutional news production, which takes into consideration "the full range of actors, actants, and audiences engaged in cross-media news work activities" (2015: 19) is in order. In this vein, a body of research has honed in on increasing collaboration between technologists and journalists (Nielsen 2012; Lewis and Usher 2013, 2014, 2016). Lewis and Usher foreground how programmers and their ethics are assuming a greater role in the journalistic field (2016) but also how the fusion between the social worlds of journalism and technology requires "significant, coordinated, and sustained effort" as the "barriers between each field's understanding of the other are real" (2014: 9). Bots, then, should not be viewed as technologies separate from their contexts of production and use. They are best analysed by locating them in – or conceiving of them as – a socio-technical assemblage that includes hardware, software, techniques and practices but also guidelines, goals and values.

Underpinned by this conceptual approach, this paper hones in on bots in the public service news sector using the BBC as a case study to explore the current state of play and potential implications. Bots raise specific questions for public service media (PSM) (Sørenson and Hutchinson 2018). The BBC is an important case study site as it is the UK's largest broadcast news organisation and a public service broadcaster with a remit to develop technology for the public good. Furthermore, its secure funding model underpins a comparatively well-resourced research and development department that is not bound by a commercial agenda and has a long history of innovating in media technologies in the public interest. The BBC is understandably highly focussed on the work of creating these new computational tools for the newsroom and this paper takes a much-needed step back from the day-to-day practical concerns with usability to critically assess these attempts.

Related Work

News Bots: Automating the Production Process

Bots have existed for almost as long as computers, and the term could technically encompass a diverse array of applications and programmes employed by newsrooms. However, it is more commonly used to describe software agents with a recognisable audience interface through which an audience/user interacts – not those agents that work solely behind the scenes. Some bots are journalist-facing and others audience-facing, though they can be both. Early bots often performed singular tasks, but many bots, or more accurately assemblages (DeLanda 2006) of bots, perform numerous interlinked tasks and straddle these categories. Their role in the production process can be further broken down according to the functions they perform: news gathering, production and distribution.

Newsgathering bots search, monitor, retrieve, alert or nudge. For example, BuzzFeed's Buzzbot for Facebook Messenger, which collected photos and stories from users at a Republican Convention in 2016, WNYC's bot that monitored federal court documents for updates, and the Associated Press bot that tracks data breaches (You 2015). These bots may flag up anomalies they find in data so journalists can investigate, or, in the case of those being developed at the Duke Reporters Lab, they may identify and suggest claims to be fact-checked (McKinney 2018). Production bots collate, analyse, create, edit, or visualise and, increasingly, they automate news writing. An early and oft-cited example of this was the LA Times Quakebot developed in 2014 to monitor earthquake magnitude and automatically write up reports before emailing an editor to alert them – both gathering and producing news. More recently, bots such as the Washington Post's Heliograph use templates written by humans combined with a source of structured data to construct stories (Keohane 2017). There has been significant investment in this area by, amongst others, Google, which in 2017 granted the UK's Press Association news agency £622,000 for its Reporters and Data and Robots (Radar) project (Ponsford 2017). Finally, distribution bots (re-)publish/broadcast, share and respond. For example, automated live tweeting of information from structured data sets by bots is commonplace around the world, e.g., for cricket games, local air quality alerts, and election results at the Hindustan Times (Wang 2017). Bots have also widely been used by both legacy organisations such as the Washington Post and digitally native providers like Quartz for news recommender systems to suggest content based on user preferences or activity.

Importantly, distribution is where chatbots and other CUIs have been most commonly applied. They are often designed with the goal of improving audience interaction and engagement with news organisations and their content by creating conversational formats that deviate from the more static, traditional modes commonly associated with journalism. For example, the New York Times Politics Bot for Facebook Messenger aimed to "combine the intimacy and charm of a human with the utility of a bot" during the Trump campaign (Phelps 2017). It sent out daily alerts with election forecasts but also hosted conversations every morning scripted by one of their political reporters, with which 25,000 people interacted (ibid.).

Conversational Journalism and the Public Service Context

News organisations, including the BBC, are responding to fragmenting audiences and rising competition from mobile, social, and digital media (Picard 2010; Anderson 2012). Whether the aim is the commercial one of more advertising revenue or the democratic one of an informed citizenry and a healthy public sphere, both commercial and public service news organisations are under pressure to reach new and under-served audiences. Like many PSM, the BBC hopes forms of digital innovation will help attract younger audiences whose changing consumption patterns reveal a shift to online and on-demand viewing (van Es 2017) and mobile and social media platforms. Sehl, Cornia, and Nielsen (2016) pinpoint three core interrelated challenges for PSM: 1) retaining younger audiences, 2) the shift to personal and mobile media and, 3) developing effective ways of delivering public service news via third-party platforms including search engines, social media, video-hosting sites, and messaging apps. These challenges have pushed PSM to publish on off-site platforms such as social media and messaging apps (ibid.) using CUIs designed to make the news more engaging and better suited to these platforms.

News chatbots exemplify a rise in "conversational journalism" approaches that aim to achieve just this by engaging people who are traditionally not users of news through the leveraging of new technologies to create formats that are informal, interactive and novel. The BBC is aiming to cultivate a youth market for "accurate but accessible" news, stating: "Our belief is that a less formal and more conversational style will be less off putting to younger readers" (BBC News Labs 2018). The ambition to create new forms of dialogue with news audiences pre-dates CUIs and has roots in broader changes to the relationship between audiences and journalism in an Internet age characterised by digital technologies that "shift the direction of communication from a one-to-many broadcasting system to a many-to-many conversational system" (Anderson 2011, 532). Recent developments in Human-Machine Communication (HMC) (see Guzman 2018; and Lewis, Guzman and Schmidt 2019) usefully move beyond conceptualising communication "as a human process through machines" to focus on "the creation of meaning among humans and machines" (Guzman 2018: 1).

The growth in news bots is also happening within larger economic processes shaping the journalism industry. Technologies like bots, which promise efficiency savings and can demonstrate increased engagement of younger audiences, resonate in public service newsrooms facing budget reductions, and they work to allay fears of declining relevance amongst future generations. Bots also represent shifts in newsroom culture, particularly towards personalisation (Helberger 2015) and the increasing measurement and tracking of audiences (Carlson 2018). The move to algorithmic personalisation in public service journalism has sparked debates focussed on either the risk it may pose to PSM values like universality, access and diversity (Bennet 2018, Sørenson and Hutchinson 2018) or the opportunities it may bring to promote diversity of supply and stimulate diversity exposure (Helberger 2015). For Sørenson and Hutchinson (2018) the five main challenges PSM face are: 1) balancing popularity and distinctiveness, 2) diversity of exposure to programming, 3) transparency of the logic underlying recommendations, 4) user sovereignty and, 5) the issue of dependence on, or independence from, commercial intermediaries. Such debates foreground difficulties in this context for the PSM "mandate to serve a full citizenry of a diverse nation while simultaneously creating common culture" (Lotz 2018, 47), facilitated through the shared media experience (Scannell 2005). Helberger argues that PSM today are "at a crossroad where they must decide how personal, persuasive, and responsive their relationship to the audience should be, and what safeguards are needed to preserve autonomy, privacy, and the public sphere" (2015: 1325).

Research Questions and Methods

This paper asks three research questions:

1. How is the BBC experimenting with bots in news?
2. What are the implications for news production and distribution?
3. What impact might this have on public service journalism?

It answers these questions by compiling a case study of news bots at the BBC, including those actually deployed into news products and those in development and testing. Importantly, we employ a mutual shaping conceptual framework that views technologies as socio-material artefacts that are constructed in situated practice. We use this approach to analyse journalists' and technologists' accounts of bots during the crucial development and testing period, during which meaning is being inscribed into, and ascribed to, the technology and the technology begins influencing, and being influenced by, journalistic practice. It is important to create site-specific understanding of how computational journalism is developing within particular organisations and sectors of the industry, and PSM are an underdeveloped area of study. As Young and Hermida point out, analysing how this technological change "combines with and emerges out of existing norms, routines, relationships, and social and material contexts," we can "discern how digital media both constitute and are constituted by practice and innovation" (2014: 381).

Initial scoping research by the authors, who are a BBC journalist and senior technology researcher[2] indicated the BBC had in total developed eleven bots – eight in-house and three outsourced to external companies. We chose to focus on the eight in-house bots, which were created by units within the BBC's Research and Development (BBC R&D) department – seven by BBC News Labs (charged with driving innovation for BBC News) and one by Connected Studio (which brings wider networks together to generate ideas for future technology).

We propose an analytical approach that interrogates how key decision-makers and actors conceive of and describe technologies, how they document and evaluate them, and how they create and appropriate narratives about them. Accordingly, we used two methods – semi-structured qualitative interviews and document analysis – and employed an iterative research process for thematic analysis based on both inductive and deductive approaches. Purposive sampling was used to identify interviewees, with the expert knowledge of the authors who work in the research context being leveraged to make a situational judgement about which individuals should be selected. Through this process we identified twelve expert interviewees. They were key actors involved in technical development (3) and in editorial production (5), and leads/strategists/managers (4), who were able to place developments in the context of broader work in voice, machine learning and the BBC's personalisation strategy. During the semi-structured interviews, conducted between October 2017 and February 2018, we asked questions relating to five areas formulated in reference to the literature, our analytical framework, and our research questions. These focussed on critical points in the life-cycle of the technology in order to draw out what influenced the material and social construction of the bots. They were: motivation for developing the bots;

technical capabilities; process of development; editorial and ethical challenges; and criteria used to evaluate and measure success.

We also conducted analysis of internal documentation, including project outlines, progress reports, and evaluations, access to which was provided by interviewees both before and after interviewing. This was supplemented with publicly accessible information, including press releases and blogs. An iterative research process allowed us to identify a sample of relevant documents from those provided and bring them together with those we had independently identified. We then coded the interview data and documentation in two stages, firstly according to the five themes previously identified and then subsequently for other emerging themes. We triangulated the data and cross-referenced analysis from each method to seek validation of findings through corroboration (Denzin 1970). Using the data from these two methods, we developed case study accounts of each bot and highlighted six themes that we situate in the organisational context and that also address wider debates in the practitioner and academic community.

We begin by providing an overview of BBC news bots and then outline six themes through which this technology can be understood in the public service context. Finally, based on that analysis, we outline future opportunities and challenges regarding CUIs in public service news at the BBC and more broadly.

Findings

Overview of Bots

BBC R&D, led by BBC News Labs, developed and ran live versions of eight bots between 2015 and 2017[3] primarily for social media sites and messenger services. Grouped by platform, four were on Twitter, two on Facebook, one on Telegram and one within articles on the BBC website. Five of the eight trials were described as chatbots, which engaged in some level of interactive, two-way dialogue or used conversational tone for chat-like interactions with users, while the other three were simply one-way distribution bots publishing information. The forms of interaction designed into the five chatbots were varied, including a Q&A, a quiz, a subscription service for push notifications and a news summary service. Most of the bots re-used previously vetted and published BBC content with a small amount of re-formatting, but two bots involved tailoring or writing bespoke material.

Third parties also developed three other bots for BBC News, namely the BBC Politics Brexit bot and 2017 General Election bot for Facebook Messenger and the NewsChatta bot for WeChat. This paper concentrates on the eight bots developed in-house but also discusses issues raised by outsourcing bot development to third parties and the emerging organisational strategy for mitigating associated risks.

The findings are organised into six overarching themes: 1) Terminology and levels of intelligence, 2) Conversational formats, 3) Working practices and organisational structures, 4) Locating automation and the journalist-in-the-loop, 5) Evaluation and measures of success, 6) Third parties and outsourcing. These themes illuminate ways in which the journalists and technologists are seeking to make sense of bots and apply them for public service news work, shedding light on how they understand the technology, act upon the possibilities it offers, and frame the decisions they make. Theme one shows that definitions of technology had yet to stabilise or formalise. Theme two illustrates how wider changes across media from one- to two-way inter-action and in favour of individualised and personalised formats were being employed by the organisation to justify the benefits of developing bots in line with the popular conversational tone prevalent on social media. It indicates that a shared organisational narrative – voiced by both technologists and journalists – was being marshalled around the value of bots in PSM for improving reach and engagement, particularly with young people. Theme three describes how technologies under construction inter-play with existing professional practice. Theme four indicates that the gains bots enable through automating news delivery are valued by technologists and journalists alike but by the latter only if they do not come at the expense of editorial control and oversight. Meanwhile, theme five explores how limited evaluation methods made it difficult to gauge public service value despite this being a stated aim. Finally, theme six highlights the significance of involving non-PSM actors in the construction of tech-nology and explicates the risks of outsourcing bots.

Terminology and Levels of Intelligence

Definitional boundaries had not yet stabilised and understandings were still being contested and under construction. Initial analysis revealed that no clear common def-inition of a bot was used consistently across the organisation and that a variety of terms were used interchangeably to denote an automated software agent, including chatbot, conversational user interface, agent, algorithm and skill. Gorwa and Guilbeault (2018) also recognise this lack of definitional clarity and foreground the problems it generates for industry, academia and policy. BBC developers described fol-lowing the naming conventions of the platforms for which they were developing soft-ware. For example, when working with Google's Alexa, they termed what could otherwise be referred to as a bot as a "skill." This convention for inheriting proprietary platforms' descriptions was prevalent among both technologists and editorial staff and framed how they thought about the technologies with which they were working. One factor that became clear, however, was that only bots that were text-based and audi-ence-facing were consistently given the moniker "bot." It was these that were chosen for analysis.

Among the eight bots identified (see Table 1), the first thing to note is that they did not use AI, ML, text-to-speech technology or NLG/NLP. Their level of "intelligent" conversation was therefore limited. They were very basic and relied on decision-tree structures to underpin their automated activity. One project lead described them as "small, lightweight, decision-tree" bots for which the content was curated by journal-ists and compared them to "a choose your own adventure story" (I-10). They were used primarily for content distribution and to gather material by searching internal pre-prepared sources, i.e., existing online articles, pre-prepared script, or internal data. There was in fact very limited modification of existing content. In these trials, the Twitter bots (UK Election 2015, EU Referendum 2016, US Election 2016 and UK Election 2017) functioned solely as an alternative distribution platform. The Telegram

Table 1. Key features and functions of bot case studies.

	Platform (BBC Online, Social Media, Messenger)	News Function (All forms of distribution)	Source Material (BBC, non-BBC)	Chatbot? (Interactive/conversational mode of address)
Newsbot	BBC Online	A chatbot placed at the end of select online articles that followed a multiple-choice question and answer format using pre-scripted material.	BBC	Yes
Mundo Bot	Social/Messenger (*Facebook*)	Subscription service. Automated push updates twice daily, linking to BBC Spanish language news site, BBC Mundo. Manual push of breaking news to subscribers.	BBC	Yes
Quiz Bot	Social/Messenger (*Facebook*)	A quiz chatbot run on Facebook and in an online article using pre-scripted material.	BBC	Yes
UK Election Bot 2015	Social (*Twitter*)	Allowed users to give the first half of their postcode in order to provide the closest matching constituency result and a link to information on the BBC website.	BBC	Yes
EU Ref Bot 2016	Social (*Twitter*)	Tweeted out EU Referendum results for each counting area by gathering results in real-time from BBC in-house system and combining with TV graphics.	BBC	No
US Election Bot 2016	Social (*Twitter*)	As above but adapted for the 2016 US Election (also tweeted in Spanish).	BBC	No
UK Election Bot 2017	Social (*Twitter*)	As above but adapted for the 2017 UK Election.	BBC	No
BBC Uzbek Bot	Messenger (*Telegram*)	Subscription service. Uses existing RSS feeds to send latest headlines/summaries/entire articles in a private message as a way to get news into a country where the BBC is blocked.	BBC	Yes

Uzbek bot summarised and distributed existing BBC articles, while the Facebook Messenger BBC Mundo bot enabled subscription to push notifications. Only the Facebook Messenger quiz format and in-article chatbots necessitated re-wording text and creating connections between pieces of content to pre-format potential pathways through the non-linear text.

This basic functionality was recognised by the News Labs team who described their work as scratching the surface of what could be achieved. When making the BBC Mundo bot, they started with the premise that users "don't always know how to interact" with an AI-powered smart bot and cited user "concern over black box algorithms and biased distribution platforms" as a motivation for giving users "clear, simple commands to control the news they receive" (He 2016). Journalists similarly pointed to the bots' limitations, explaining, for example: "It doesn't have AI – it doesn't learn … it just has selective answers, for example saying 'sorry, I don't understand' etcetera" (I-2), and "It was an early try" and "was a bit clunky" (I-1). Some expressed a desire for higher functionality, including a "need to improve communication skills, be clever, give more possibilities … I want to improve it, give the user more options." (I-2). This limited functionality is not dissimilar to that of chatbots developed by other PSM, such as Australia's ABC Newsbot.

It is clear that AI/ML-driven bots have not yet been incorporated into BBC News and that a cautious approach to bot capabilities has been adopted but that the organisation is learning from the challenges faced during these experiments to refine the format with a view to applying ML technologies. Prototypes built for hackathons have been more ambitious, for example using text-to-speech and experimenting with multilingual API services, but these had not been trialled for BBC News.

Conversational Formats

The main area of innovation was in chatbots, which exemplify a move towards more individualised and personalised formats in news by way of user interfaces designed to mimic conversation. The five chatbot trials reveal experimentation with new technical capabilities and editorial approaches with the explicit goal of creating a more personal tone for news and an individual mode of address, aimed at increasing reach and engaging less traditional news audiences, particularly the young. BBC developers intended chatbots to be more *conversational, personal, and interactive* – departing from traditional linear and formal modes of news presentation and distribution. The experiments were used to "measure public enthusiasm for chat-like interactions" (Document 1). One project lead said: "there's been a convergence around personalisation, customisation, and interaction" (I-10). Journalists conceived of the conversational approach as a means to an end – to get more people viewing their work. One explained: "I think we need to experiment with new ways of telling stories and if it's allowing you to explain quite technical things in a more accessible way, that's clearly important for our job" (I-1), whilst another said: "It's a novelty … it goes to another platform that is quite shareable so content can potentially reach many people" (I-2). This indicates a shared organisational narrative around the value of bots in PSM for improving reach and engagement.

The descriptor "conversational" was used by developers rather than journalists to describe two interlinked elements of the bots – the tone of voice that deviated from formal news presentation and the interactive back-and-forth through which the bot would respond to user prompts. The Q&A and quiz chatbots exemplify hybridised news formats whereby a tried and tested format is adapted to fit the capabilities, style and tone of social media and/or messenger apps. Even though the Q&A was placed inside conventional BBC online stories, it was designed to feel like a conversation instead of a linear explainer, sidebar, or fact box, greeting users with an informal: "Hello, I'm an experiment from BBC News Labs." Only the Uzbek bot diverged from this design goal, driven as it was by the need to provide BBC news to an audience who were blocked from accessing it by national authorities. However, it too adopts a deliberately conversational mode of address consistent with the Telegram messaging platform for which it is built. Whilst not mainstream, the bots sit within the BBC's push towards becoming a "pioneer" of personalisation with a publicly stated ambition to provide a "more personal and relevant" BBC that is more "about you" (Hall 2017). This only recently became viable through the move to a sign-in model, marking a significant change in the BBC's relationship with its audience. BBC news chatbots currently tailor the information they provide to users in a way more akin to explicit customisation than implicit personalisation (Zuiderveen Borgesius et al. 2016, 3). At the stage of development encountered during this study, the level of personalisation was extremely limited. For example, the BBC Mundo bot addressed users by name and varied the expressions used in messages to make the messages seem more like human conversation but then served each subscriber the same selection of news, working in a way that resembled the traditional broadcast function despite being accessed through a personal device. Though viewed by developers and journalists as a more interactive way to deliver news, the bots, in some circumstances, have new forms of passivity built into their structure. For example, the BBC Mundo bot and the Uzbek bot push information to users, removing any need to search it out, which might preclude serendipitous content discovery.

The BBC is re-thinking and redefining how audiences/publics can engage with public service news. Chatbots were designed specifically to foster new relationships that feel more like an informal one-to-one dialogue as opposed to a more formal public broadcast. As one journalist said: "the more friendly, the better" (I-1). Early research indicated that more people engaged with a bot when it was presented in the form of a person as "an expert" rather than as the organisation or simply a bot (Document 1). Chatbots on social media and messenger services blur the boundaries between public spheres of news and private, personal interactions. One project lead said private messenger services have fostered an environment where "you expect people to talk back to you" (I-10). In doing so, they make public news consumption akin to a personal and private experience, by design. This feeds into wider concerns around the collapse of public and private boundaries brought about by social media (Baym and boyd 2012) and around algorithmic personalisation in public service media (Bennet 2018; Helberger 2015; Sørenson and Hutchinson 2018). A personal message from the BBC arriving in the user's Facebook inbox is notably different to the user landing on the same BBC website index pages as other people and being exposed to the wider content on those pages. PSM understandably want to leverage the new opportunities offered by social media but also need to be cautious of ways platform logics might compromise public value (van Dyke and Poell 2015, 149). Developers recognised potential conflicts in making journalism conversational "while maintaining trust – off platform and on" (I-6).

Working Practices and Organisational Structures

The case studies show new forms of collaborative working between editorial and technical teams – a trend found more widely across the news media industry (Holton and Belair-Gagnon 2018; Nielsen 2012; Lewis and Usher 2013, 2014, 2016). Both editorial and technical teams commissioned the bots, however, there was a clear partitioning of responsibilities between developer and journalist, and output remained under editorial control, revealing how bot technology interacts with existing structures of professional practice. Editorial teams proposed the idea for six of the bots, while the two Facebook Messenger bots were suggested by developers, indicating that both editorial needs or desires and technical opportunities are driving bot innovation. Particularly in the early stages, developers and journalists would work together closely – uncommon in the newsroom. For example, the reporter who worked with the first Twitter bot, and called it "quite hacky" and "improvised," described how he sat up all night through the election: "It was me, a developer, and a laptop … If there are editorial changes, I can make them or if anything breaks down, the developer can rewrite the programme" (I-4).

Whilst working on these bots, journalists had to learn new skills and either take time out of their usual working routines or modify them. Changing work practices around the introduction of new technologies is not uncommon in news as journalists are regularly required to revise their skills in the light of institutional, economic, and technological change (Willnat, Weaver, and Choi 2013). As Powers notes, although evolving journalistic work processes are not new, they often force "new tasks on reporters and editors alike" (2012: 27). New tasks in these experiments included, for example, monitoring the performance of a live bot, responding to audience enquiries, and writing into new production software. Studies looking at more technically advanced conversational technology, such as natural language generation, in journalism (Dörr 2015) have pointed to journalists "migrating from a direct to an indirect role" (Napoli 2014, 350). Journalists working with the BBC bots continued to play a key role in the editorial and creative process, though work with bots remained only a small part of their job.

Journalists reported altered workflows – particularly having to set aside time to learn how to set up and work with the bots – but some considered this a part of their role and weighed it in relation to the benefits the bot brings. For example, the Mundo Facebook Messenger bot journalist noted an increase in his work – "It was a lot of work, I had to develop different scenarios, work iteratively with developers" – remarking on the process of "sending, reviewing and amending content" alongside technical development (I-2). This is in part because chatbots impose different requirements to traditional editorial creative practice, as a more modular form of content is needed to fit the technical format. Though the content creation work is not entirely new (e.g., Q&As already exist in linear formats in news), content needs to be further transformed to support the appearance of an unfolding dialogue. In order to get journalists on board, developers produced guidelines and advice for non-linear storytelling, including, for example, the importance of allowing the user to "stop at any point" and of leaving "no dead ends" (I-10). This exemplifies the impact of computational forms of journalism which necessitate content that can be easily queried, traversed and re-assembled according to computational logics as part of the trend to individualise and personalise media. However, bots were not always seen as placing an increasing demand on time. The Newsbot journalist said the content for the bot "took the same, if not less, time to create" as "the Q&As the BBC already runs" and was "more engaging" (I-1). A project lead explained that bot testing has led to "informal groups of journalists interested in bots now," and new positions have been created that fuse editorial and technical skills, such as a Senior Journalist role as Bot Development Producer.

Locating Automation and the Journalist-in-the-Loop

Bots were valued by technologists and journalists alike for their role in distributing news but journalists were clear that this should not come at the expense of editorial control and oversight of content. The role of the bots in the news production process was limited to distribution and a small amount of processing (i.e., re-formatting). The gathering of information and initial creation of news remained in the hands of the journalist. Moreover, only two bots had what can be described as bespoke material made for them. The more creative part of the journalistic process, i.e., the knowledge work, therefore remained in the purview of the human. One project lead explained that "it [the content and bot script] is all curated. All written by journalists." Journalists additionally felt the need to maintain oversight over the published product. For instance, the editorial lead of the Twitter EU Referendum bot remarked sitting up all night to "watch the updates go live" in order to monitor output and "work out what to do when there was a mistake in terms of corrections" (I-4). This suggests that with the benefits of scalability, i.e., the ability to increase the scale of the audience, comes a desire to maintain editorial control and ensure the automated tasks performed by the bot are subject to quality control. It highlights the perceived importance, particularly as automation in bots increases, of having a "journalist-in-the-loop."

When journalists were asked about their views on more technically sophisticated conversational bots, they acknowledged this needed "more thought" and expressed concerns about "accountability" and "editorial balance," and the need "to get the balance of automation and curation right" (I-1). The in-article Newsbot journalist, for example, warned that if the bot was to be used more widely or on topics with polarised views such as politics, then "we should spend time thinking about which questions are put first" and therefore most likely to be accessed, and asked, "are you offering a balance?" (I-1), adding that he thinks it is crucial to always have editorial oversight. If chatbots with more algorithmic complexity are developed to tell a full news story (e.g., in the form of a "conversation" through a messaging app), they would have to ensure that the core elements needed for an editorially robust and balanced report are presented to all users despite varying user journeys. Furthermore, this suggests that if chatbots become more common, changes to workflow and potentially the creation of new roles may be required for oversight. This was a point made by BBC technology strategists who were thinking about how to manage the step change from small scale and ad hoc experiments to what they describe as a more scalable, consistent and resilient approach that would support an integrated chatbot ecosystem. This finding exemplifies a challenge for public service journalism: preserving control over the final outputs of an editorial process (as was possible with a standardised broadcast) when there are multiple variations (afforded by personalised news, enabled by automation).

As conversations become more "intelligent" (e.g., employing NLP and capable of becoming more implicitly and highly personalised), issues around balance, universality, diversity, accountability and transparency etc. are likely to become more pressing and pronounced, while at the same time there is a risk of their becoming more concealed (e.g., behind algorithmic decision-making or voice interfaces). The amalgamation of algorithmic processes, audience data and semantic markup of content that enables personalised or responsive conversations will take place behind an interface, which, unless due process is in place, will make scrutiny of when, why and to whom content is shown increasingly difficult. The BBC has been discussing these issues broadly across its application of ML (O'Donnell 2017; BBC 2017).

Evaluation and Measures of Success: What Makes a Good Bot?

Evaluation during trial periods of prototype technologies plays an important role in justifying their continued development and use. However, methods for determining the success of bots were limited and made it difficult to gauge public service value despite this being a stated aim. There were no clear criteria for measuring value and success across the trials, yet these evaluations play an important role in informing the organisation's understanding of the potential of bot technology. One technologist said she would ask "can we get something technically up and running?" and then "did we learn anything?" (I-7). Across the case studies there was no systematic gathering of comparable statistics, comprehensive application of analytics or common instruments for measuring success, meaning evaluation lacked common criteria for deciding whether a bot experiment was successful and whether it had public value. One manager said public service values were "built into everything we do" and come into the team's thinking "right at the beginning" of any project (I-11). However, the only consistent criterion prioritised and applied to all trials was technical: did the bots perform the task they were supposed to and were there any bugs or problems? This is perhaps unsurprising given the remit in R&D concerns the technical side of innovation. The manager explained that for each bot he would ask, "does it increase engagement and reach, especially with underserved audiences?" (I-11) – a central tenet of public service provision, with underserved audiences including, amongst others, the young and black and minority ethnic communities. Methods for assessing how well some of the bots performed did include audience engagement in terms of "reach" and "clicks," but metrics were not detailed enough to indicate whether the bots actually appealed to these target audiences or helped with their comprehension of the subject matter. Those involved in development acknowledged a need for improved measures and metrics to evaluate if the bots "add value" for public service news (I-11, I-7).

Members of editorial staff were asked for feedback – sometimes as short written reports or verbally. Developers and journalists put different weights on aspects used to evaluate success, with the former more focussed on whether/how efficiently the bots performed their assigned function. The latter – perhaps often taking for granted that the technology should work – focussed on the impact on their workflow and whether this impact, if cumbersome, was outweighed by the benefits they assumed the bot brought for audience reach and engagement. For example, the reporter working on the in-article Newsbot said it was "very difficult to measure success from such a small trial" but that, from an editorial perspective, "the primary measure for me would be longer engagement time… if they kept clicking" (I-1). He added: "It needs to pass two tests: Add something for the reader, which it did, and be realistic for the journalists, which with some reservations, it did" (I-1). It was important for him that bots in future should "free us up to do other things" that require journalistic skill by taking care of routine and repetitive tasks, a view found in other studies of automation in news (Van Dalen 2012). Developers, meanwhile, considered that "measuring the usefulness" was "not within the scope of the experiment" as they were looking to gauge "enthusiasm" for the bots (Document 1). It is important to note that both journalists and developers were making some assumptions about the success of the bots with the audience. Audience attitudes towards, and experiences of, the bots, were not formally or comprehensively assessed, and nor were the implications for journalistic workflow.

The lack of formalised benchmarks for determining what success in a public service context would look like meant it was difficult to determine not only how each bot performed in comparison to the others but also what the wider public value of chatbots in journalism over other formats might be. This is an area where ambitions were stated but no rigorous assessment made of the extent to which those ambitions were met. For example, one project lead said bots should be about "relationship building" with the audience, getting them "engaged and developing trust over time" and giving a person "agency" to "follow their own paths" (I-10). Limited research at this stage of development can have wider implications as developers risk misunderstanding the impact of novel formats and technologies on editorial staff, audiences and public service journalism. Given the increasingly important role of technology in the delivery of PSM, preliminary research and evaluation should extend beyond technical matters, user experience and reductive measures of audience engagement such as clicks and time spent – standard measures of engagement in the media industry (Baym 2013) – to include evaluations based on how much these technologies help achieve PSM goals.

Third Parties and Outsourcing

In addition to these findings, it is important to take account of the issues raised by the BBC's engagement of third parties to develop three news bots – the BBC Politics Brexit bot, the 2017 General Election bot and NewsChatta[4]. Outsourced bot development raises questions about how much control is ceded to third parties (Sørenson 2007), whether their technologies are open to scrutiny or "black-boxed" and whether they align with public service values. BBC strategists had begun assessing risks posed by bots and were aware of the constraints of working with third parties (I-12), highlighting issues ranging from security compliance, and access to APIs, to "black boxing" (1-12). Assessments highlighted the BBC's need to be able to access, audit and approve algorithms and access raw audience data collected by bot platforms (I-12), which is particularly important for PSM because they must be accountable to regulators and the public.

Outsourcing, by nature, requires PSM to cede control and oversight of the development of that technology to third parties. Editorial independence is a core public service value, but increasing reliance on commercial software "solutions" and third-party distribution platforms raises issues around dependence on, and independence from, commercial intermediaries and around transparency and accountability. Sørenson and Hutchinson see this as a potential "strategic vulnerability" (2018: 99) for PSM. Belair-Gagnon and Holton (2018) highlight for example how web analytics companies employed by news organisations have fostered disruptive, profit-oriented norms and values in newsrooms. In-house development in this study's cases ensured the BBC retained technical and editorial control, but in instances where external companies are used it is vital that appropriate partnership strategies are put in place that ensure they adhere to BBC values and standards.

These case studies distributed pre-published and pre-approved BBC material, thus avoiding many editorial and ethical issues associated with delegation of content generation to algorithmic and automated processes. The overarching challenge identified by interviewees was how to make journalism conversational using automated techniques while still maintaining trust and preserving editorial control – it was both about "relationship building" with the audience and "developing trust over time" (I-10) by balancing automation with curation (I-1). Bennet (2018, 118) comments on the importance of aligning algorithmic and editorial logics in PSM. As bots and other automated software shift the balance of responsibility for content from the editorial to the technological side, journalists must consider how these technologies are mediating content in order to exert meaningful control over output.

Chatbots: Moving the Conversation Forward

These bot experiments were solely trials, and only the in-article chatbot had been rolled out into BBC newsrooms. Conscious of risk to trust and brand, BBC News bot development has so far been measured and shows a desire to master basic capabilities before rushing to keep up with the industry's drive towards AI in the market. The research identified an ambition to develop more intelligent, conversational and automated journalism that does not appear to match the reality on the ground, partly due to a cautious approach taken to avoid undermining trust and partly to the difficulty of integrating new technology (particularly ML) into legacy systems. The BBC's circumspect approach is in line with other PSM and contrasts with more highly automated, algorithmic and ML-driven experiments amongst commercial media and bot platforms.

Taken individually, the bots might not have a significant impact. However, they form part of the organisation's wider moves towards algorithmically personalised news and individually-oriented modes of addressing audiences, and further consideration of potential cumulative impacts and challenges to public service journalism is necessary to provide a counterpoint to the immediately perceptible opportunities. If conversational journalism becomes a dominant paradigm in news provision without due critical assessment, what appear to be isolated and negligible transformations may end up shaping public service news in unforeseen ways. This research indicates that in the process of experimentation, the BBC is developing new infrastructure, skills and technologies for bots and other CUIs and is shaping future formats for engaging with news. New job roles have been created fusing editorial and technical skills, and, importantly, rules, guidance and policy are being developed to standardise currently disparate approaches to CUIs and the use of third-party companies – an important area which PSM must think about critically and which is ripe for future research.

Following these trials, the BBC has begun investing in tools that can scale up use of bots, for example by creating a "BotBuilder" that "automatically generates a database of questions and answers from an inputted article URL" or from bespoke text to quickly make a bot and simplify the process for journalists (BBC News Labs 2018). It is also looking to enhance the technical capacity of CUIs, for example by building a chatbot with which a human can "converse" using free text. Meanwhile, the recent turn towards voice interaction – exemplified by Microsoft's Cortana, Apple's Siri and HomePod, Amazon's Alexa and Echo, and Google's Assistant and Home – has seen BBC R&D expand into this area (Barot 2017). It is exploring the potential of combining voice technology (using ML applications such as NLP), with more sophisticated audience data analytics and recommender algorithms[5]. Exploring "meaning-making" in these news contexts of human-machine communication will be crucial to understanding how technology can be conceptualised as more than a channel or medium, entering into the role of a communicator (Guzman 2018; Lewis, Guzman and Schmidt 2019).

Ensuring scrutiny of these processes and putting methods of accountability in place will be difficult but a vital part of applying public service values to future BBC journalism and, ultimately, of maintaining trust with the audience. More ML in content production and distribution creates opportunities for broadcasters but also introduces further challenges, some of which the BBC is already familiar with, such as transparency, bias, accountability, and trust. However, there are distinctly new dimensions to these challenges as they become increasingly interwoven into the design and development of new data-driven technologies. For example, in order to apply ML to conversational agents in ways that do not undermine trust in PSM news (Waddell 2017), there will need to be: transparency around training data sets – making them available for scrutiny; explainability regarding the role of algorithms in editorial output – making algorithmic aspects visible and providing explanations that justify their use; accountability built into new processes and new forms of distributed responsibility – identifying who is responsible when things go wrong (Weeks 2014; Montal and Reich 2017); and conversational agents that do not unintentionally discriminate – ensuring personalisation treats people fairly. Reliance on commercial ML "solutions" and third-party platforms raises important questions around degrees of dependence on, or independence from, commercial interests and around degrees of commercial interference. The BBC must develop in ways that ensure its values are embedded and preserved in the application of these technologies as part of its public service. The key question for the BBC is not simply a technical one; it is about developing applications of conversational technologies and machine learning that enshrine and bolster the public purpose.

These developments, alongside others occurring across the BBC, are changing the way journalists, managers and developers think about what is possible and may be altering the expectations that audiences have of their engagement with the BBC and news more generally. Further research is needed to analyse bots in contexts where they are beyond the trial stage and embedded in news production in order to gain insight into how they are shaping, and shaped by, journalists' routines, professional identity, and perception of bots and automated technology. This should be complemented by audience research probing the relationship with, and impact on, news consumption.

Conclusion

This study sheds light on how the BBC has experimented with bots, and particularly chatbots, primarily for news distribution rather than for meaningful interaction with audiences. Recognising that technologies, as socio-material artefacts, are enacted in material-discursive practices (Bucher 2018) through a process of mutual shaping in context, our analysis illuminated not only the functions of BBC news bots but also the ways in which key actors conceived of, documented, and evaluated them. It indicated consensus over the meaning of bots was yet to stabilise and illustrated how bots were being mobilised as a vehicle to test out novel forms of individualised, personalised and two-way interaction, reflecting the popular conversational tone prevalent on social media. It suggested a shared organisational narrative – voiced by both technologists and journalists – was being marshalled around the value of bots in PSM for improving reach and engagement, particularly with underserved audiences including young people, but also suggested that limited evaluation did not adequately assess this. It highlighted concern that increased automation and the increased algorithmic complexity of bots should not undermine editorial control and oversight. These bots are concrete examples of how the BBC is translating evolving notions of journalism as a more accessible and less abstract public good into the technologies it is developing. In future, bots – particularly chatbots and CUIs – seem likely to play a part in revising the relationship between public service broadcasters such as the BBC and their audience. BBC News bots at the time of this research were not AI- or ML-driven and their limited technical capabilities and reliance on pre-written BBC sourced text did not predispose them to some of the ethical issues foregrounded by more algorithmically generated content. However, this study captures an important moment in the changing face of BBC News, which plans to build from its experiences developing these bots to experiment with AI for conversational journalism. We find evidence of efforts to stabilise this form of technology as the BBC begins to rein in the ad hoc elements of development and pin down a strategy for future work on conversational agents by formalising development processes, relationships with platforms and, importantly, with partners. Decisions about whether to develop in-house or outsource are likely to be of increasing importance and pose one of the most pressing challenges in ensuring public service values are preserved, warranting further research. Bots – specifically chatbots – at the BBC were seen as an opportunity to reach and engage underserved audiences by making the news more accessible to young people and those who are typically turned off by the formality of journalism. But their contribution to achieving PSM goals is unclear due to limited organisational research into audience responses. This is fertile ground for enquiry, particularly as the levels of intelligence and algorithmic complexity of bots increase.

Notes

1. A distinction can be made between AI and ML, the latter being any technology that allows computers to learn directly from examples and experience in the form of data, and the former being an umbrella term for the science of making machines "intelligent." There is no agreed definition of AI, but most stress that AI systems are those that automate aspects of human intelligence. ML is a sub-field or narrow application of AI. The BBC is currently thinking about AI largely in terms of ML.
2. Author one is a BBC Broadcast Journalist for BBC News Online and author two is a Senior Researcher in BBC Research & Development.
3. Additionally, there is ongoing work on a "breaking news bot" but this has not yet advanced to trial stage.
4. In 2017, BBC Politics commissioned UK-based bot technology agency The Bot Platform to produce a Brexit Facebook Messenger bot, which used push notifications (e.g., for constituency results), a quiz and news updates. It then hired the same company for the 2017 UK General Election bot, which provided the latest news on the campaign, and information about the parties and their policies. Also in 2017, it launched the NewsChatta chatbot on WeChat for a Nigerian audience, developed again by a third party – Nigerian company Codulab.
5. See https://www.bbc.co.uk/rd/projects/talking-with-machines and http://bbcnewslabs.co.uk/projects/voice-user-interfaces/.

Acknowledgements

We would like to acknowledge the help of the BBC, where both authors are employed and in particular the team at BBC News Labs.

Disclosure statement

In accordance with Taylor & Francis policy and our ethical obligation as researchers, we are reporting that we are both employed by the BBC, which may be affected by the research reported in the enclosed paper. I have disclosed those interests fully to Taylor & Francis, and I have in place an approved plan for managing any potential conflicts arising from this employment.

Funding

No grants were used to support this research.

ORCID

Bronwyn Jones http://orcid.org/0000-0003-2482-5181
Rhianne Jones http://orcid.org/0000-0002-8749-9953

References

Anderson, Chris W. 2011. "Deliberative, Agonistic, and Algorithmic Audiences: Journalism's Vision of its Public in an Age of Audience Transparency." *International Journal of Communication* 5: 529–547.

Anderson, Chris W. 2012. "Towards a Sociology of Computational and Algorithmic Journalism." *New Media and Society* 15 (7): 1005–1021.

Barot, Trushar. 2015. "The Botification of News". *Nieman Lab*. December. http://www.niemanlab.org/2015/12/the-botification-of-news/

Barot, Trushar. 2017. "The Future of News is Humans Talking to Machines". *Nieman Lab*, September. http://www.niemanlab.org/2017/09/the-future-of-news-is-humans-talking-to-machines/.

Baym, Nancy K. 2013. "Data Not Seen, the Uses and Shortcomings of Social Media Metrics." *First Monday* 18 (10).

Baym, Nancy K., and Boyd, Danah. 2012. "Socially Mediated Publicness: An Introduction." *Journal of Broadcasting & Electronic Media* 56 (3): 320–329.

BBC. 2017. Written Evidence (AIC0204). *Artificial Intelligence Committee* Submission. http://data.parliament.uk/writtenevidence/committeeevidence.svc/evidencedocument/artificialintelligence-committee/artificial-intelligence/written/70493.pdf Accessed 18 June 2018.

BBC News Labs. 2018. "Scripting chatbots is hard. Here's how we made it easier for BBC journalists: In our toolkit: BBC News BotBuilder". *Medium*. June. https://medium.com/bbc-news-labs/bbc-botbuilder-ba8e09b6a2e9.

Belair-Gagnon, Valerie, and Holton, Avery E. 2018. "Boundary Work, Interloper Media, and Analytics In Newsrooms." *Digital Journalism*, 6 (4): 492–508.

Bennet, James. 2018. "Public Service Algorithms." In *A Future for Public Service Television*, edited by Des Freedman and Vana Goblot. London: Goldsmiths Press.

Bucher, Taina. 2018. *If… Then: Algorithmic Power and Politics*. New York, N.Y: Oxford University Press.

Carlson, Matt. 2015. "The Robotic Reporter: Automated Journalism and the Redefinition of Labor, Compositional Forms, and Journalistic Authority." *Digital Journalism* 3 (3): 416–431.

Carlson, Matt. 2018. "Confronting Measurable Journalism". *Digital Journalism*, 6 (4): 406–441.

Caswell, David, and Dörr, Konstantin. 2017. "Automated Journalism 2.0: Event-Driven Narratives: From Simple Descriptions to Real Stories." *Journalism Practice* 12 (4): 477–496.

Coddington, Mark. 2015. "Clarifying Journalism's Quantitative Turn: A Typology for Evaluating Data Journalism, Computational Journalism, and Computer-Assisted Reporting." *Digital Journalism* 3 (3): 331–348.

DeLanda, Manuel. 2006. *A New Philosophy of Society: Assemblage Theory and Social Complexity*. London: Continuum.

Denzin, Norman K. 1970. The Research Act: A Theoretical Introduction to Sociological Methods. New York: Aldine.

Dörr, Konstantin. 2015. "Mapping the Field of Algorithmic Journalism." *Digital Journalism*. 4 (6): 700–722.

Flew, Terry, Spurgeon, Christina, Daniel, Anna, and Swift, Adam. 2012. "The Promise of Computational Journalism." *Journalism Practice* 6 (2): 157–171.

Gehl, Robert W., and Bakardjieva, Maria (Eds.). 2016. *Socialbots and Their Friends: Digital Media and the Automation of Sociality*. New York, N.Y: First Edition. Routledge.

Gillespie, Tarleton, Boczkowski, Pablo and Foot, Kirsten. 2014. *Media Technologies: Essays on Communication, Materiality, and Society*. Cambridge, MA: The MIT Press.

Graves, Lucas. 2018. "Boundaries Not Drawn." *Journalism Studies* 19 (5): 613–631.

Gorwa, Robert, and Guilbeault, Douglas. 2018. "Unpacking the Social Media Bot: A Typology to Guide Research and Policy." *Policy & Internet*. doi:10.1002/poi3.184.

Guzman, Andrea. 2018. "What is Human-Machine Communication, Anyway?" In *Human-Machine Communication: Rethinking Communication, Technology, and Ourselves*, edited by Andrea Guzman. Chapter: Introduction, 1–28. New York, NY: Peter Lang.

Hall, Tony. 2017. "Tony Hall's speech at the launch of the Annual Plan for 2017/18." *BBC website*. July. http://www.bbc.co.uk/mediacentre/speeches/2017/tony-hall-annual-plan#heading-a-personalised-uniquely-tailored-bbc

He, Lei. 2016. "Behind the BBC's Messenger News Bot." *BBC News Labs Blog*. November http://bbcnewslabs.co.uk/2016/11/16/mundo-for-messenger/.

Helberger, Natali. 2015. "Merely Facilitating or Actively Stimulating Diverse Media Choices? Public Service Media at the Crossroad." *International Journal of Communication* 9: 1324–1340.

Holton, Avery and Belair-Gagnon, Valerie. 2018. "Strangers to the Game? Interlopers, Intralopers, and Shifting News Production". *Media and Communication* 6 (4): 70–78.

Jones, Rupert. 2018. "NatWest Bank tests Cora, an AI bot that will answer customer questions." *Guardian Online*. https://www.theguardian.com/money/2018/feb/21/natwest-bank-tests-cora-an-ai-bot-that-will-answer-customer-questions.

Keohane, Joe. 2017. "What news-writing bots mean for the future of journalism" *Wired*. February. https://www.wired.com/2017/02/robots-wrote-this-story/.

Lewis, Seth C., Guzman, Andrea and Schmidt, Thomas. 2019. Automation, Journalism, and Human–Machine Communication: Rethinking Roles and Relationships of Humans and Machines in News. *Digital Journalism*. 1–19. doi:10.1080/21670811.2019.1577147.

Lewis, Seth C., and Usher, Nikki. 2013. "Open Source and Journalism: Toward New Frameworks for Imagining News Innovation." *Media, Culture & Society*, 35 (5): 602–619.

Lewis, Seth C., and Usher, Nikki. 2014. "Code, Collaboration, and the Future of Journalism: A Case Study of the Hacks/Hackers Global Network". *Digital Journalism*. 2 (3): 383–393. doi: 10.1080/21670811.2014.895504

Lewis, Seth C., and Usher, Nikki. 2016. "Trading Zones, Boundary Objects, and the Pursuit of News Innovation: A Case Study of Journalists and Programmers." *Convergence: The International Journal of Research into New Media Technologies* 22 (5): 543–560.

Lewis, Seth C., and Westlund, Oscar. 2015. "Actors, Actants, Audiences, and Activities in Cross-Media News Work". *Digital Journalism* 3 (1): 19–37.

Lokot, Tetyana and Diakopoulos, Nick. 2015. "News Bots: Automating News and Information Dissemination on Twitter." *Digital Journalism* 4 (6), 682–699. doi:10.1080/21670811.2015.1081822.

Lotz, Amanda D. 2018. "Inventing Public Service Media." In *A Future for Public Service Television*, edited by Des Freedman and Vana Goblot. London: Goldsmiths Press.

McKinney, Sydney. 2018. "Tech & Check Alerts aim to ease the workload of fact-checkers." *Duke Reporters Lab*. April. https://reporterslab.org/tech-and-check-alerts-automated-fact-checking/

Montal, Tal and Reich, Zvi. 2017. "I, Robot. You, Journalist. Who is the Author?" *Digital Journalism* 5 (7): 829–884.

Napoli, Philip M. 2014. "Automated Media: An Institutional Theory Perspective on Algorithmic Media Production and Consumption." *Communication Theory* 24 (3): 340–360.

Neff, Gina and Nagy, Peter. 2016. "Talking to Bots: Symbiotic Agency and the Case of Tay." *International Journal of Communication* 10: 4915–4931.

Newman, Nic. 2018. "Digital News project 2018. Journalism, Media, and Technology Trends and Predictions 2018." *Reuters Institute for the Study of Journalism*. https://reutersinstitute.politics.ox.ac.uk/sites/default/files/2018-01/RISJ%20Trends%20and%20Predictions%202018%20NN.pdf

Nielsen, Rasmus Kleis, 2012. "How Newspapers Began to Blog: Recognizing the role of technologists in old media organizations' development of new media technologies". *Information, Communication, and Society* 15 (6): 959–978.

O'Donnell, Fionntán. 2017. "What We Talk About When We Talk About Fair AI." *Medium*, https://medium.com/bbc-news-labs/what-we-talk-about-when-we-talk-about-fair-ai-8c72204f0798

Phelps, Andrew. 2017. "This is How The New York Times is Using Bots to Create More One-To-One Experiences with Readers." *Nieman Lab.* http://www.niemanlab.org/2017/04/this-is-how-the-new-york-times-is-using-bots-to-create-more-one-to-one-experiences-with-readers/

Picard, Robert. 2010. "The Future of the News Industry." In *Media and Society*, edited by J. Curran, 365–379. London: Bloomsbury Academic.

Ponsford, Dominic. 2017. "First Robot-Written Stories from Press Association Make it into Print in 'World-First' for Journalism Industry." *Press Gazette* http://www.pressgazette.co.uk/first-robot-written-stories-from-press-association-make-it-into-print-in-world-first-for-journalism-industry/

Powers, Matthew. 2012. "In Forms That are Familiar and Yet-to-be Invented': American Journalism and the Discourse of Technologically Specific Work." *Journal of Communication Inquiry* 36 (1): 24–43.

Scannell, Paddy. 2005. "The Meaning of Broadcasting in the Digital Era." In *Cultural Dilemmas in Public Service Broadcasting*, edited by Gregory Ferrell Lowe and Per Jauert, 129–142. Göteborg: Nordicom.

Sehl, Annika, Cornia, Alessio, and Nielsen, Rasmus Kleis. 2016. "Public Service News and Digital Media. Digital News Project 2016." *Reuters institute for the Study of Journalism.*

Sørenson, Jannick Kirk. 2007. "The Paradox of Personalisation." *PhD Thesis.* Available at https://www.researchgate.net/publication/295825824_The_Paradox_of_Personalisation_Public_Service_Broadcasters%27_Approaches_to_Media_Personalisation_Technologies . Accessed 20.5.2018.

Sørenson, Jannick Kirk, and Hutchinson, Jonathon. 2018. "Algorithms and Public Service Media. In Public Service Media in the Networked Society" *RIPE* 2017, pp. 91–106.

Thurman, Neil, Dörr, Konstantin, and Kunert, Jessica. 2017. "When Reporters Get Hands-On with Robo-Writing: Professionals Consider Automated Journalism's Capabilities and Consequences." *Digital Journalism* 5 (10): 1240–1259.

Van Dalen, Arjen. 2012. "The Algorithms Behind the Headlines: How Machine-Written News Redefines the Core Skills of Human Journalists". *Journalism Practice* 6 (5–6): 648–658.

Van Dyke, Jose and Poell, Thomas. 2015. "Making Public Television Social? Public Service Broadcasting and the Challenges of Social Media." *Television & New Media* 16 (2): 148–164.

Van Es, Karen. 2017. "An Impending Crisis of Imagination Data-Driven Personalization in Public Service Broadcasters." *Media@LSE working papers.* 43: 1–18. https://dspace.library.uu.nl/handle/1874/358206

Waddell, T. Franklin. 2017. "A Robot Wrote This? How Perceived Machine Authorship Affects News Credibility." *Digital Journalism* 6 (2): 236–255.

Wang, Shan. 2017. "From Election Results to Sports, The Hindustan Times is Trying Out Twitter Bots for Live Coverage." *Nieman Lab.* http://www.niemanlab.org/2017/06/from-election-results-to-sports-the-hindustan-times-is-trying-out-twitter-bots-for-live-coverage/

Weeks, Lin. 2014. "Media Law and Copyright Implications of Automated Journalism." *NYU Journal of Intellectual Property and Entertainment Law* 4: 67–94. https://jipel.law.nyu.edu/vol-4-no-1-3-weeks/

Willnat, Lars, Weaver, David H. and Choi, Jihyang. 2013. "The Global Journalist in the Twenty-First Century: A Cross-National Study of Journalistic Competencies." *Journalism Practice* 7 (2): 163–183.

Woolley, Samuel and Howard, Philip N. 2017. "Computational Propaganda Worldwide: Executive Summary". Edited by Samuel Woolley and Philip N. Howard, eds. Working Paper No. 11. Project on Computational Propaganda. Oxford Internet Institute. University of Oxford, UK.

You, Jia. 2015. "ONA15: How News Organizations Build Simple Bots to Help Report the News. Northwestern University Knight Lab." https://knightlab.northwestern.edu/2015/10/09/ona15-how-news-organizations-build-simple-bots-to-help-report-the-news/

Young, Mary-Lynn, and Hermida, Alfred. 2014. "From Mr and Mrs Outlier to Central Tendencies: Computational Journalism and Crime Reporting at the Los Angeles Times." *Digital Journalism* 3 (3): 381–397.

Zuiderveen Borgesius, Frederik J., Trilling, Damian, Möller, Judith, Balázs, Bodó, de Vreese, Claes H., Helberger, Natali. 2016. "Should We Worry About Filter Bubbles." *Internet Policy Review* 5 (1): 1–16.

Selling News to Audiences – A Qualitative Inquiry into the Emerging Logics of Algorithmic News Personalization in European Quality News Media

Balázs Bodó ⓘ

ABSTRACT
How do news organizations design and implement algorithmically personalized news services? We conducted 16 in-depth interviews with professionals working in European public service broadcasting and commercial quality news media to answer this question. The news business is undergoing rapid transformations regarding how news production is financed, how news is produced and delivered to audiences and how citizens consume news. In all of these changes algorithmic recommender systems play a role. We focus on news organizations' own personalized news services, and analyze how they define the role of personalization in contributing to the financial success of the organization, in reaching and retaining audiences, and in fulfilling their editorial mission. We interviewed editors, journalists, technologists and business intelligence and publishing professionals to gain a structural understanding of the often conflicting goals of personalization. We found that rather than focusing on increasing short-term user engagement, European quality news media try to use news personalization to increase long-term audience loyalty. In distinction to the "platform logic of personalization", which uses personalization to produce engagement and sell audiences to advertisers, they have developed a "news logic of personalization", which uses personalization to sell news to audiences.

Introduction

The idea of personalized news is more than 20 years old (Negroponte 1995). Digital technologies enable newsreaders to reveal their interests, preferences, values, location and other news consumption-specific individual features. Based on this information, news organizations can deliver tailor-made news packages to readers. To use the language of Negroponte, news personalization is an "interface to news", or a window to the world, which selects, highlights and filters individual news items, and compiles and aggregates them into news packages in a different manner for each individual newsreader. Similarly, Thurman and Schifferes (2012, 776) define news personalization as a "form of user-to-system interactivity that uses a set of technological features to adapt the content, delivery and arrangement of a communication to individual users' explicitly registered and/or implicitly determined preferences".

Personalized news services started to gain traction in the early 2000s. Lacking more sophisticated technologies, first-generation personalized news services asked users to explicitly reveal their news consumption-related preferences. Thurman and Schifferes (2012) list a number of these early news products that were based on explicit personalization: customizable newsletters and RSS feeds; different front pages based on geographical location; widgets; and customizable "My news" sections. Despite the widespread use of such explicit personalization options, many of these first-generation personalized news services remained marginal and largely unsuccessful (Sørensen 2013), mainly because users were reluctant to invest time and energy in explicit personalization.

The second generation of news personalization incorporates implicit personalization techniques. This approach builds digital profiles out of indirect user signals, such as clicks, third-party user information and transaction history, and uses these as an input for algorithmic agents that provide personalized recommendations. Such agents were first developed and successfully deployed in various commercial domains, such as by Amazon for e-commerce, by Google in the search and digital advertising sectors, by YouTube and Facebook to promote engagement with the platforms, etc. These services proved that it is possible to algorithmically match users to content that they appreciate, provoking interest in their application also in the business of news.

The arrival of second-generation implicit personalization technologies within the news business raised serious questions about whether, and how, the commercial personalization logics as developed by platforms could be applied in the newsroom. Personalization embodies and brings together a number of distinct developments that affect the business of news production and delivery. First, personalization relies on the quantification of audiences, linking personalization to the decades-old debates on how newsrooms should reconcile readers' demands with editors' journalistic mission and editorial judgement (Turow 2005; Zamith 2018). Second, algorithms require the formalization of editorial decisions on news and entertainment value, serendipity, diversity, social relevance and importance into specific algorithmic arrangements. How to conceptualize these dynamic, subjective and often deliberately weakly defined considerations in the language of computer science poses challenges (Helberger, Karppinen, and D'Acunto 2018; Reviglio 2019). Third, the same technologies and data that are used to personalize news are used to deliver online advertising. Therefore, at least on the surface, news personalization and free, ad-financed news production are intrinsically linked. The issues around personalized digital advertising, such as users' resistance to commercial surveillance, may affect news personalization, and the fact that the same traffic data and user profiles can be used to personalize both ads and news may lead to conflicts between commercial and editorial considerations (Bodó et al. 2019). Fourth, information-personalizing algorithms are believed to have their own agency, for example through their ability to create filter bubbles, echo chambers and polarization, if left unchecked (Borgesius et al. 2016). And last, but not least, personalization technologies are also used by online platforms, albeit with very different goals. Platforms upset the logics of news production, delivery and consumption in more than one way: they compete for advertising revenues with news organizations; through their control of access to audiences, they play an increasingly important role in news delivery; and through their own personalization efforts, they are able to set their own agendas, at the expense of news media.

When news organizations embark upon implementing implicit, data-driven, algorithmic news personalization services, they have to navigate a complex landscape in which these different questions all come together in the design of the personalized service. For this reason, we set out to study how news organizations implement algorithmic news personalization services. In particular, we asked the following questions:

RQ 1: How do different news organizations design and implement algorithmically personalized news services?

RQ 2: How do they reconcile potentially competing goals and identify and address the challenges?

RQ 3: How does personalization fit into the wider, economic, journalistic strategies of news organizations?

We studied these questions in two particular contexts. First, our geographic focus was on Europe, to balance the US-centric literature with insights from a diverse media landscape where public service media organizations are strong and important constituents of media markets; where fundamental legal rules, like data protection and privacy laws, are markedly different from those in the USA; and where the development of media has followed a path that differs slightly from that of North American media. Second, we focused on quality news organizations, namely public service media, and often long-standing legacy media with established reputations and a clearly defined journalistic mission to serve the public. Such quality media face significant challenges and opportunities in the current era of digital transformation. On the one hand, they can serve as reliable sources of verified information in the age of fake news, propaganda and weaponized social media (Bodó, Helberger, and de Vreese 2017). On the other hand, digital broadsheets are struggling to maintain their relationship with audiences, and alongside most other commercial news companies face economic challenges due to falling advertising revenues (Newman et al. 2016, 2017).

Personalized news seems to be in direct competition with the personalization efforts of platforms for audiences, revenues and relevance. This competition defines news organizations' technological, business, editorial approach to personalization. We set out to analyze the forces that shape the development of such news personalization logics within the European quality media, and identify what we call the "news logic of personalization" in contrast to how platforms personalize – often the very same – information.

Literature review

The existing literature on news personalization, especially in Europe, offers limited insight into how algorithmic news personalization relates to the overall strategic challenges experienced by quality news organizations.

Many studies focus on the impact of modern audience metrics on the journalistic profession (Anderson 2011; Turow and Draper 2014; Cherubini and Nielsen 2016; Hindman 2017; Zamith 2018). Audience feedback (de Sola Pool and Shulman 1959) shapes journalistic production in terms of content, form, selection, headlines, titles, etc. While audience measurement dates back to the 1930s, and news organizations were already actively incorporating a quantified and rationalized image of the audience in their practices (Napoli 2011, 26), it was only with the arrival of digital technologies that quantified audiences became highly visible and often centrally situated fixtures in newsrooms. The proliferation of low-cost automated systems to measure audiences reignited age-old debates about the conflict between editorial integrity and commercial pressures (Loosen and Schmidt 2016; Zamith 2018). Metrics revealed the gap between what audiences read and what editors think is societally relevant (Boczkowski and Mitchelstein 2013; Wendelin, Engelmann, and Neubarth 2017). Audiences seem to prefer content that is usually associated with print tabloid media (Wendelin, Engelmann, and Neubarth 2017). Empirical studies showed that editorial decisions are affected by audience metrics, resulting in the pushing of stories that already do well (Lee, Lewis, and Powers 2014; Vu 2014; Christin 2015; Welbers et al. 2016; Tandoc 2015; Cherubini and Nielsen 2016; Schlemmer 2016; Hanusch 2017; Hindman 2017; Wendelin, Engelmann, and Neubarth 2017) and the deselection of poorly performing articles (Tandoc 2014). Algorithmic news personalization automates the process of turning audience metrics into editorial decisions. Yet there is little research on whether that automation pushes news organizations further to serve the demand revealed by the metrics, and how they are able to resist that pressure, if indeed they are.

A second strand of inquiry discusses news organizations' response to the changes in the economic environment of news production, the loss of audiences and the general crises in the news business (Napoli 2011; Lowrey and Gade 2012; Siles and Boczkowski 2012; Coddington 2015) in the digital world and following the 2008 financial crisis. Usher (2015), for example, traces U.S. newspapers' response to the economic crisis, while Kaye and Quinn (2010) offer a comprehensive report on the different organizational responses to the economic challenges and changing technology landscape. Lowrey and Woo (2010) distinguish two different coping strategies. In "tight coupling", news organizations respond to the uncertainties of the field by being more responsive to the demands of their customers (readers and advertisers) and adjust their resources (such as the size and composition of the newsroom) and their practices (such as what and how they publish) to the demands of their customers. In "loose coupling", they "maintain and demonstrate the accepted forms and practices that have brought them institutional legitimacy" (Lowrey and Woo 2010, 42). There is little research on whether algorithmic news personalization is used by news organizations to better detect and serve audience demand under a tight coupling strategy or, on the contrary, whether they reject such use and define the role of personalization in terms that better fit with the loose coupling approach.

A third line of research offers insight into the actual news personalization practices. Pioneering work on news personalization (Thurman 2011; Thurman and Schifferes 2012) offered an early insight into news personalization practices. While these studies describe the outcome of news personalization projects as visible from the outside, either they do not deal with the process of creating them or they only discuss the internal design and implementation process from a narrow, public service media focus (Sørensen 2013). While algorithmic news personalization has grown to be a powerful technology in terms of its impact on both content and the success of particular business models, there are very few studies that discuss how algorithmic news personalization is reconciled with the business challenges and professional considerations of quality news organizations.

Methods

In 2017, we conducted sixteen 60- to 90-minute, in-depth, semi-structured interviews with individuals working for 12 European quality news organizations. We did our best to diversify our sample in terms of geography, media type and expertise. We approached people from different units within different types of news organization, namely broadcasters, newspapers, digital native organizations and public service media. We interviewed representatives of news organizations in the Netherlands, the UK, Switzerland, Germany and Finland. To build our sample, we visited relevant industry events[1] and used the referral sampling technique to get further leads to professionals working on algorithmic news personalization services. The complete list of interviewees is included in Appendix A.

We identified the topics relevant for the interviews through a review of previous research, the analysis of industry documents, such as "New York Times: Innovation" (New York Times 2014), and our pre-existing engagement with local news organizations. An interdisciplinary team of researchers working on news personalization[2] prioritized the topics to be addressed. The detailed list of interview questions is included in Appendix B.

We coded the interviews to identify recurring patterns and refined the coding in two subsequent waves to identify and consolidate concepts. A number of concepts emerged from the codes. Issues related to the transformation of news production and different approaches to the use of algorithms started to aggregate under the concept of *strategic challenges*: short-term vs long-term goals, difficulties reaching (especially young) audiences and issues with social media. Several concepts emerged specific to the *design and operation of news personalization* services, such as their *stated goals* (engagement, loyalty, etc.), their *design* (for free and premium, print or audio-visual content), the *recommendation logics* used (depth, diversity, breadth, etc.), the *key performance indicators* (individual, societal, business) and the *conflicts/problems* they lead to (ethical issues, loss of editorial control, user experience, etc.). Legal and ethical issues emerged around privacy, data protection and editorial independence.

We followed an inductive approach (Thurman 2018) and used grounded theory to arrange the concepts into new theories applicable to the wider economic and technological conditions of news production at the end of the 2010s (Strauss and Corbin 1990).

After the analysis, we organized a one-day symposium to verify our findings (van Drunen et al. 2018). We presented the findings of this and other related research

(Bodó et al. 2019; Helberger, Karppinen, and D'Acunto 2018; Möller et al. 2018), and discussed them with the invited interview subjects and academic experts. This verification process helped us to address the most obvious shortcoming of our sample, namely that we could not contrast editorial and non-editorial perspectives in each organization. The symposium enabled our interviewees to reflect upon the experiences of their colleagues from other organizations and to qualify or corroborate those experiences. We used the feedback we gathered to refine our analysis and conclusions.

Despite its breadth in terms of geographic scope, media organization types and professional expertise, our study had a number of limitations. We did not interview high-level executives, as we wanted to stay close to the loci of practical dilemmas and decisions. We tried but failed to reach tabloid news organizations and others with exclusively ad-based business models. We did not approach southern or eastern European news media because we saw limited use of news personalization among them. Further research is needed to address these shortcomings.

Also, this study lacks a detailed account of the personalization services implemented by the media organizations. Such a catalogue would have required the formal description of a wide range of factors constituting a personalization algorithm, including the details of the data used in the personalization process, the algorithmic primitives deployed, their parameterization, the shape and form of recommendations and the Key Performance Indicators (KPIs) used to assess them. Personalization technologies are inherently unstable, and their individual constituents may change quickly and substantially, as parameters, input data, or KPIs are continuously adjusted during A/B tests, software updates, etc. The internal workings of machine-learning models are even less penetrable. This also means that however detailed, a single snapshot of the personalized services would have been outdated the moment after it was taken, substantially limiting its usefulness for scholarly research. In contrast, an account of how the personalization technologies change in all the relevant dimensions over a longer period of time would certainly be useful. However, such a study was beyond the scope of this paper.

Results

The 16 interviews that we present in Results section offer a comprehensive insight into the processes through which news organizations harmonize personalization logics, and news recommender technologies with editorial considerations, business objectives and organizational constraints. The analysis revealed that if we try to present our findings in the structure of the three original research questions, we lose sight of important temporal and structural interdependencies cross-cutting the three questions. Consequently, Results section describes the process of how news organizations design and implement algorithmically personalized news services (RQ1), and discusses the findings related to the two other questions in the context of this process.

The personalized news services in our sample cover a wide range of approaches. Some are more basic (offering recommendations on general content popularity), and others are more sophisticated (offering recommendations based on individual profiles). At the time of our interviews, personalized article recommendations on web properties were at various stages of implementation, from experimental proof of concept services to ongoing wide-scale deployment. These were based on complex, individual profile-based recommendation technologies. The digital native organizations in our sample had personalization at the core of their service designs, and built their products around highly sophisticated algorithmic systems.

The algorithms used to provide these personalized services are technological black boxes that are intelligible only to technical experts (and sometimes not even to them) (Pasquale 2015; Diakopoulos and Koliska 2017). Most lay users usually deal with the input and the output of personalization algorithms, but need not concern themselves with how one is turned into the other. Such ignorance is not an option for news organizations that implement personalized services. Personalization logics need to be adjusted to the profile, limitations, goals and resources of the organization, such as the scope, quality, frequency and content of the data that are available on users and content; the results the organization wants to achieve, etc. Given that the technology of algorithmic personalization originates in computer science, the challenge of news personalization is always also a challenge regarding what kind of understanding other organizational stakeholders, such as journalists, editors, executives and marketing/business people, are able and willing to form around the highly technical process of transforming data into recommendations.

The interviews revealed that this interpretation process has several stages. Personalization starts with defining the input data that the algorithms will use. Personalization ideally needs as much high-quality data as possible on the content and on the users. Due to recent advances in audience quantification in newsrooms, such data tend to be already available (Carlson 2018).

In the second stage, news organizations need to formulate the goals they want to reach with their personalized services. Editorial concerns, values and priorities, such as diversity, societal relevance, etc., need to be expressed in algorithmic terms and balanced against other considerations, such as technical feasibility, profitability, scalability, data availability, etc. The result of this process is a set of key performance indicators (KPIs) that quantitatively express the consolidated organizational goals and serve as a means to measure and improve the performance of the algorithms.

Finally, the different personalization logics, their particular design and ultimately their performance are constantly evaluated from multiple (user, business, editorial) perspectives, and the results are fed back into the design of the personalization service. This feedback loop creates a continuously evolving system, in which the subsequent iterations of the personalized news service are defined by how its current version manages to navigate the complex, and not always easily reconcilable, editorial, user and business expectations.

In the following section, we discuss specific challenges at each stage of this process to highlight how news organizations succeed (and sometimes fail) in their attempts to personalize news personalization technologies.

Measuring the audience

News personalization rests on the assumption that the more is known about the tastes, preferences, interests and attitudes of individuals, as well as the circumstances in which they read news (time of day, location, device, occasion, available time for news consumption, etc.), the more precisely personalization technologies can recommend relevant articles to users. A soccer-loving male adolescent browsing the latest news on his mobile during his morning commute is assumed to be interested in a set of news articles very different from those his expat middle-aged female intellectual mother wants to read while browsing the digital weekend edition of a newspaper. Audience quantification technologies made such data available to newsrooms even before algorithmic personalization projects needed them. The impact of these data on news production and distribution is well documented, and our interviewees repeatedly mentioned both the dangers and the opportunities associated with audience measurement. The interviewees reported having access to one or more audience measurement tools, and confirmed that such data are used in the newsroom. The exact nature of the data that are available to editors and journalists varied case by case, as did the use of such data in editorial decisions. In one newsroom, audience metrics were displayed on one screen at the entrance. In another, the digital distribution department circulated by email the analysis of the traffic data from the previous day. Elsewhere, journalists had direct access to dashboards showing data in real time. One way or another, each organization was seen by our interviewees as a "data-informed" organization. When asked specifically about that topic, both editors and non-editors were keen to insist that audience metrics do not guide short-term editorial decisions, which are still driven by a professional understanding of what counts as societally important, relevant quality information. The following is how IP3, a data scientist responsible for digital distribution, put it:

> Editors have a dashboard in which they can see which item was sent how many times, and then how it was read. I actually don't want them to use it, because I don't think they should base their decisions on that. I don't mind them looking at it, but I don't want them to completely base all their decisions on such a dashboard. *If we need that, we can make an algorithm that does exactly that, make decisions based on the dashboard.* [emphasis added]

While exploring the true extent to which data shape editorial decisions in each of these organizations was beyond the scope of this research, our interviews confirmed that such knowledge was seen as important enough for each organization to set up specialized units to gather and analyze such data for distribution decisions. In each organization, the optimization of the digital distribution of news was done in a unit separate from the newsroom, by digital distribution professionals with backgrounds in publishing, marketing, technology, or business intelligence. The task of making sure that the output of the newsroom reaches the right audience at the right moment on the right platform was described as somewhat separate from the traditional roles assigned to audience-oriented editors (Ferrer-Conill and Tandoc 2018), whose task is to optimize content for digital consumption. IP15 explained the difference and interaction between the two types of approach:

> We use editorial analytics to optimize the content where we think it's important that people know about it. So if the algorithm is only serving the funny stories or celebrity news, then we focus on those important stories and see how we can present them better to people so they read them. Like changing the header or changing the video, changing things and putting effort into those stories. If we want to be relevant, then

we have to tell you something which makes you think that you've learnt something and understand a subject better. If we only serve you cat videos, you probably won't come back to the public service media anymore, because for cat videos you go to YouTube.

We found that the news personalization projects were situated within the digital distribution efforts in the organizations we talked to. Sometimes they were directly under the organizational units responsible for digital distribution, and sometimes they were organizationally separate, but they always involved both editors and distribution professionals. In theory, this organizational separation of editorial and distribution considerations means that potentially conflicting goals do not have to be resolved by the editor or journalist alone. Instead, conflicts are raised and resolved in specialized professional for a setup to deal with such issues. As IP16, a professional responsible for digital distribution, put it:

> I will never argue about what editors ask us to send out in our daily newsletter. Never. It's a journalist's decision. I will never argue today about that article. After it has been published, I will sometimes ask "Was this the smartest move?"

We were specifically interested in how conflicts are handled and resolved under such conditions, because we wanted to find out how much autonomy newsrooms enjoy in their editorial goals vis-à-vis data-supported decisions; in other words, whether there is anything similar to the "news-business wall" between the publisher and the newsroom of an earlier era (Coddington 2015). The interviewees stressed that the distribution unit and the newsroom have a shared interest in the wide reach and circulation of news, and that both work to "to maximize the audience for civically valuable content" (Hindman 2017, 185). The analysis and interpretation of audience metrics were said to take place retrospectively, and the process in which data are reconciled with practical editorial decisions was described as artisanal, deliberate and ad hoc. The interviewees suggested that this process takes place in complex organizational frameworks, where the conclusions are formed through the coordinated efforts of editors and distribution professionals. The answers to this question also revealed that there are more or less formalized channels of conflict resolution. IP14 said the following about this:

> Most of the time we'll [reach a decision] very quickly; it's an open company, so we talk to each other. Let's say we have something we cannot align on. [Such a conflict] automatically goes to the highest level. We have a CEO, and we have a chief editor who is also a member of the board. They discuss things. And we have learned not to let [conflicts escalate] so far. You never get the right answers, everybody loses. Instead, let's see this as a joint operation.

Algorithmic news personalization requires the automation of this deliberate balancing between editorial and distribution considerations. Instead of the artisanal cooperation of editors and the distribution professionals, abstract formulas interpret the audience metrics on an industrial scale. The automation transfers the task of translating audience metrics into who-gets-to-see-what decisions from humans to machines. This transfer of responsibility is also an at least partial transfer of authority: from human to machine, and from the traditional, in-house editorial expertise of a news organization to technologists who shepherd the algorithms, often as external contractors.

Since algorithmic news personalization automates these previously human decisions, it is reasonable to think of the design and implementation of personalized news
services as a process during which the professional editorial norms and business considerations are turned into choices regarding the technical design and parameterization of recommender algorithms. This translation process usually takes place in the
second step of news personalization.

Setting KPIs and defining recommendation logics

The biggest challenge in news personalization is that although it is easy to measure
some aspects of news consumption, such as clicks or reading time, it is hard to measure others, such as user satisfaction, loyalty (to a news brand, or to consuming quality
news as part of one's daily routine), or the health and functioning of the public
sphere. Consequently, it is much easier to come up with algorithms that increase the
former. Measuring clicks or time spent, and increasing these forms of user engagement with algorithmic recommendations is not just a low hanging fruit for computer
science, but it can also be nicely aligned with some of the short-term considerations
of news organizations (Ferrer-Conill and Tandoc 2018).

In the context of ad-financed free news, where economic uncertainty prompts news
organizations to pursue a tight coupling strategy (Lowrey and Woo 2010) and align
themselves better with the demands of their customers, the logic of personalization
looked simple. Measure simple engagement metrics, such as the number of clicks or
page views, or time spent on the page, and try to increase these numbers using algorithmic recommendations that are based on the harvested data on the individual user.
And use the same data and technology to sell the audience to advertisers to finance
the newsroom. In the early 2010s, the role of personalization was to increase reader
engagement to support the free, ad-financed business model by collecting data to aid
ad profiling and targeting and by building an audience to sell to advertisers. The
underlying recommender logic increased reader engagement through the algorithmic
identification and satisfaction of user demand.

For a while, this strategy seemed to produce results. Thurman and Schifferes found
a significant and consistent increase in personalized news services provided by major
publishers after 2008, which they explain by the desire of news organizations to
deploy a business model "that aligns better with the nature of Internet advertising,
where the importance of the cost-per-click (CPC) revenue model and the dynamic,
contextually-aware, serving of advertisements means that online news providers, more
than ever, need to maximize the relevance of content to individual users" (2012, 785).

By 2017, however, many limitations of this approach became apparent. News
organizations' digital advertising revenues were shrinking due to the increasing competition from platforms, the move to mobile with smaller screens and the widespread
use of ad-blockers by users (Newman et al. 2016, 2017). Platforms captured an increasing swathe of the audience, turning into exclusive news sources for some users and
important traffic sources for some news organizations. Taken together, these developments made the ad-based free-news business models less appealing, and forced news
organizations to experiment with other revenue-generation models.

By the same year, the commercial news organizations in our sample were already moving away from the free, digital advertising-based business models and working on alternative modes of financing news production. As IP2, the personalization project manager at a legacy print newspaper, put it:

> The old ways of distributing media, and of making money with them, have been disrupted. We are now looking for new ways to find our audience, to reach our audience and to get paid by our audience. Ultimately, we need some kind of monetization and the way we like it the most is if people have a subscription.

IP13, the editor-in-chief from an online-only news organization, agreed: "The business is a challenge even for us. We're profitable, but we need to find other revenue streams, because advertising is not going to take us another ten years". IP14, from another print legacy organization, explained more: "Google and Facebook are sucking up the whole Dutch advertising market. So let's not compete against them. Let's try to compete on the subscription side. It's something we understand better and something we've done longer than competing on the advertising side".

These claims are in line with the wider industry trends. Reports suggest that in the last two years there has been an increase in people's willingness to pay for news, as concerns about fake news, manipulation and the inadequacy of social media-mediated news grew after the 2016 U.S. elections and the Brexit referendum (Cornia et al. 2017; Newman et al. 2016, 2017). These developments reinforced the position of quality news organizations as a source of authentic information and allowed them to justify their experimentation with business models that try to replace digital advertising revenues with subscription-based ones.

As we suggest elsewhere, turning casual, free-website visitors into paying customers requires personalization strategies that are different from those used to generate ad revenues (Bodó et al. 2019). In line with scholarly research on the topic (Kammer et al. 2015; Fletcher and Nielsen 2017; Newman 2017), our interviewees agreed that long-term customer loyalty, satisfaction, and trust are key to making customers pay for news. Public service media, which do not rely on ad revenues but have also been struggling to keep their audiences, and continuously have to justify their tax-based funding, were the first to recognize the importance of these long-term factors and realize that short-term engagement metrics, such as clicks, do not necessarily accurately represent, or effectively foster, long-term commitment (Costera Meijer and Groot Kormelink 2016). IP11, from the BBC, described the goals they wished to achieve with personalization:

> Ultimately what we're trying to do is make people feel that they're getting good value for money, for their license fees, from the BBC. The key to that is the breadth of content they consume from the BBC. Our research shows that the more breadth that they get from the BBC, the more value they feel they have.

This approach reveals two important dimensions that were largely absent from the earlier models of news personalization. First, it reflects the recognition that in addition to the easily measurable short-term engagement metrics, there are also other long-term factors of user engagement that are important but cannot be easily captured through web-based audience analytics (Cherubini and Nielsen 2016). Information about the drivers of user satisfaction and the willingness to pay for a "free" service necessitates surveying long-term trends and user attitudes. Second, there is a tension between long-term and short-term goals. As IP2 put it:

> Our goal with personalization for now is engagement, but also trust, how people perceive the quality of the newspaper. If we narrow down the selection of our articles to the reader, because we only are giving him the news that he likes, then we are on the wrong path. Our goal as a news organization is to inform people about what is happening and there are things that are not always fun.

Despite their differences, the different types of news organization in our sample, public service and commercial, digital-born, or with broadcast or print legacies, expressed their strategic goals regarding personalization along similar lines. Increasing short-term engagement expressed in quantitative metrics is desirable, but it is not the ultimate goal of the organization. The survival, legitimacy and commercial success of quality news organizations, and their ability to retain old audiences and attract new ones, depend on the achievement of long-term goals expressed in qualitative terms: trust, user satisfaction, relevance, authenticity. Personalized services need to serve these goals; otherwise, they are not only not useful, but also detrimental.

The interviews provided us with a rudimentary catalogue of how these organizations see the role of algorithmic personalized news services in the aforementioned context. At the time of the study, these personalization goals were at various stages of implementation: for some organizations they were still aspirational; for others they already manifested themselves in widely used services. In any case, the roles described below were consistently raised by more than one interviewee, and, accordingly, we regard them as structural forces that shape the development of personalized news services across a wide range of different news media organizations:

Showcase the hidden richness and diversity of content. Recommenders are used to display news that does not make it to the front page, items that have not been seen by the user but have serendipity value (Reviglio 2019), or that are important (by editorial standards), or just different (i.e., niche content). Algorithmic recommenders can also be used to prove that newsrooms do their job properly and keep track of the news of the world, even if that news does not interest a particular individual. IP2 spoke about using personalization to address the issues stemming from the sheer volume of news:

> Recommendation is one of the ways of presenting articles to our audience. We use it to help them to find articles they are interested in, but which they may not see because they cannot look at the news 24 hours a day, and articles may already be gone or they may be deeper in our website, so they can't find them.

IP6 discussed the use of recommenders to funnel traffic to less popular content:

> You have niche content and you have hero content. Hero content will be able to provide new audiences for niche content in a totally new way. Recommendations are a very simple means of transferring audiences from one piece of content to the other. This changes the way niche content is produced and is delivered to an audience.

Push important stories that did not get to enough people. Many editors see algorithmic recommenders as a tool to execute editorial decisions. If editors think something is important and should reach as many people as possible, they can use algorithms to "push articles to the public" (IP2) to make sure that the news item gets through people's natural filters and reaches them even if they had it algorithmically filtered out. This approach considers recommender algorithms as a tool whose usefulness goes beyond the short-term satisfaction of user interests, and uses them to address societal level considerations. IP11 put it this way:

> We must make sure we are not just going to recommend the next most likely click. My job as an editor is to offer breadth and also to say, "Do you know what? This matters. This is just important, so let's wait and see when Theresa May triggers Article 50, that's going to be everywhere and we're just going to do it". I don't care if you say: "Don't show me anything about Brexit, it depresses me". You're going to learn, you're going to hear about it. It's important we tell the story.

Serve underserved audiences with specific interests. Personalization is also used by some organizations to identify and cater to niche audiences. In the non-personalized paradigm, they would not have been big or specific enough to be recognized, but with personalization they can be identified and may be commercially or societally relevant enough to be served by the newsroom. Local editions, and certain verticals (for example content specific to the real estate market), were mentioned as examples. IP13 suggested:

> The algorithm could send me a message saying hey, actually there's x number of people who want tennis on the front page, but we can't do that right now because we don't publish enough articles on that. So we can have a debate about what we want to do. Can we do it? Do we need extra investment in this? A lot of people might want more news that we don't have right now.

Focus on selling articles and subscriptions. Selling stories to potential buyers became a prominent use of personalization for organizations that have implemented paywalls or produce premium content. All the commercial media in our sample already sold content or subscriptions, or were planning to launch premium products. IP2 belongs to the former group: "Netflix is one of the pioneers of recommendation and they learned that if they recommend the right movies, the perception of the brand is going up and users will not cancel their subscriptions. That's what we learned from Netflix".

Re-aggregate disaggregated news and re-create context. Personalization can re-create context around news that is disaggregated on digital media. IP8 pointed out that "News brands deliver the most value by putting information into context. For news brands, the highest value is not to personalize it down to each and every article, but to create a context to what's happening out there". IP11 explained more:

> If we start optimizing around people's interests and beliefs, are we still being impartial? If someone says, "I'm very pro-Brexit, very anti-immigration", should we feed them a diet of "Europe is bad, immigration is bad" – style stories, and don't challenge that picture of the world? That's an enormous problem to never once challenge one's world view and present someone else's.

IP8 told us that they use personalization to select and arrange individual news items according to an emotional pattern:

> We have been a news company since World War II, so we have another understanding of news consumption. We don't try to recommend the perfect article. We try to find the perfect session, we try to create what we call a symphony for the user which tackles

different needs, like sadness, laughing, trending, serendipity, we have surprise, we have what the fuck, we have outrage, we have these different type of symphonies throughout the day, as your needs are different in the morning than when you have a coffee break or in the evening, and when you go to bed.

This approach requires a more detailed machine-readable description of news articles in dimensions such its topic, tone, sentiment, or position in the political spectrum. Such metadata (added by humans, or guessed by algorithms) can be taken into account by algorithmic recommenders to provide more diversity in recommendations (Helberger, Karppinen, and D'Acunto 2018).

These different personalization goals point in the same direction: the quality news organizations we interviewed are keen to maintain their authority and reinforce their position as sources of reliable, trustworthy information in society. To achieve this, they try to use the new technologies of algorithmic personalization to "maintain and demonstrate the accepted forms and practices that have brought them institutional legitimacy" (Lowrey and Woo 2010, 42). In the earlier model, personalization was seen as a tool in the hands of news organizations to sell ads to their audiences and to sell audiences to advertisers. In the new model, where digital advertising has less relevance, personalization is seen as a tool to sell news to audiences.

Evaluation

In the last, evaluation stage of the implementation process, news organizations need to compare the actual and the desired use and the actual and the desired impact of the personalized news service. The feedback loop that is created at this stage may necessitate the readjustment of the design of the personalized service, the readjustment of expectations, or both. This feedback loop ensures that the factors that contribute to the success of the personalized service, namely user satisfaction, editorial integrity and financial viability, are all taken into account and, if found to be in conflict, renegotiated.

Earlier work on news personalization highlighted a number of issues that emerged during the evaluation of the first generation of personalized services. Users were found to be reluctant to explicitly reveal their preferences, which is the prerequisite for explicit personalization (Sørensen 2011; Thurman 2011; Thurman and Schifferes 2012; Sørensen 2013). It also turned out to be technologically challenging to design algorithmic personalization services that provide diverse, societally valuable recommendations (Bozdag and van den Hoven 2015; Sørensen and Schmidt 2016; Helberger, Karppinen, and D'Acunto 2018).

The news organizations we interviewed were working on the second generation of personalized news services. During the evaluation of their personalization efforts, they revealed some shared experiences and concerns:

News organizations find that users have a conflicted, complex relationship with personalization. Elsewhere, we have demonstrated that Dutch news readers expect more depth and more diversity from personalized news services, and that they are concerned about the potential negative impact of news personalization on a shared, societal knowledge base – the "common core" (Bodó et al. 2019). Our interviews confirmed that many news organizations also share that latter concern. For example, IP5 said that: "I see personalization as a threat to the public service that we are supposed to deliver. Because once it's too personal, it's no longer public".

Other studies show that users do not always embrace personalized news services (Sørensen 2013), and this was echoed in our interviews. Our interviews suggest that news organizations are at least partially aware of these user concerns, so they do extensive testing and adjust the role of personalized services in their portfolios accordingly. Our sources agreed that audiences visit news websites because they want to read the latest news and see the breaking headlines, and they want to understand the context around the most recent news via opinion pieces, background reports, etc. The editor-compiled front page fulfils that role, while personalized services are used to retain users with more tailor-made offerings. IP10 described this process as follows:

> We've tried, like, half a dozen personalization models for the news website front page, but we abandoned every single one after the initial user tests. Everything was faulted to some extent. All the personalization is in our news app [where] we have several tabs, and only one is personalized. Headlines, latest news, sports, none of these are personalized, but you can personalize the "For You" tab to the max. The user is really the king there. Earlier, the personalized tab was the default tab to open when users opened the app. We've changed that to the headline stories, so we've sort of taken a step or two back with personalization.

Filter bubbles are not seen as a major issue and they are actively dealt with. Though in the academic and popular discourse filter bubbles are a major concern (Borgesius et al. 2016), few news organizations are worried about them, because they feel they understand the nature of the threat and are prepared to address it. Editors expressed their understanding that "[n]othing is more boring than more of the same. [Perfect personalization makes] a perfectly boring, very foreseeable, very cold and technology driven product, that doesn't feel like a proper journalistic product". – as IP8 put it. In-house recommendation technology developers, like IP3, are also aware of the dangers of diversity-reducing filter bubbles: "We look at engagement, we do see that engagement correlates with diversity and if we make more diverse recommendations, we see higher engagement. So, I'm not worried there". As we have seen above, personalized services are also offered in addition to human-edited front pages and headline sections, often as ancillary products, so users are less in danger of losing access to a shared news baseline.

Algorithmic personalization requires continuous human oversight to mitigate side effects. Algorithms can fulfil their KPIs in unexpected ways, which may lead to undesirable side effects. For example, the Dutch public service broadcaster wanted people to watch recommended videos to the end, so it parameterized its algorithm accordingly. Human editors realized that this KPI led the algorithm to recommend only short videos, which have a higher chance of being watched till the end. It requires continuous human oversight and judgement to ensure that the increases in the easily quantifiable dimensions do not produce unforeseen and undesirable side effects in other, less visible, less easily quantifiable dimensions. IP1 shared the following dilemma:

> In principle you should be informed. So if you're watching a lot of sports, then you should also watch a documentary. That's good for you, and for society. We can build this into [our personalized video recommender]. But, can we change [the whole approach to

public service recommendations]? After I've seen you watching three hours of television, should we stop showing you recommendations so people shut it off and go outside? Is that one of our responsibilities? Or are we there just to keep you glued to the screen? Is that what we are optimizing for?

Third-party personalization technologies have particular values embedded in them that limit their applicability for quality news personalization. During the verification event, our interviewees expressed their concern that third-party personalization technologies arrive with certain values embedded in them (van Drunen et al. 2018). In recent years, personalization and the provision of algorithmic recommendations have become an industry of their own, with multiple firms offering services that turn data into recommendations. The news organizations in our sample varied in whether they develop their recommendation engines in-house, or as a member of a consortium,[3] or use third-party systems. News organizations that rely on external parties for their personalized services are becoming increasingly aware of the values that come embedded in the technologies they use. Many commercially available personalization services, their recommendation algorithms, the data they rely on, the logics they employ, their embedded KPIs and the defaults of the software were developed for other, usually e-commerce, uses and reflect choices optimized for the particular use of ad click-through or sales optimization. To what extent these embedded values are incongruent with the values that different news personalization approaches prefer to rely on is an open question.

Personalizing algorithms do not have to lead to the loss of editorial control. A purely editorial control of news personalization was rare in the organizations we interviewed. This is probably due to the complexity of the task and the fundamentally different challenges the long-term development poses vis-à-vis the daily operation of a recommender system. On the development level, we found shared or multi-centred control of personalization. The model described by IP9 was shared by others in our sample:

> In terms of organization, the development of personalized news services is driven by the online department of the company, which is a mix of journalists, engineers and developers. The head of the department is a journalist. So I cannot say [that personalization is] IT driven because it would be false. But I don't think it's journalist driven either, because we are only a part of the equation. It's really both of them.

IP7, who works for an organization that operates a similar model, elaborated further:

> The personalization on iPlayer is not the same as personalization on news, and shouldn't be. So all major products have a "product direction group" where the editorial, the product lead, the marketing and others with a role meet every month and review the product strategy and its execution. This group is accountable for the budget for the product and for the KPIs in the product. The result of the strategic alignment is the alignment of KPIs.

On the other hand, newsrooms play an important role in the daily operation of recommender systems. Our interviewees agreed that it takes time and effort to get journalists and editors acquainted with the technology and its use, power and implications, but once that happens, editors can assert control over the technology and include it in their editorial decisions. This is how IP7 described this process:

> We need to define personalization in a way that resonates with [journalists]. If I go there and say "Look, I've got tools that will help you to get your content to people who care about it", that leads to an interesting and productive conversation. Technology journalists get this right away. The political journalists are like, "Okay, there are things I want everybody to know and there are things that are more in-depth and kind of only a subset of people will want to know. If you let me make those decisions then I get how personalization can help me".

However, some of our interviewees also acknowledged that from the perspective of journalists, who may fear that automation will take their jobs, this process might seem less uncontroversial, and even outright threatening.

Conclusions

The economic, technological and sociocultural conditions of the production, distribution and consumption of news have been in flux for more than three decades. The algorithmic control of information flows and the customization of the information environment around each of us constitute the latest development in that process.

In this paper, we documented the shifting landscape of news personalization. First, it turned out that personalization cannot be reduced to a conflict between editorial values and user demand. Personalization is deeply embedded in the wider economic, social, political and technological contexts of news production and distribution, as well as in how society sees the role of (algorithmically personalized) media in the democratic processes (see Natali Helberger's analysis in this special edition). As the business of news moves away from free, ad-financed models and starts to focus on paid models, both the design and the use of personalized news services change. In the ad-based model, the role of personalized services was to sell audiences to advertisers. In the paid news models, their role is to sell paid news to audiences, or in the case of public service media, justify the public spending on PBM in the eyes of the tax payers and elected politicians. These different goals imply fundamentally different technological and organizational designs for news personalization.

Second, it has become clear that personalization is not a monolithic technology/ idea/approach. Driven by different values, at least two markedly different strands of personalization seem to have emerged by the end of 2017. One type of personalization is done by major platforms. The "platform logic of personalization" is characterized by an abundance of user data; an immense user and content base; an aggressive and successful ad-based business model; almost limitless financial and technological resources; and a strong resistance to any editorial control or oversight of the algorithmic recommendations. In contrast, the "news logic of personalization" is characterized by a limited set of data on users (curtailed by limited financial resources and concerns about trust); a limited user base and content base; a struggling ad-based business model, with paying news emerging as an alternative; limited financial and technological resources; strong editorial control and a professional culture.

The conditions in which news is produced gave birth to personalization logics that deviated from the platform-based personalization logics. It needs further work to map the landscape of "news-based personalization logics" across different jurisdictions and across different media types.[4] But one thing is clear: we need to better distinguish between the two types of personalization, as they differ substantially in their threats and the opportunities they create.

Third, for a while people wondered whether personalization would emerge as an autonomous agent within the news organization, with the power to ultimately replace human editors. We found two strong factors that limit the autonomy of the algorithm. User emancipation and audience gatekeeping turned out to be less desirable than imagined. Audience metrics revealed that, left to their own devices, audiences tend to make societally suboptimal choices about what news or information they consume, especially if technologies are deployed to exploit human weakness in order to turn a profit (Webster 2010; Boczkowski and Mitchelstein 2013; Bucher 2017; Hanusch 2017; Wendelin, Engelmann, and Neubarth 2017). In response, journalists and editors began to build up their competences and started to develop ways to use and control personalization technologies. The development of personalized news services can also be read as a process through which news professionals claim certain algorithmic tools to counter the dominance of personalization technologies deployed by platforms and ad companies, and mitigate their negative impact on the news business.

Ultimately, the most important change we witnessed was that algorithmic news personalization technologies changed from being a tool to serve audience demand into being a tool to control it (Beniger 1986). Personalization has always been a technology to manipulate demand in a way that serves the goals of the organization. What has changed is that news organizations realized that for them this manipulation of demand is about selling quality information, cultivating a taste for hard news (Hindman 2017, 192), justifying public investment, or maintaining journalistic authority and reliability in the age of fake news, rather than competing with platforms in chasing audience engagement and selling ads.

In order to fulfil these goals, news organizations, their editors, journalists, distribution professionals are struggling to gain control over news personalization, as a technology of controlling the demand for news.

Notes

1. Such as the big data conference of the European Broadcasting Union, Geneva, 21–22 March 2017 (https://www.ebu.ch/events/2017/03/big-data-week).
2. The research is part of a wider effort at the University of Amsterdam to study the normative implications of news personalization (ERC StG Grant #638514 PersoNews: Profiling and targeting news readers – implications for the democratic role of the digital media, user rights, and public information policy), and the practice and implications of personalized communication in general. See http://personalised-communication.net/ for details.
3. See, for example, the coalition of European public service media working on a shared recommendation technology: https://peach.ebu.io/
4. We expected news personalization by public service media to be unique, mostly because of their lower exposure to commercial pressures and their well-established role. It was more surprising to see how similarly commercial quality news organizations thought about the role of personalization. One reason for that might be that in both cases, it is long-term audience loyalty that is of value, resulting in either public legitimacy or subscriptions.

Acknowledgements

The author wishes to thank the participants of the 2018 Amsterdam Workshop on News Personalization, and the Algorithms, Automation and News Conference for their insights. I am also indebted to my colleagues at the Personalized Communications Project at UvA, the anonymous reviewers and the editors of the special issue for their useful comments.

Disclosure statement

No potential conflict of interest was reported by the author.

Funding

The research was conducted as part of the PERSONEWS ERC-2014-STG, European Research Council project, [grant no: 638514]. PI: Prof. Dr. N. Helberger.

ORCID

Balázs Bodó ⓘ http://orcid.org/0000-0001-5623-5448

References

Anderson, C W. 2011. "Deliberative, Agonistic, and Algorithmic Audiences: Journalism's Vision of Its Public in an Age of Audience Transparency." *International Journal of Communication* 5 (2011): http://ijoc.org/index.php/ijoc/article/view/884.

Beniger, James R. 1986. *The Control Revolution: Technological and Economic Origins of the Information Society*. Cambridge, Mass: Harvard University Press.

Boczkowski, Pablo J, and Eugenia Mitchelstein. 2013. *The News Gap: When the Information Preferences of the Media and the Public Diverge*. Cambridge, MA: MIT Press.

Bodó, Balázs, Natali Helberger, Sarah Eskens, and Judith Möller. 2019. "Interested in Diversity," *Digital Journalism* 7 (2), 206–229. doi:10.1080/21670811.2018.1521292.

Bodó, Balázs, Natali Helberger, and Claes H de Vreese. 2017. "Political Micro-Targeting: A Manchurian Candidate or Just a Dark Horse?" *Internet Policy Review* 6 (4).

Bozdag, Engin, and Jeroen van den Hoven. 2015. "Breaking the Filter Bubble: Democracy and Design." *Ethics and Information Technology* 17 (4): 249–265.

Bucher, T. 2017. "'Machines Dont Have Instincts: Articulating the Computational in Journalism." *New Media & Society* 19 (6): 918–933. doi:10.1177/1461444815624182

Carlson, Matt. 2018. "Confronting Measurable Journalism." *Digital Journalism* 6 (4): 406–417.

Cherubini, Federica, and Rasmus Kleis Nielsen. 2016. *Editorial Analytics: How News Media Are Developing and Using Audience Data and Metrics*. Oxford, UK: Reuters Institute for the Study of Journalism. Available at SSRN 2739328.

Christin, Angèle. 2015. "'Sex, Scandals, and Celebrities'? Exploring the Determinants of Popularity in Online News." *Sur Le Journalisme About Journalism Sobre Jornalismo* 4 (2): 28–47.

Coddington, Mark. 2015. "The Wall Becomes a Curtain." In *Boundaries of Journalism: Professionalism, Practices and Participation*, edited by Matt Carlson and Seth C. Lewis, 67–82. London: Routledge.

Cornia, Alessio, Annika Sehl, Felix Simon, and Rasmus Kleis Nielsen. 2017. *Pay Models in European News*. Reuters Institute Factsheet. Oxford, UK: Reuters Institute for the Study of Journalism.

Costera Meijer, I., and T. Groot Kormelink. 2016. "Revisiting the Audience Turn in Journalism: How a User-Based Approach Changes the Meaning of Clicks, Transparency and Citizen

Participation." In *The Routledge Companion to Digital Journalism Studies*, edited by B. Franklin, 345–353. London, New York: Routledge.

Diakopoulos, Nicholas, and Michael Koliska. 2017. "Algorithmic Transparency in the News Media." *Digital Journalism* 5 (7):809–828. doi:21670811.2016.1208053.

Drunen, Max van, Balázs Bodó, Jannick Kirk Sørensen, and Natali Helberger. 2018. *News Personalization Symposium Report*. Amsterdam. http://personalised-communication.net/wp-content/uploads/2018/05/Report-2018-Amsterdam-News-Personalisation-Symposium-1.pdf.

Ferrer-Conill, Raul, and Edson C Tandoc. 2018. "The Audience-Oriented Editor." *Digital Journalism* 6 (4): 436–453.

Fletcher, Richard, and Rasmus Kleis Nielsen. 2017. "Paying for Online News." *Digital Journalism* 5 (9): 1173–1191.

Hanusch, Folker. 2017. "Web Analytics and the Functional Differentiation of Journalism Cultures: Individual, Organizational and Platform-Specific Influences on Newswork." *Information Communication and Society* 20 (10): 1571–1586.

Helberger, Natali, Kari Karppinen, and Lucia D'Acunto. 2018. "Exposure Diversity as a Design Principle for Recommender Systems." *Information, Communication & Society* 21 (2): 191–207.

Hindman, Matthew. 2017. "Journalism Ethics and Digital Audience Data." In *Remaking the News: Essays on the Future of Journalism Scholarship in the Digital Age*, edited by Pablo J. Boczkowski and C. W. Anderson, 177–195. Cambridge, MA: MIT Press.

Kammer, Aske, Morten Boeck, Jakob Vikaer Hansen, and Lars Juul Hadberg Hauschildt. 2015. "The Free-to-Fee Transition: Audiences' Attitudes toward Paying for Online News." *Journal of Media Business Studies* 12 (2): 107–120.

Kaye, Jeff, and Stephen Quinn. 2010. *Funding Journalism in the Digital Age: Business Models, Strategies, Issues and Trends*. New York, NY: Peter Lang.

Lee, Angela M, Seth C Lewis, and Matthew Powers. 2014. "Audience Clicks and News Placement: A Study of Time-Lagged Influence in Online Journalism." *Communication Research* 41 (4): 505–530. doi:10.1177/0093650212467031.

Loosen, Wiebke, and Jan-Hinrik Schmidt. 2016. "Between Proximity and Distance: Including the Audience in Journalism (Research)." In *The Routledge Companion to Digital Journalism Studies*. edited by B. Franklin and A. E. Scott II, 354. London, New York: Routledge.

Lowrey, Wilson, and Peter J Gade. 2012. *Changing the News: The Forces Shaping Journalism in Uncertain Times*. London, New York: Routledge.

Lowrey, Wilson, and Chang Wan Woo. 2010. "The News Organization in Uncertain Times: Business or Institution?" *Journalism & Mass Communication Quarterly* 87 (1): 41–61.

Möller, Judith, Damian Trilling, Natali Helberger, and Bram van Es. 2018. "Do Not Blame It on the Algorithm: An Empirical Assessment of Multiple Recommender Systems and Their Impact on Content Diversity." *Information, Communication & Society* 21 (7): 959–977.

Napoli, Philip M. 2011. *Audience Evolution: New Technologies and the Transformation of Media Audiences*. New York, NY: Columbia University Press.

Negroponte, Nicholas. 1995. *Being Digital*. 1st ed. New York, NY: Knopf.

New York Times. 2014. "New York Times: Innovation." *New York Times*.

Newman, Nic. 2017. *Attitudes to Paying for Online News*. Oxford, England: Reuters Institute for the Study of Journalism.

Newman, Nic, Richard Fletcher, Antonis Kalogeropoulos, David A. L. Levy, and Rasmus Kleis Nielsen. 2017. *Digital News Report 2017*. Oxford: Reuters Institute.

Newman, Nic, Richard Fletcher, David A. L. Levy, and Rasmus Kleis Nielsen. 2016. *Digital News Report 2016*, 1–124. Oxford: Reuters Institute for the Study of Journalism, University of Oxford.

Pasquale, Frank. 2015. *The Black Box Society: The Secret Algorithms That Control Money and Information*. Cambridge, MA: Harvard University Press.

Reviglio, Urbano. 2019. "Serendipity as an Emerging Design Principle of the Infosphere: Challenges and Opportunities." *Ethics and Information Technology* 21 (2), 151–166. doi: 10.1007/s10676-018-9496-y.

Schlemmer, Christoph. 2016. *Speed Is Not Everything: How News Agencies Use Audience Metrics*. Oxford, England: Reuters Institute Fellowship Paper.

Siles, Ignacio, and Pablo J Boczkowski. 2012. "Making Sense of the Newspaper Crisis: A Critical Assessment of Existing Research and an Agenda for Future Work." *New Media & Society* 14 (8): 1375–1394.

Sola Pool, Ithiel de, and Irwin Shulman. 1959. "Newsmen's Fantasies, Audiences, and Newswriting." *Public Opinion Quarterly* 23 (2): 145–58.

Sørensen, Jannick Kirk. 2011. "The Paradox of Personalisation: Public Service Broadcasters' Approaches to Media Personalisation Technologies." PhD diss., University of Southern Denmark.

Sørensen, Jannick Kirk. 2013. "PSB Goes Personal: The Failure of Personalised PSB Web Pages." *MedieKultur: Journal of Media and Communication Research* 29 (55): 28.

Sørensen, Jannick Kirk, and Jan-Hinrik Schmidt. 2016. "An Algorithmic Diversity Diet? Questioning Assumptions behind a Diversity Recommendation System for PSM." Paper presented at *RIPE@2016*. University of Antwerp, Antwerp. http://ripeat.org/library/2016.

Strauss, Anselm, and Juliet M Corbin. 1990. *Basics of Qualitative Research: Grounded Theory Procedures and Techniques*. Los Angeles, CA: SAGE.

Tandoc, Edson C. 2015. "Why Web Analytics Click: Factors Affecting the Ways Journalists Use Audience Metrics." *Journalism Studies* 16 (6): 782–799.

Tandoc, Edson C. 2014. "Journalism Is Twerking? How Web Analytics Is Changing the Process of Gatekeeping." *New Media & Society* 16 (4): 559–575.

Thurman, Neil. 2011. "Making 'The Daily Me': Technology, Economics and Habit in the Mainstream Assimilation of Personalized News." *Journalism* 12 (4): 395–415.

Thurman, Neil. 2018. *Mixed-Methods Communication Research: Combining Qualitative and Quantitative Approaches in the Study of Online Journalism*. London, UK: SAGE. doi:10.4135/9781526428431.

Thurman, Neil, and Steve Schifferes. 2012. "The Future of Personalization at News Websites: Lessons from a Longitudinal Study." *Journalism Studies* 13 (5–6): 775–790.

Turow, Joseph. 2005. "Audience Construction and Culture Production: Marketing Surveillance in the Digital Age." *The ANNALS of the American Academy of Political and Social Science* 597 (1): 103–121.

Turow, Joseph, and Nora Draper. 2014. "Industry Conceptions of Audience in the Digital Space: A Research Agenda." *Cultural Studies* 28 (4): 643–656.

Usher, Nikki. 2015. "Newsroom Moves and the Newspaper Crisis Evaluated: Space, Place, and Cultural Meaning." *Media, Culture & Society* 37 (7): 1005–1021.

Vu, Hong Tien. 2014. "The Online Audience as Gatekeeper: The Influence of Reader Metrics on News Editorial Selection." *Journalism* 15 (8): 1094–1110.

Webster, James G. 2010. "User Information Regimes: How Social Media Shape Patterns of Consumption." *Nw. UL Rev.* 104. HeinOnline: 593.

Welbers, Kasper, Wouter Van Atteveldt, Jan Kleinnijenhuis, Nel Ruigrok, and Joep Schaper. 2016. "News Selection Criteria in the Digital Age: Professional Norms versus Online Audience Metrics." *Journalism* 17(8):1–17. doi:10.1177/1464884915595474.

Wendelin, Manuel, Ines Engelmann, and Julia Neubarth. 2017. "User Rankings and Journalistic News Selection: Comparing News Values and Topics." *Journalism Studies* 18 (2): 135–153.

Zamith, Rodrigo. 2018. "Quantified Audiences in News Production." *Digital Journalism* 6 (4): 418–435.

Zuiderveen Borgesius, F. J, Damian Trilling, Judith Möller, Balázs Bodó, Claes H. de Vreese, and Natali Helberger. 2016. "Should We Worry about Filter Bubbles?" *Internet Policy Review* 5 (1). doi:10.14763/2016.1.401

Appendix A: List of interviewees

ID	Country	Media	Field	Role (may be redacted to ensure anonymity)
IP1	NL	Public service	Broadcast	Business Intelligence Manager
IP2	NL	Commercial	Print	Innovation Manager
IP3	NL	Commercial	Online	CTO
IP4	NL	Commercial	Online	Editor-in-chief
IP5	NL	Public service	Broadcast	Digital Media Manager
IP6	NL	Consulting	Broadcast	Management
IP7	UK	Public service	Broadcast	Director
IP8	DE	Commercial	Print	Chief Executive
IP9	CH	Public service	Broadcast	Digital Innovation Manager
IP10	FI	Public service	Broadcast	Head of Development
IP11	UK	Public service	Broadcast	Managing Editor
IP12	UK	Public service	Broadcast	Legal counsel
IP13	NL	Commercial	Online	Editor-in-chief
IP14	NL	Commercial	Print	Head of Digital
IP15	NL	Public service	Broadcast	Head of Digital
IP16	NL	Commercial	Print	Head of Digital

Appendix B: Topics covered during the semi-structured interview and the most important questions

Topics	Sample questions
The use and interpretation of audience metrics	• What kind of data do you currently take into consideration to support your decisions as editor, distribution professional or publisher?
Data use in news dissemination	• How do you plan, monitor and assess the dissemination of your news articles? • What kind of performance metrics do you use to assess the performance of news production/distribution?
The design of the personalized news product of the organization	• Does your organization have a news personalization project/service (planned or in operation)? • What are the editorial, business and technological goals of the project? • How were these goals defined? • What are the challenges, opportunities, threats and benefits of news personalization?
The organizational set-up of personalization projects	• Who is leading the project? • What kind of expertise is present in the project? • Were there any substantial misunderstandings, differences or conflicts within the group regarding the design and implementation of the system? • How were these differences/conflicts resolved?
Potential threats to editorial independence by personalization	• How did the power balance between the publisher and the editor change under the new (datafied, algorithmic, digital) conditions?
Ethical and legal challenges related to personalization, including the collection and analysis of personal data, the need for the regulation of social media and legal safeguards of editorial independence	• Are you aware of any unfair data practices by others that should be tackled? • Do you develop self-regulation regarding your uses of data? • Do you feel editorial independence is sufficiently guaranteed?

Making Artificial Intelligence Work for Investigative Journalism

Jonathan Stray (iD)

ABSTRACT
Many have envisioned the use of AI methods to find hidden patterns of public interest in large volumes of data, greatly reducing the cost of investigative journalism. But so far only a few investigative stories have utilized AI methods, in relatively narrow ways. This paper surveys what has been accomplished in investigative reporting using AI techniques, why it has been difficult to apply more advanced methods, and what sorts of investigative journalism problems might be solved by AI in the near term. Journalism problems are often unique to a particular story, which means that training data is not readily available and the cost of complex models cannot be amortized over multiple projects. Much of the data relevant to a story is not publicly accessible but in the hands of governments and private entities, often requiring collection, negotiation, or purchase. Journalistic inference requires very high accuracy, or extensive manual checking, to avoid the risk of libel. The factors that make some set of facts "newsworthy" are deeply sociopolitical and therefore difficult to encode computationally. The biggest near-term potential for AI in investigative journalism lies in data preparation tasks, such as data extraction from diverse documents and probabilistic cross-database record linkage.

Introduction

Investigative journalism may be one of the most effective ways to discourage corruption and reveal wrongdoing across society, and recent analyses suggest that it is one of the most cost-effective as well (Hamilton 2016). If machine intelligence were applied to investigative journalism, it might monitor global feeds for important news, find socially relevant patterns among diverse data sets, and maybe even write up the resulting stories (Hansen et al. 2017; Marconi and Siegman 2017). However, AI is not currently widely used in investigative journalism, despite its supposed promise.

This paper contributes to the study of journalism and automation by unpacking, investigating, and re-developing the common assumption that AI can increase the power and reach of investigative journalists. Typically, the idea is that AI will reduce the cost of investigative journalism production by replacing certain types of tedious or expensive human labor with cheap computation. While this is a real possibility, there are several key roadblocks, and the most significant potential applications of AI in investigative work may not look much like previous speculation.

We start by discussing the handful of uses of AI techniques in investigative work to date. An analysis of these cases and others suggests some fundamental reasons why it is hard to successfully apply AI in an investigative journalism context. However, there are some very interesting possibilities which seem like they could be tackled in the next few years with a program of applied research. Data ingestion and cleanup, which are often glossed over in AI research, consume a great deal of journalists' time and are good candidates for automation.

The intersection of investigative journalism and artificial intelligence is a small part of the intersection between computation and journalism generally.

The classic textbook *The Elements of Journalism* says that investigative journalism "puts emphasis on the role of the press as activist, reformer, and exposer" (Kovach and Rosenstiel 2014, 169). Hamilton's (2016) study of the economics of the practice says that "investigative reporting involves original work, about substantive issues, that someone wants to keep secret" (10). Contemporary investigative reporting also frequently involves working with large volumes of public records and data, which is a natural opening for automation.

Artificial intelligence is an active field of computer science research, and also a wide set of engineering practices (Russell, Norvig, and Davis 2010). Some branches of AI, such as algorithms for playing chess, do not have obvious applications in journalism. Here, we are especially interested in those methods which might "lower the costs of discovering watchdog stories" (Hamilton 2016). In practice, these methods will be "narrow AI" and not "general AI" (Broussard 2018).

These definitions usefully exclude other types of journalism automation. For example, breaking news is not typically investigative reporting because there is no time for in-depth research, while journalistic data visualization is not typically an application of artificial intelligence because such work does not employ the computational methods developed by AI researchers. This paper also does not consider AI methods built into widely applicable tools. For example, email spam filtering and automated grammar checkers are used in every industry. Instead, *our focus is the application of AI theory and methods to problems that are unique to investigative reporting, or at least unsolved elsewhere.*

I start by reviewing related work, and collecting the various hopes that have been expressed for AI in journalism. Then I survey stories where AI methods were used successfully. These stories are not as numerous or as sophisticated as the hopes, so I examine why investigative journalism is a hard problem for AI, including detailed examples of unsolved problems. There are a variety of technical, legal, political, and philosophical challenges to build better AI for investigative journalism. One key interdisciplinary question is the algorithmic description of what counts as news—that is, what should we design our story-finding AI to find? Despite fundamental challenges, there remains great promise for AI in investigative journalism. I end by suggesting several ways that near-future AI could be applied productively, by helping with data preparation and cleaning.

Investigative AI in the Context of Journalism Automation

The subject of this paper is AI applied to investigative reporting, that is, story *production* as opposed to story distribution or promotion. AI methods are now commonly applied to the other areas of news work but are still relatively rare in story production. Conversely, automation is increasingly common in investigative work, but most of this would not be considered AI.

Many news organizations use machine learning techniques to solve a variety of business problems, including predicting the popularity or "virality" of stories in order to decide what to promote, modeling user behavior to increase subscriptions and minimize churn, and so on (Stone 2014; Prakash 2017). Machine learning-based news personalization systems are widely used by news publishers such as *The New York Times* (Spangher 2015) and news aggregation apps such as *Google News* (Das 2007).

Conversely, news articles are widely used as test data sets in AI research for problems such as named entity recognition, topic modeling (Newman et al. 2006), recommendation, and summarization (Paulus, Xiong, and Socher 2018). These techniques are relevant to investigative journalism tasks, but the AI models created in this line of research are trained on the *output* of journalists. This is unlikely to yield good results for journalism applications as the source material used in reporting is substantially more diverse and messy than most NLP training sets (Stray 2016a).

Automated story production techniques have come into wide use in the last few years, with major newsrooms, including the AP, Reuters, and Forbes producing thousands of stories a month based on structured data feeds of corporate earnings and sports scores (LeCompte 2015; Marconi and Siegman 2017). The process is akin to filling out a form, with some conditional elements to select from a finite set of sentences based on data values (e.g., "the home team emerged victorious" vs. "it was a sorry loss for the home team.") While automated story production fundamentally challenges conceptions of the roles of humans and machines in journalism (Lewis, Guzman, and Schmidt 2019), automating the writing of investigative stories seems as if it would require artificial general intelligence, so we should not expect it soon.

The "computational journalism" literature gets closest to discussing the use of AI in story production. This relatively new term has been used in a variety of ways (Coddington 2015), including the use of computational techniques to find stories in data, and conversely the journalistic investigation of the properties of algorithms used by government and industry (Diakopoulos 2016). Both might be accelerated by AI. The 2011 definition of Cohen, Hamilton, and Turner is most relevant here:

> Stories will emerge from stacks of financial disclosure forms, court records, legislative hearings, officials' calendars or meeting notes, and regulators' email messages that no one today has time or money to mine. With a suite of reporting tools, a journalist will be able to scan, transcribe, analyze, and visualize the patterns in these documents. (Cohen, Hamilton, and Turner 2011)

Computational methods are today routine in journalism, if unevenly distributed (Berret and Phillips 2016). There are now widely used journalism-specific tools for analyzing unstructured documents (such as DocumentCloud (Mor and Reich 2018), Overview (Brehmer et al. 2014; Stray 2016a), Tadam (Plattner, Orel, and Steiner 2016), and Tabula (Aristarán et al. 2013)) and data wrangling (such as CSVkit (Christopher et al.

2018), Open Refine (openrefine.org n.d.), and Dedupe.io (DataMade 2016)). Pioneering organizations such as the International Consortium of Investigative Journalists (ICIJ) and the Organized Crime and Corruption Reporting Project (OCCRP) are fusing diverse data sets in graph databases to facilitate network analysis (Cabra 2016; Stray 2017).

For the most part, current computational journalism efforts would not be considered "artificial intelligence" in the sense that they do not use AI methods. Admittedly, this distinction can be fuzzy. One practical question—and a key economic consideration—is whether or not these applications require the services of a developer trained in contemporary AI technology. So far, that has rarely been the case.

Hamilton and others have suggested cost-effectiveness as a core rationale for applying AI (Hamilton 2016; Cohen, Hamilton, and Turner 2011) and we explore this consideration below. But this does not specify what AI should be doing. Broussard articulates a remarkable role for AI in investigative journalism: to analyze data for differences between what is and what ought to be (Broussard 2015), an idea to which we will return.

The Assumption of AI Advantage

We start from the idea that AI will prove transformative for investigative journalism, which is widely held in both industry and academia. This is the core assumption that this paper explores. A report from Columbia Journalism School concludes that "AI tools can help journalists tell new kinds of stories that were previously too resource-impractical or technically out of reach" (Hansen et al. 2017). An Associated Press report says AI will "empower the creation of entirely new types of journalism" (Marconi and Siegman 2017).

In such discussions, AI is typically described as being able to "identify a pattern" (Hansen et al. 2017), "uncover social problems" (Broussard 2015), "tell the stories hidden in the data" (Holmes 2016), or otherwise illuminate previously unknown connections. This is exciting, but vague. Without the grounding of story case studies, it will be difficult define the function of such pattern detection systems.

The other major claim is that AI will speed up investigative work. An example comes from the ICIJ:

> The ICIJ didn't utilize any AI technology during the investigative process [on the Panama Papers], but Matthew Caruana Galizia, the organization's web applications developer, wishes they did.

> "We were dealing with a vast amount of documents, and ICIJ just didn't have the resources to investigate them all," Galizia said. "But by using artificial intelligence, we would have been able to make that process much faster for all the journalists involved and end up with the same result." (Marconi and Siegman 2017)

What type of "AI" is useful here, and which part of the investigative workflow will it accelerate, or what new types of stories will be possible? There are few concrete examples. In part, these questions are difficult to answer because there are surprisingly few descriptions of data-driven investigative journalism processes, that is, what investigative journalists actually do with data in the course of their work. Although journalists often discuss the methods they used to complete an individual story, systematic summaries of investigative data practice are rare. There are detailed process descriptions of document mining in (Stray 2016a) and network analysis in (Stray 2017).

What Investigative AI Looks Like Now

The current uses of AI in investigative journalism are modest. To an AI researcher they may even seem trivial. Even so, these examples are important lessons in what journalists actually do, and may point the way to more ambitious applications.

Previous successful uses of AI in journalism fall into a few broad categories: document classification, language analysis, data cleaning, lead generation, and breaking news detection. Not all of these examples are investigative, but all have potential investigative applications. The stories produced in these ways might not have been possible without AI techniques, typically because they would have required too much manual labor. The seven stories and one system discussed in this section include many of the examples discussed within the data journalism community.

There are perhaps another dozen instances that might also be considered AI used for investigative reporting in (Stray 2016a; Stray 2017). The most comprehensive work on journalism automation lists about two dozen examples (Diakopoulos 2019) including most of those discussed here. This same small set of examples is repeatedly discussed at data journalism conferences such as NICAR (Shorey et al. 2018). The high overlap between sources suggests that there are a relatively small number of cases in total; no doubt there are others, but certainly not an order of magnitude more. In other words, AI methods are not yet commonly used for investigative reporting, and I will explore the reasons why below.

Document Classification

The most common use of machine learning in investigative journalism so far is supervised document classification. For the story "License to Betray" the Atlanta Journal Constitution scraped over 100,000 doctor disciplinary records from every state, looking for instances where doctors who had sexually abused patients were allowed to continue to practice (Teegardin et al. 2016). Logistic regression reduced the likely cases to 6000 documents, which they then read and coded manually (Stray 2016a).

The Los Angeles Times story "LAPD underreported serious assaults, skewing crime stats for 8 years" (Poston, Rubin, and Pesce 2015) was based on comparing the narrative descriptions of more than 400,000 incident reports with the category assigned by police, e.g. "aggravated assault." They found that there was a systematic misclassification of assaults as less serious than they actually were, according to LAPD's own definitions. Fortunately the reporters had manually reviewed one year's worth of data for a previous story, providing a training set of over 20,000 incidents (Stray 2016a).

Language Analysis

Some stories have relied on NLP techniques such as topic modeling, clustering, word embeddings, sentiment analysis, etc.

In their 2014 story "The Echo Chamber," Reuters reporters showed how a small group of elite lawyers have argued most of the cases before the US Supreme Court (Biskupic, Roberts, and Shiffman 2014). The reporters also broke down the number of accepted cases by type, for example, whether filed by a business, individual, or government agency. They accomplished this mostly by hiring 20 freelancers to read 10,300 petitions over a period of three months, but were able to gain some additional information through LDA topic modeling (Stray 2016a).

For the 2013 story "DHHS downplayed food stamp issues" (Dukes 2013), a WRAL-TV reporter used Overview (Brehmer et al. 2014) to automatically cluster 4500 pages of state government emails obtained through a Freedom of Information Act request. One large cluster corresponded to messages posted to an inter-county government email list. The reporter manually read this cluster and found messages showing the government officials knew that a web browser compatibility problem was causing delays, ultimately affecting 70,000 people (Dukes 2014).

Sentiment analysis has been used by journalists on social media data as a proxy for public opinion, but investigative journalism use is rare. For the Washington Post story "Whistleblowers say USAID's IG removed critical details from public reports" (Higham and Rich 2014) reporters compared 12 draft reports with their final versions. Using sentiment analysis, they found that more than 400 negative references were removed before publication (Stray 2016a).

Monitoring for Breaking News

The advent of global public social media such as Twitter seems to offer enormous opportunity to find previously obscure news. It has taken some time and effort to successfully exploit this data stream for journalism. While monitoring for breaking news is not usually an investigative journalism application, this is one of the only production examples of more general "story finding" AI.

The Reuters Tracer system continuously ingests Twitter data, filters out spam and tweets which are not about events, then clusters tweets by event and ranks them for review by journalists (Liu et al. 2016; Stray 2016b). The system employs a number of trained models for tweet classification, clustering, and newsworthiness ranking, as shown in Figure 1. Out of a sample of 31 news events, in 27 cases Tracer found a corresponding tweet cluster faster than Reuters journalists were able to issue an alert using traditional reporting methods, often by a half hour or more.

Lead Generation

Several authors have noted that AI could be especially useful for journalistic lead generation, generating lines of inquiry rather than definitive conclusions (Hansen et al. 2017; Diakopoulos 2019; Shorey et al. 2018). Human involvement also avoids the potential accuracy and relevance problems of directly publishing automated output.

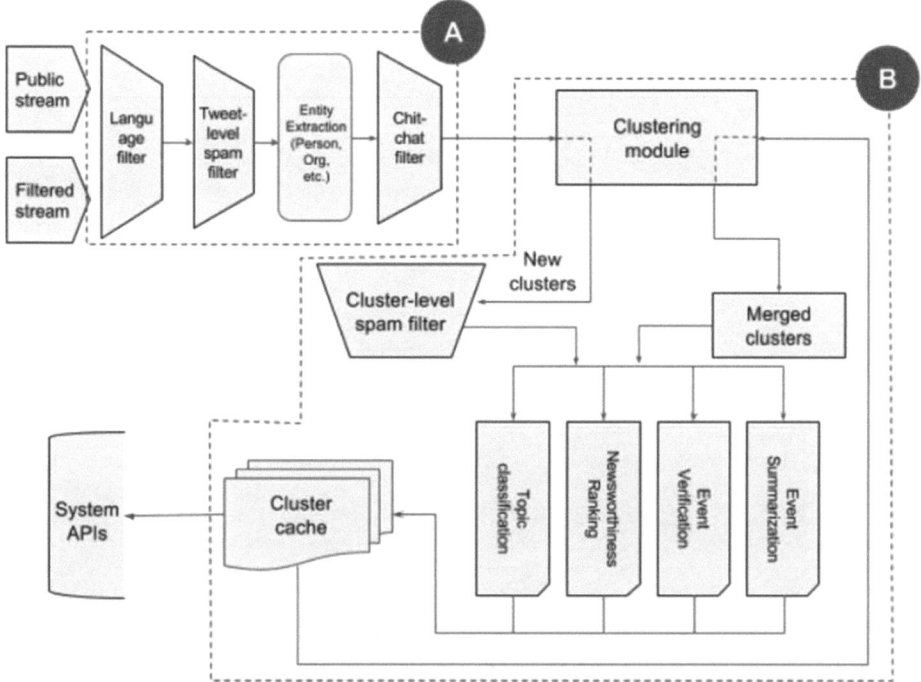

Figure 1. Machine learning system architecture for Reuters Tracer: (A) tweet processing module; (B) event detection module. Many of the stages in this diagram involve custom built and trained models. From Liu et al. (2016).

The *New York Times' Who The Hill* was designed to recognize the faces of US members of congress (Shorey et al. 2018) in images uploaded by readers. It was more of a curiosity than a serious reporting tool, but it contributed to at least one story when congresswoman Claudia Tenney was identified in a photograph taken at a fundraising party (Vogel and Shorey 2018).

Buzzfeed's story on US government surveillance planes is one of the most intriguing uses of machine learning in journalism. Reporters knew from previous stories that law enforcement would sometimes circle over major cities to take surveillance footage or capture cell phone signals (Aldhous and Seife 2016) (Figure 2). By training on the flight paths of known law enforcement planes, using features describing the flight path bounding box and flight speed and direction histograms, Buzzfeed was able to identify many planes for further investigation (Aldhous 2017).

This seems like a great success for machine learning on an important story. However, machine learning was not really necessary. In independent work, Bastien identified most of the same planes by ranking flights according to a simple metric designed to detect circling: the percentage of points on the flight path within 10 miles of the centroid (Bastien 2017). As several practitioners have pointed out, there are often simpler alternatives to machine learning (Shorey et al. 2018). In any case, the hard work of this story is not finding the planes, but the subsequent time-consuming investigation of who owns them, what they are doing, and whether it is legal and ethical.

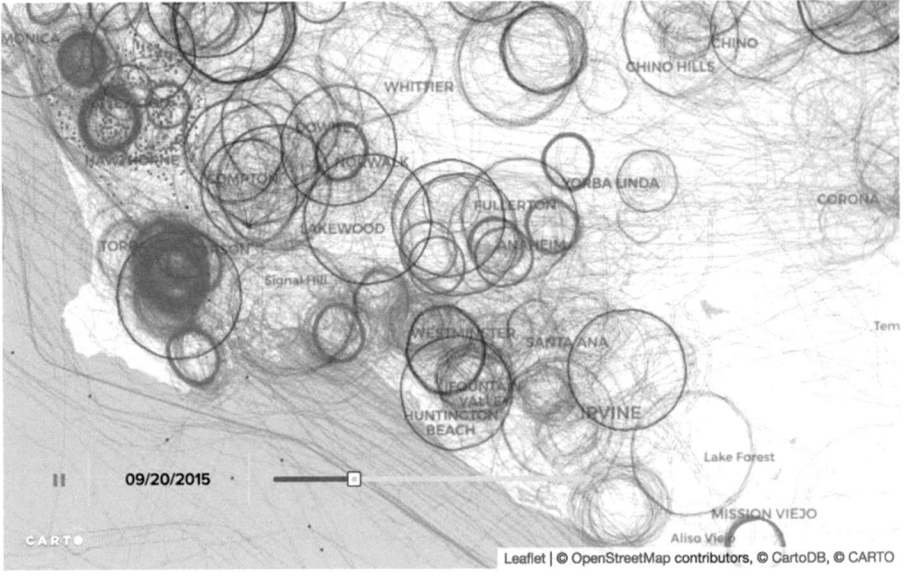

■FBI ■DHS

Figure 2. US government surveillance plane flight paths identified by machine learning (Aldhous and Seife 2016).

Why AI for Investigative Journalism Is Hard

So far, AI methods in investigative journalism have produced useful but modest results. There are perhaps a perhaps a few dozen examples to date, and there is a wide gap between these cases and the ambitious visions quoted above. AI has barely touched investigative journalism, let alone transformed it.

This failure could be an issue of technology diffusion or inadequate investment. Or perhaps the problem is simply difficult. There are a number of domain-specific issues that make it challenging to apply AI techniques to investigative journalism. Some of these appear to be fundamental, and unlikely to be solved quickly.

Data Availability

"Public data," meaning data that is legally required to be accessible to citizens, is not necessarily publicly available. Often it must be requested, negotiated, scraped, or purchased. Certain national corporate registries, especially in tax havens such as Cyprus and Hong Kong, require company registration records to be purchased one at a time, meaning that it is impractically expensive to acquire the complete "public" data set. Surprisingly often, public records are not even digital. Fully a third of the document sets in a recent survey of document-driven investigative journalism projects arrived on physical paper (Stray 2016a).

The bad news is that journalists spend an enormous amount of time gathering data from a variety of sources. The good news is that, armed with suitable metadata

and integrations with existing data provider search systems, an AI assistant could propose scraping or purchasing the records required to answer a query, or help file and
track public records requests as MuckRock already does (MuckRock 2018). Human
sources will remain out of reach of automated methods for the foreseeable future;
despite recent dramatic advances in conversational systems, such as Google's Duplex
AI which can make simple phone calls to book services (Leviathan and Matias 2018),
it will be a long time before machines can talk to people in an investigative context.

Journalism AI research is also hindered by the lack of standard training data sets.
While "general" AI efforts such as question answering and document summarization
may prove themselves valuable to journalists, investigative reporters also face some
unique and uniquely complex data tasks. Creating specialized training and evaluation
data repositories may be an important first step in producing AI research that leads to
useful journalism applications. ProPublica's Free The Files project (ProPublica 2012),
discussed below, is one labeled investigative journalism corpus that could be packaged and promoted as a research data set.

Unique Stories

When AI is used in a commercial setting there is typically an ongoing business problem to be solved. Transactional data such as clicks and purchases arrives in continuous
streams, and a model trained on this data can be used as long as the underlying
stream is stable.

By contrast, many data-driven investigative stories are never repeated. The Atlanta
Journal-Constitution's model for finding documents describing sexual abuse by doctors will never be useful again, because there is not another backlog of 100,000
reports to examine. In such cases the cost of building a custom AI solution cannot be
amortized over multiple stories.

I am aware of only one set of experiments on the time/cost/accuracy of machine
learning vs. human information extraction in a journalism context, which suggests that
the break-even point is on the order of a few hundred documents (Giorgi 2015). For
document classification tasks, the domain of legal e-discovery is perhaps most similar to
investigative journalism, and one vendor addresses the problem of fixed costs by noting
that machine learning (called "predictive coding" in this domain) "has been successfully
leveraged in cases with only a few hundred or thousand documents"(Robinson 2018).
A survey of machine-assisted document-driven investigative journalism projects gives a
median document set size of 4000 documents (Stray 2016a). This lower limit of hundreds to thousands of documents suggests that many document sets in journalism are
simply too small to benefit from AI methods.

Challenging Problems

As part of an investigation of Donald Trump's business deals, students at Columbia
Journalism School examined New York City real estate public records pertaining to
several Trump properties. These records are available from the city's ACRIS database,
covering a variety of contracts including mortgages and liens between dozens of

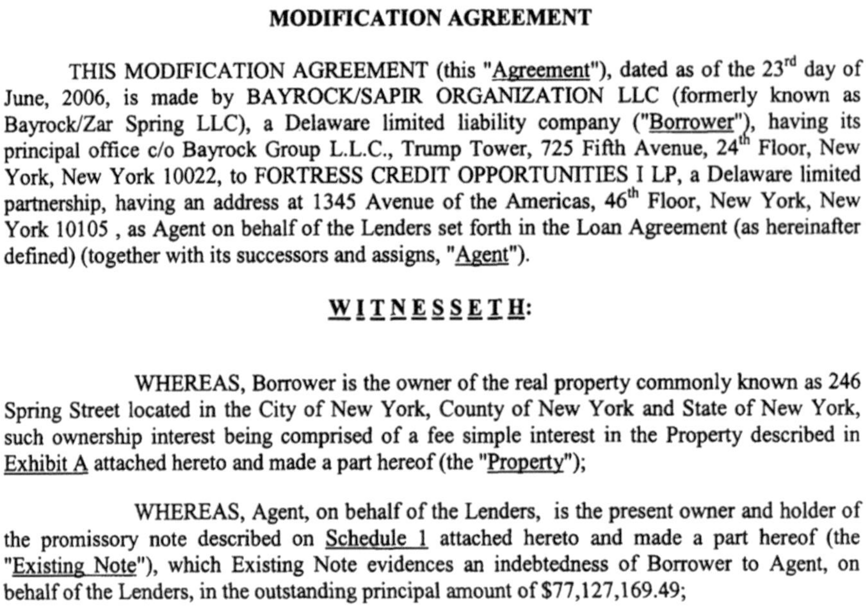

MODIFICATION AGREEMENT

THIS MODIFICATION AGREEMENT (this "Agreement"), dated as of the 23rd day of June, 2006, is made by BAYROCK/SAPIR ORGANIZATION LLC (formerly known as Bayrock/Zar Spring LLC), a Delaware limited liability company ("Borrower"), having its principal office c/o Bayrock Group L.L.C., Trump Tower, 725 Fifth Avenue, 24th Floor, New York, New York 10022, to FORTRESS CREDIT OPPORTUNITIES I LP, a Delaware limited partnership, having an address at 1345 Avenue of the Americas, 46th Floor, New York, New York 10105 , as Agent on behalf of the Lenders set forth in the Loan Agreement (as hereinafter defined) (together with its successors and assigns, "Agent").

W I T N E S S E T H:

WHEREAS, Borrower is the owner of the real property commonly known as 246 Spring Street located in the City of New York, County of New York and State of New York, such ownership interest being comprised of a fee simple interest in the Property described in Exhibit A attached hereto and made a part hereof (the "Property");

WHEREAS, Agent, on behalf of the Lenders, is the present owner and holder of the promissory note described on Schedule 1 attached hereto and made a part hereof (the "Existing Note"), which Existing Note evidences an indebtedness of Borrower to Agent, on behalf of the Lenders, in the outstanding principal amount of $77,127,169.49;

Figure 3. The beginning of a document describing a modification to one of the loans used to finance the Trump Soho hotel (New York City ACRIS document 2006083000784001).

parties over more than a decade. Figure 3 is an example document concerning the Trump Soho hotel (later renamed The Dominick). The investigative questions are

- Who are the parties that currently own the building?
- What was the equity and outstanding debt of each party at each point in time?
- Who did they owe these debts to?

This can only be determined by painstakingly reading and reconstructing the series of documents filed for this property, which range from standardized forms to complex natural-language contracts. Figure 4 shows part of a hand-built spreadsheet of the transactions contained in these documents, used by the reporters to answer these questions. The task is deterministic in the sense that there is a definite answer, though that answer may involve descriptions of financial relationships that fall outside of the simple categories in the above questions.

This is a multi-document comprehension problem that is well beyond the current state of the art of AI. Progress is likely to be slow: training data is scarce, expensive to produce, and unlikely to generalize. There are perhaps ten thousand New York City real estate developments of this size and complexity (New York City Department of Finance 2017), each one would require a dozen or so hours to generate a spreadsheet like the one above, and even a complete data set would not be large enough for current deep learning approaches. By comparison, the data sets used for much simpler "question answering" or "reading comprehension" AI research are orders of magnitude larger. The Stanford Question Answering Dataset includes 130,000 examples (Rajpurkar, Jia, and Liang 2018) and the CNN/Daily Mail training data set is over a million examples (Chen, Bolton, and Manning 2016).

Recorded / Filed	Document Type	Pages	Party1	Party2	Doc Amount
5/3/06 16:44	MORTGAGE AND CONSOLIDATION	14	BAYROCK/SAPIR ORGANIZATION LLC	FORTRESS CREDIT OPPORTUNITIES I LP	74,298,931.00
5/3/06 16:44	UCC3 AMENDMENT	14	BAYROCK/SAPIR ORGANIZATION LLC	FORTRESS CREDIT OPPORTUNITIES I LP	.
5/3/06 16:44	UCC3 AMENDMENT	13	BAYROCK/SAPIR ORGANIZATION LLC	FORTRESS CREDIT OPPORTUNITIES I LP	.
6/13/06 15:39	MISCELLANEOUS	1	246 SPRING STREET, LLC		.
8/23/06 11:43	MISCELLANEOUS	29	BAYROCK/SAPIR ORGANIZATION LLC		
9/5/06 13:57	AGREEMENT	10	BAYROCK/SAPIR ORGANIZATION LLC	FORTRESS CREDIT OPPORTUNITIES I LP	9,884,807.00
5/3/07 11:00	ZONING LOT DESCRIPTION	12	BAYROCK/SAPIR ORGANIZATION LLC		.
9/24/07 14:19	MORTGAGE	33	BAYROCK/SPAPIR ORGANIZATIONLLC,	ISTAR FINANCIAL	87,000,000.00
9/24/07 14:19	ASSIGNMENT OF LEASES AND RENTS	13	BAYROCK/SPAPIR ORGANIZATIONLLC,725	ISTAR FINANCIAL	.
9/24/07 14:19	ASSIGNMENT, MORTGAGE	9	BAYROCK/SPAPIR ORGANIZATIONLLC,725	ISTAR FINANCIAL	.
9/24/07 14:19	UCC3 TERMINATION	16	BAYROCK/ZAR SPRING LLC C/O BAYROCK GROUP L.L.C.	FORTRESS CREDIT CORP.	.
9/24/07 14:19	MORTGAGE	31	BAYROCK/SAPIR ORGANIZATION LLC,	ISTAR FINANCIAL INC,	28,237,515.00
9/24/07 14:19	ASSIGNMENT OF LEASES AND RENTS	14	BAYROCK/SAPIR ORGANIZATION LLC,	ISTAR FINANCIAL INC,	.
9/24/07 14:19	INITIAL UCC1	10	BAYROCK/SAPIR ORGANIZATION LLC,	ISTAR FINANCIAL INC,	.
9/24/07 14:19	MORTGAGE	31	BAYROCK/SAPIR ORGANIZATION LLC,	ISTAR FINANCIAL INC,	9,762,485.00
9/24/07 14:19	ASSIGNMENT OF LEASES AND RENTS	13	BAYROCK/SAPIR ORGANIZATION LLC,	ISTAR FINANCIAL INC,	.
9/24/07 14:19	INITIAL UCC1	10	BAYROCK/SAPIR ORGANIZATION LLC,	ISTAR FINANCIAL INC,	.
9/24/07 14:19	INITIAL UCC1	10	BAYROCK/SAPIR ORGANIZATION LLC,	ISTAR FINANCIAL INC,	.
9/28/07 16:58	ADDITIONAL MORTGAGE TAX	1	BAYROCK/ SPAPIR ORGANIZATION LLC		2,816,263.00

Figure 4. Excerpt of the hand-built chronological list of New York City real estate public records concerning the Trump Soho hotel. Color coding indicates documents on the same date (Giannina Segnini/Columbia Journalism School).

The Need for Accuracy

Imagine a news organization which uses AI to examine public records to find suspected money laundering. Inaccurately suggesting that someone is involved in criminal activity is not only a serious violation of journalistic ethics, but it can also lead to an expensive libel lawsuit—even if the other 99% of inferences are correct. Although this has yet to be tested in court, it seems likely that US publishers will be liable for algorithmic errors: "news organizations should be concerned about liability for libelous automated journalism content affecting private plaintiffs, who can recover by proving the negligence on the part of the news organization" (Lewis, Sanders, and Carmody 2019).

It is unlikely that any AI system used in investigative journalism will reach 100% accuracy, in part because of the usual sources of error in AI systems (variance, generalization error, etc.) but more fundamentally because the available data is usually ambiguous. For example, there is no algorithm to determine whether the same name in two different databases actually refers to the same person or not. This requires more data, for example, the person's address, but even then errors are possible: there could have been two people with the same name living at the same address at different times, or "Jr." and "Sr." suffices could be missing, or it could simply be an error in the data. Only manual research—perhaps a phone call to the landlord—can ultimately resolve such questions.

Thus, AI-generated results cannot be directly published if an incorrect result might injure someone's reputation. This is not an issue when AI is used to rank items for human follow-up, as in Buzzfeed's identification of potential surveillance flights. But if algorithmic results are to be published, they may first need to be individually checked by hand, in which case the computational advantages of scale and speed may be lost.

Image available in original journal article

An alternative is to publish only aggregate information, which can sometimes be corrected for algorithmic uncertainty—though quantification of that uncertainty usually requires human review. For the LAPD crime misclassification story, the reporters reviewed a random sample of 2400 machine-labeled incidents and discovered that the classifier error rate was a hefty 24%. Rather than attempting to improve the classifier, they simply adjusted their yearly totals of misclassified crimes to produce more conservative estimates (Postin and Pesce 2015).

Cost-Effectiveness

If there is an underlying thread to the problems so far, it is the issue of cost-effectiveness. AI may be able to help journalists find and produce stories that would otherwise be impossible; if it does not, it must help journalists do their work faster and cheaper. As Cohen Hamilton, and Turner (2011) point out, talking to human sources is often just as efficient as data analysis.

> Journalists often collect records to address a specific question, which, when answered, marks the end of the analysis and the beginning of the story. This suggests a strict limit on the time and money invested in any document or data; it must be more effective or newsworthy than the alternative path of asking whistle-blowers or partisan insiders for the material. (Cohen, Hamilton, and Turner 2011)

The issue of time is multiplied by the relative market rates of different types of work. According to US salary data from job site Glassdoor, the average "reporter" salary is around $50,000 while the average "artificial intelligence engineer" is closer to $150,000. This constrains the amount of time that can be shifted from reporting to engineering, if automation is to increase efficiency in terms of stories per dollar. It also means that AI talent developed in the newsroom is in danger of leaving for better paid jobs.

Moreover, most of the data analyses performed in contemporary journalism can be done with a spreadsheet. AI will only be cost-effective for a subset of stories where:

- Data is a substantial and important source of information for the story.
- There is a data subtask which is at least partially automatable.
- Straightforward (non-AI) computational techniques are not sufficient.
- It would be faster and/or cheaper to apply an AI method instead of doing it manually.
- There is no good alternative, such as talking to a domain expert or inside source.

Today this is a rather small set of stories. Yet AI may still have enormous impact, if it can truly help find stories that a human alone would miss. Even one story can have an outsized impact. Money laundering investigations by the Sarajevo-based OCCRP have uncovered over 5 billion dollars stolen from public funds in Eastern European countries (OCCRP 2018). If an AI can marshal evidence that a human reporter missed, a single story might benefit thousands or millions of people.

What Is News?

Perhaps, the most complex challenge in AI-assisted investigative story production is the technical systematization of the concept of "news." The description of "news values" by sociologist Stuart Hall seems as fresh today as when it was written in 1973:

> News values are one of the most opaque structures of meaning in modern society. All 'true journalists' are supposed to possess it; few can or are willing to identify and define it. Journalists speak of 'the news' as if events selected themselves. Further, they speak as if which is the 'most significant' news story, or which 'news angles' are most salient are divinely inspired. Yet of the millions of events which occur every day in the world, only a tiny portion ever become visible as 'potential news stories,' and of this proportion, only a small fraction are actually produced as the day's news in the news media. We appear to be dealing, then, with a 'deep structure' whose function as a selective device is un-transparent even to those who professionally most know how to operate it. (Hall 1973)

Of course, "news values" are not completely opaque even if they are hard for journalists to articulate, and decades of research have attempted to learn from journalists and their stories what counts as news. A recent review (Harcup and O'Neill 2017) suggests over a dozen criteria, such as *the power elite*, *conflict*, *surprise*, *magnitude*, *shareability*, *bad news*, and *celebrity*. Investigative journalism may or may not encode the same set of values as news generally, but it certainly uses *some* set of values to decide what is worth reporting. Embedding these values into code—teaching a computer to identify the fact patterns that constitute a "story"— is poorly explored. It is a major technical, political, and ethical challenge.

One approach is to design algorithmic definitions of newsworthiness from first principles. The Los Angeles Times' earthquake reporting bot used data from the USGS Earthquake Notification Service to "automatically generate short reports on earthquakes above the 'newsworthy' threshold of a 3.0 magnitude" (LeCompte 2015). Others have used more sophisticated methods to interpret incoming data. The Marple system monitors Swedish crime data for potential stories and flags anomalous data points. It models the average number of crimes per month from historical data, but there must still be a newsworthiness threshold. In this case, the researchers chose a statistical significance threshold (p value) of 0.0001, meaning that only data points with less than a 1-in-10,000 chance of being generated by the historical model will be flagged. The researchers found that this struck a good balance between missing "obvious" peaks and overwhelming the reporters with notifications—an approach they described as "ad-hoc" (Magnusson, Finnäs, and Wallentin 2016).

How should one decide on these thresholds? How to elicit them from reporters? Newsroom automation practitioners frequently describe this as a problem. For the Associated Press' automated story production efforts,

> Translating even the simplest data means converting the loose guidelines a human reporter might follow into concrete rules a computer can follow. For example, a human reporter might have a general idea of when a company's performance was very different from analyst expectations, based on their knowledge of the industry. But for the algorithm, the AP had to specify exact ranges for which the spread between actual earnings and expectations is considered large or small. (LeCompte 2015)

The development of the Reuters Tracer system encountered similar obstacles:

> Newsroom standards are rarely formal enough to turn into code. … 'The interesting exercise when you start moving to machines is you have to start codifying this,' says Chua. 'Much like trying to program ethics for self-driving cars, it's an exercise in turning implicit judgments into clear instructions.' (Stray 2016b)

Instead of trying to come up with explicit rules for newsworthiness, some researchers and practitioners have used human journalists' output as training data. To train their Tracer system to decide whether an event is newsworthy, Reuters engineers created a set of 300 clusters of tweets around specific events, 63 of which were identified as newsworthy by journalists. And to evaluate the recall of the system, they collected all major news events over a period of one week as reported by Reuters, AP, and CNN (Liu et al. 2016).

Asking journalists to label training data or evaluate automated output avoids the problem of articulating explicit rules for newsworthiness. It also replicates any biases in existing reporting. For example, it is well established that crime reporting is biased. Metropolitan newspapers in the US report somewhere between 30% and 70% of the homicides in their city. Generally, a crime is more likely to be covered if the victim is young, female, white, and/or rich, or if the killing is particularly gruesome or involves multiple victims or sex. This produces a distorted picture of crime in the public imagination. Also, the focus on individual incidents as opposed to trends may explain why the majority of Americans believe that violent crime is increasing when it has been decreasing for decades in most cities (Stray 2012).

The codification of newsworthiness provides a unique opportunity to reflect on what investigative journalists cover and what they should cover. Rather than simply replicate what newsrooms do now, journalism AI researchers could entirely re-imagine reporting. However, this re-imagining will run into constraints. One team discovered that finding breaking news on social media requires monitoring active accounts with large audiences, and this means attending to "men in the media" even if one might wish to highlight other, less heard voices (Thurman et al. 2016). Investigative AI designers will be forced to think deeply about both the goals and the practicalities of story detection.

Near-Term Promise for Investigative AI: Data Wrangling

So far, we have looked at the challenges to the grand visions of AI in investigative journalism. There are also problems that could be solved with near-future AI techniques. The biggest opportunity is speeding up data preparation and cleaning.

Data "wrangling" and cleaning makes up a large fraction of the time spent most data projects, with surveys showing numbers between 30% and 80%, yet it is not a particularly well-studied research topic (Kandel et al. 2011; Furche et al. 2016; Press 2016). The problem is particularly acute for investigative journalism because of the huge variety of different source document and data formats, even for the same type of data. The next sections give two real-world examples of data preparation tasks that AI could help with: data extraction from documents and cross-database record linkage.

Data Extraction from Heterogeneous Documents

While every TV station in the United States must disclose political ad sales, there is no requirement on format or standardization. This leads to a dizzying array of different form types, nearly as many as there are TV stations, three of which are reproduced in Figure 5. Standard OCR cannot cope with all these layouts, the need for high accuracy, and the required standardization and merging. The problem is so resistant to automation that for the 2012 election, ProPublica enlisted its readers in a crowd-sourced data transcription effort called Free The Files, which eventually manually entered data for about 17,000 of the 43,000 disclosure documents they obtained (ProPublica 2012).

There are deep learning methods to extract structured data from richly formatted documents (Wu et al. 2018) which could, in principle, be applied to document sets relevant to journalism. Services such as Amazon's Textract are starting to offer similar capabilities commercially. It is not clear how AI trained on one document domain—such as corporate ownership records, financial disclosures, or court filings—would generalize to the others, which makes this a challenging research problem.

Record Linkage

Fusing databases has long been a basic investigative journalism technique. One early example is a 1985 story in which reporters cross-referenced a list of school bus drivers with a list of felons to find a disturbing amount of overlap. The resulting story led to policy changes, and 65 drivers had their licenses revoked (DeFleur 2013).

Record linkage is the process of determining that two records refer to the same entity, typically a person or company. When a database must be linked to itself—as in the case of identifying unique donors in campaign finance data—this is also known as deduplication. Because names are not unique, record linkage depends on the existence of other fields such as addresses, but even then it is often not possible to match

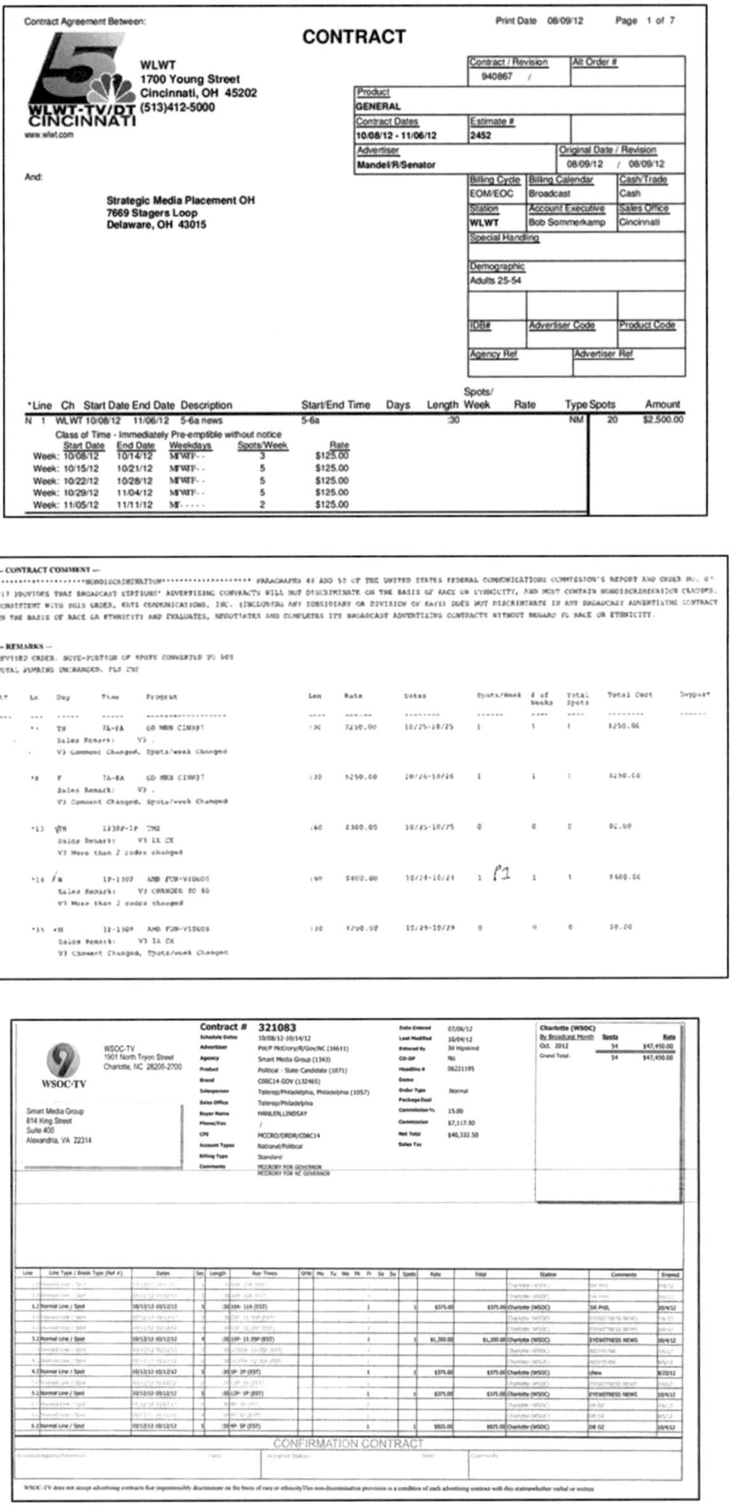

Figure 5. Three different political ad buy disclosures from the 2012 US election, from ProPublica's Free The Files (ProPublica 2012).

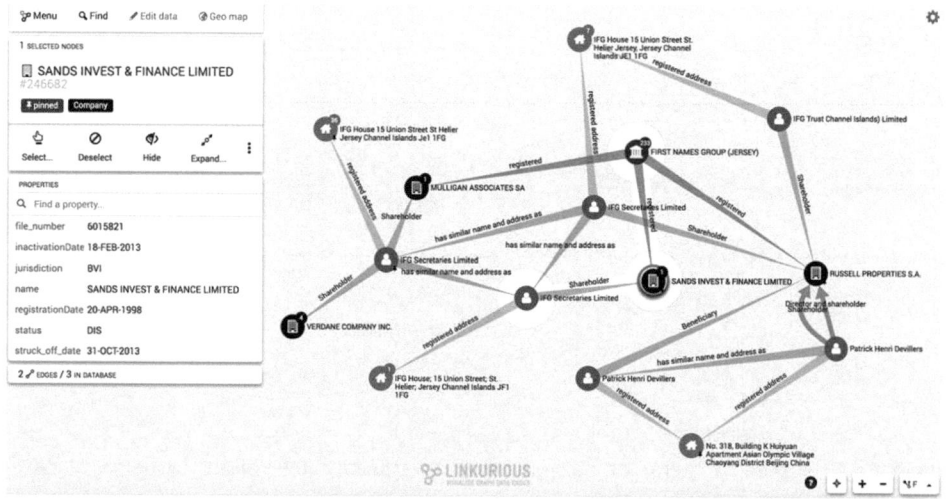

Figure 6. A subset of the Panama papers structured data, in a graph created by a reporter. Note the duplicate records from different databases, and also machine-generated linkages such as "has similar name and address as" (reproduced from Cabra 2016).

names with 100% certainty. Probabilistic record deduplication is already in use in journalism (DataMade 2016).

Recently, there have been a series of increasingly ambitious data fusion projects carried out by organizations such as ICIJ and OCCRP. The prototypical example is the Panama Papers. The structured data sets (which comprised only one part of the total leak) were loaded into the Neo4j graph database, then entities with similar names and addresses were given a "soft linkage" by adding edges, as shown in Figure 6. Journalists reported on the data by graphically exploring the networks around specific people and companies of interest (Stray 2017).

Automated linkage judgments must still be validated manually before publishing, because a crucial link which forms the basis of a public accusation of wrongdoing cannot rest on the vagaries of a particular model. Previous work proposes a hybrid model where the computer links records automatically and shows merged entities to the user, which can be expanded as needed to evaluate the underlying linkages (Stray 2017). One possible system, including an un-merged graph data store, is shown in Figure 7.

Conclusion

This paper has unpacked the idea that AI can be useful in investigative journalism, proceeding in three parts: case studies demonstrating how AI has been used to date, an analysis of the challenges that have prevented wider use, and a proposed near-term research focus on data wrangling, which is immediately useful and sidesteps many of the greatest difficulties.

Previous discussions of AI in investigative journalism have often dodged the details of exactly how it would be used. Generally, authors have imagined that AI could be used for

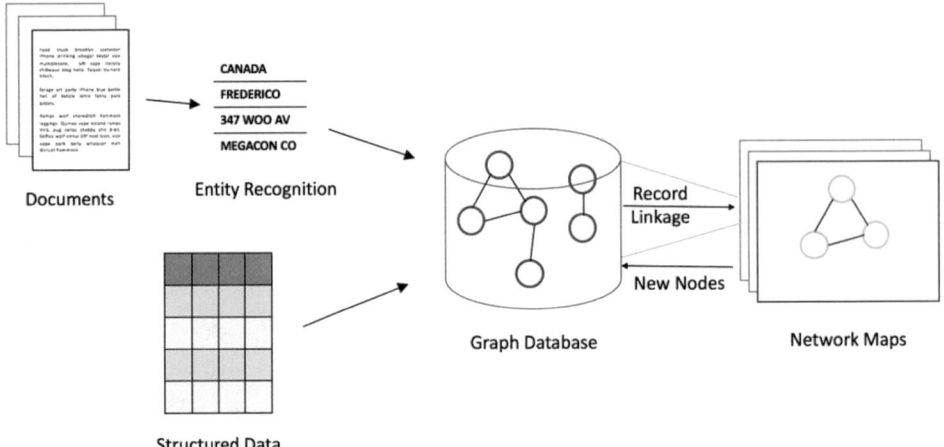

Figure 7. A proposed system for network-based investigative journalism, including AI-assisted record linkage. From Stray (2017).

"pattern recognition" within large data sets of public interest, greatly reducing the human effort required to produce investigative stories. There are several reasons why this will be difficult:

- Data access is a continual problem. Even public records frequently need to be requested, scraped, purchased, or negotiated.
- Investigative projects are often unique or "one off," so the development costs of AI models cannot be amortized across stories.
- Investigative journalism problems are often well beyond the state of the art of current methods, such as complex multi-document summarization tasks.
- Professional ethics and libel law necessitate essentially perfect accuracy in any published inferences. This usually means AI output requires human checking.

Human labor is always an option, so these can all be understood as issues of cost-effectiveness. AI engineers are also substantially more expensive than reporters, which further constrains the economics. Even for tasks such as document classification, where existing AI methods are effective, problem set-up costs currently favor manual work for smaller data sets, perhaps up to a few thousand documents.

AI could also help find stories that humans would miss, either because it would be too expensive to have reporters read all of the relevant data or because the required pattern recognition is a cognitive task better suited to machines. Unfortunately, specifying which sorts of fact patterns constitute a "story" is an extremely challenging problem. It is difficult to translate notions of "newsworthiness" into code. The alternative is to have machine systems learn newsworthiness from human examples, but this will replicate any existing biases in coverage. Should investigative story-finding algorithms come into wide use, we should expect that they will be subjects of social and political controversy, as news recommendation algorithms already are.

There is at least one area where AI methods are likely to benefit investigative journalism in the near term: data cleaning and "wrangling." This work typically consumes a substantial fraction of the time required to produce a data-driven investigative story, yet the required operations tend to be simpler and less open-ended than other investigative tasks. The primary source records that journalists must rely on are maddeningly diverse and messy, which makes data extraction and probabilistic record linkage promising targets for AI automation.

Beyond that, if the above challenges should prove surmountable, we are faced with the question of what, ultimately, investigative journalism AI should be used to accomplish. At the highest level of abstraction, "an investigation often arises when a reporter perceives a difference between what is (the observed reality) and what should be (as articulated in law or policy)" (Broussard 2015). In principle, AI could be used to evaluate both the *is* and the *ought*. This is an enormously complex task. Determining what *is* is the core, hard task of investigative reporting. What *should* be is an even more complex question. Law and policy only capture part of what is right, people disagree for good reasons, and the answers are unavoidably political. Ultimately, investigative journalism AI requires not just vast quantities of public records and deep contextual understanding, but opinions on right and wrong.

Disclosure statement

No potential conflict of interest was reported by the author.

ORCID

Jonathan Stray (iD) http://orcid.org/0000-0003-4467-1239

References

Aldhous, Peter. 2017. "How BuzzFeed News Revealed Hidden Spy Planes in US Airspace." *Columbia Journalism Review*. Accessed August 7 2017. https://www.buzzfeed.com/peteraldhous/hidden-spy-planes?utm_term=.oyox5J8g6#.nik4pQLYZ.

Aldhous, Peter, and Charles Seife. 2016. "Spies in the Skies." *Buzzfeed*. Accessed April 6 2016. https://www.buzzfeed.com/peteraldhous/spies-in-the-skies?utm_term=.ae7VDwyKL#.rhyKAN7bD.

Aristarán, Manuel, Mike Tigas, Jeremy B. Merrill, and Jason Das. 2013. "Tabula: Extract Tables from PDFs." 2013. http://tabula.technology/.

Bastien, Laurent. 2017. "Finding Every Government Surveillance Flight." 2017. https://github.com/laurentbastien/spyplanes/blob/master/laurent_bastien_DATA_SAMPLE.pdf.

Berret, Charles, and Cheryl Phillips. 2016. "Teaching Data and Computational Journalism." https://journalism.columbia.edu/system/files/content/teaching_data_and_computational_journalism.pdf.

Biskupic, Joan, Janet Roberts, and John Shiffman. 2014. "The Echo Chamber." *Reuters*. Accessed December 8 2014. https://www.reuters.com/investigates/special-report/scotus/.

Brehmer, Matthew, Stephen Ingram, Jonathan Stray, and Tamara Munzner. 2014. "Overview: The Design, Adoption, and Analysis of a Visual Document Mining Tool for Investigative Journalists." *IEEE Transactions on Visualization and Computer Graphics* 20 (12): 2271–2280.

Broussard, Meredith. 2015. "Artificial Intelligence for Investigative Reporting." *Digital Journalism* 3 (6): 814–831.

Broussard, Meredith. 2018. *Artificial Unintelligence : How Computers Misunderstand the World*. Cambridge: MIT Press.

Cabra, Mar. 2016. "How the ICIJ Used Neo4j to Unravel the Panama Papers." *Neo4j Blog*. 2016. https://neo4j.com/blog/icij-neo4j-unravel-panama-papers/.

Chen, Danqi, Jason Bolton, and Christopher D. Manning. 2016. "A Thorough Examination of the CNN/Daily Mail Reading Comprehension Task." arXiv preprint arXiv:1606.02858.

Christopher Groskopf 2018. "Csvkit 1.0.3." 2018. https://csvkit.readthedocs.io/en/1.0.3/.

Coddington, Mark. 2015. "Clarifying Journalism's Quantitative Turn." *Digital Journalism* 3 (3): 331–348.

Cohen, Sarah, James T. Hamilton, and Fred Turner. 2011. "Computational Journalism." *Communications of the ACM* 54 (10): 66.

Das, A S. M. Datar, A. Garg, and S. Rajaram. (2007, May). "Google news personalization: scalable online collaborative filtering" In Proceedings of the 16th international conference on World Wide Web, 271–280. ACM.

DataMade. 2016. "Introducing Dedupe.Io." 2016. https://datamade.us/blog/introducing-dedupeio.

DeFleur, Margaret H. 2013. *Computer-Assisted Investigative Reporting: Development and Methodology*. Abingdon: Routledge.

Diakopoulos, Nicholas. 2016. "Accountability in Algorithmic Decision Making." *Communications of the ACM* 59 (2): 56–62.

Diakopoulos, Nicholas. 2019. *Automating the News*. Cambridge, MA: Harvard University Press.

Dukes, Tyler. 2013. "Records: DHHS Downplayed Food Stamp Issues." *WRAL*. Accessed December 9 2013. http://www.wral.com/records-dhhs-downplayed-food-stamp-glitches/13173174/.

Dukes, Tyler. 2014. "Human-Assisted Reporting Gets the Story." Source: An OpenNews Project. 2014. https://source.opennews.org/articles/human-assisted-reporting/.

Furche, Tim, Georg Gottlob, Leonid Libkin, Giorgio Orsi, and Norman W. Paton. 2016. "Data Wrangling for Big Data: Challenges and Opportunities." Paper presented at Proceedings of the 19th International Conference on Extending Database Technology (EDBT), Bordeaux, France.

Giorgi, Ariana. 2015. "An Analysis of Methods for Information Retrieval." 2015. https://github.com/arianagiorgi/masters-proj/blob/master/Giorgi_MP2015.pdf.

Hall, Stuart. 1973. "The Determinations of News Photographs." In *The Manufacture of News: Social Problems, Deviance and the Mass Media*, edited by Stanley Cohen and Jock Young London, 226–247. Constable.

Hamilton, James. 2016. *Democracy's Detectives: The Economics of Investigative Journalism*, Cambridge, MA: Harvard University Press.

Hansen, Mark, Meritxell Roca-Sales, Jon Keegan, and George King. 2017. "Artificial Intelligence: Practice and Implications for Journalism." Tow Center for Digital Journalism, Columbia Journalism School, New York. https://towcenter.org/research/artificial-intelligence-practice-and-implications-for-journalism/.

Harcup, Tony, and Deirdre O'Neill. 2017. "What Is News?" *Journalism Studies* 18 (12): 1470–1488.

Higham, Scott, and Steven Rich. 2014. "Whistleblowers Say USAID's IG Removed Critical Details from Public Reports." *The Washington Post*. Accessed October 22 2014. https://www.washington-post.com/investigations/whistleblowers-say-usaids-ig-removed-critical-details-from-public-reports/2014/10/22/68fbc1a0-4031-11e4-b03f-de718edeb92f_story.html?utm_term=.df962e16a5d3.

Holmes, Jonathan. 2016. "AI Is Already Making Inroads into Journalism but Could It Win a Pulitzer?" *The Guardian*. Accessed April 3 2016. https://www.theguardian.com/media/2016/apr/03/artificla-intelligence-robot-reporter-pulitzer-prize.

Kandel, Sean, Jeffrey Heer, Catherine Plaisant, Jessie Kennedy, Frank Van Ham, Nathalie Henry Riche, Chris Weaver, Bongshin Lee, Dominique Brodbeck, and Paolo Buono. 2011. "Research Directions in Data Wrangling: Visualizations and Transformations for Usable and Credible Data." *Information Visualization* 10 (4): 271–288.

Kovach, Bill, and Tom Rosenstiel. 2014. *The Elements of Journalism*. 3rd ed. New York, NY: Three Rivers Press.

LeCompte, Celeste. 2015. "Automation in the Newsroom." *Nieman Reports*. Accessed September 2015. http://niemanreports.org/articles/automation-in-the-newsroom/.

Leviathan, Yaniv, and Yossi Matias. 2018. "Google Duplex: An AI System for Accomplishing Real-World Tasks Over the Phone." *Google AI Blog*. 2018. https://ai.googleblog.com/2018/05/duplex-ai-system-for-natural-conversation.html.

Lewis, Seth C., Amy Kristin Sanders, and Casey Carmody. 2019. "Libel by Algorithm? Automated Journalism and the Threat of Legal Liability." *Journalism & Mass Communication Quarterly*. 96 (1): 60–81

Lewis, Seth C., Andrea L. Guzman, and Thomas R. Schmidt. 2019. "Automation, Journalism, and Human–Machine Communication: Rethinking Roles and Relationships of Humans and Machines in News." *Digital Journalism* 1–19.

Liu, Xiaomo, Ramdev Wudali, Robert Martin, John Duprey, Arun Vachher, William Keenan, Sameena Shah, et al. 2016. "Reuters Tracer: A Large Scale System of Detecting & Verifying Real-Time News Events from Twitter." Paper presented at Proceedings of the 25th ACM International on Conference on Information and Knowledge Management - CIKM '16, 207–216. New York, NY: ACM Press.

Magnusson, Måns, Jens Finnäs, and Leonard Wallentin. 2016. "Finding the News Lead in the Data Haystack: Automated Local Data Journalism Using Crime Data." Paper presented at *Computation + Journalism Symposium*. Stanford University, Palo Alto, CA http://journalism.stanford.edu/cj2016/files/Finding the news lead in the data haystack.pdf

Marconi, Francesco, and Alex Siegman. 2017. "The Future of Augmented Journalism: A Guide for Newsrooms in the Age of Smart Machines." New York, NY: Associated Press.

Mor, Niv, and Zvi Reich. 2018. "From "Trust Me" To "Show Me" Journalism: Can Document Cloud Help to Restore the Deteriorating Credibility of News?" *Journalism Practice*, 12 (9). 1091–1108.

MuckRock. 2018. "About MuckRock." 2018. https://www.muckrock.com/about/.

New York City Department of Finance. 2017. "Annual Property Tax Report." http://www1.nyc.gov/site/finance/taxes/property-reports/property-reports-annual-property-tax.page.

Newman, David, Chaitanya Chemudugunta, Padhraic Smyth, and Mark Steyvers. 2006. "Analyzing Entities and Topics in News Articles Using Statistical Topic Models." In *International conference on intelligence and security informatics*, 93–104. Berlin, Heidelberg: Springer.

OCCRP. 2018. "About Us." Organized Crime and Corruption Reporting Project. 2018. https://www.occrp.org/en/about-us.

openrefine.org. n.d. "OpenRefine." Accessed April 8 2018. http://openrefine.org/.

Paulus, Romain, Caiming Xiong, and Richard Socher. 2018. "A Deep Reinforced Model for Abstractive Summarization." Paper presented at Sixth International Conference on Learning Representations, Vacncouver, Canada. https://arxiv.org/pdf/1705.04304.pdf.

Plattner, Titus, Didier Orel, and Olivier Steiner. 2016. "Flexible Data Scraping, Multi-Language Indexing, Entity Extraction and Taxonomies: Tadam, a Swiss Tool to Deal with Huge Amounts of Unstructured Data." Paper presented at Computation + Journalism Symposium, Palo Alto, CA: Stanford University.

Postin, Ben, and Anthony Pesce. 2015. "How We Reported This Story." *Los Angeles Times*. 2015. http://www.latimes.com/local/cityhall/la-me-crime-stats-side-20151015-story.html.

Poston, Ben, Joel Rubin, and Anthony Pesce. 2015. "LAPD Underreported Serious Assaults, Skewing Crime Stats for 8 Years." *Los Angeles Times*. Accessed October 15 2015. http://www.latimes.com/local/cityhall/la-me-crime-stats-20151015-story.html.

Prakash, Shailesh. 2017. "Journalism and Technology: Big Data, Personalization, Automation." Paper presented at Computation + Journalism Symposium. Evanston: Northwestern University. https://www.youtube.com/watch?v=PqMvxo89AQ4.

Press, Gil. 2016. "Cleaning Big Data: Most Time-Consuming, Least Enjoyable Data Science Task, Survey Says." *Forbes*. 2016. https://www.forbes.com/sites/gilpress/2016/03/23/data-preparation-most-time-consuming-least-enjoyable-data-science-task-survey-says/#38052d456f63.

ProPublica. 2012. "Free the Files." ProPublica. 2012. https://projects.propublica.org/free-the-files/.

Rajpurkar, Pranav, Robin Jia, and Percy Liang. 2018. "Know What You Don't Know: Unanswerable Questions for SQuAD." arXiv preprint arXiv:1806.03822.

Robinson, Eric. 2018. "The Ultimate Predictive Coding Handbook." *The Ediscovery Blog*. 2018. http://www.theediscoveryblog.com/2018/01/03/the-ultimate-handbook-for-mastering-predictive-coding/.

Russell, Stuart Jonathan, Peter Norvig, and Ernest Davis. 2010. *Artificial Intelligence : A Modern Approach*. Upper Saddle River, NJ: Prentice Hall.

Shorey, Rachel, Anthony Pesce, Chase Davis, and Peter Aldhous. 2018. "Getting Started with Machine Learning for Reporting." IRE NICAR. Chicago. 2018. http://paldhous.github.io/NICAR/2018/machine-learning.html.

Spangher, Alexander. 2015. "Building the Next New York Times Recommendation Engine." *The New York Times*. Accessed August 11 2015. https://open.blogs.nytimes.com/2015/08/11/building-the-next-new-york-times-recommendation-engine/.

Stone, Martha L. 2014. "Big Data for Media." https://reutersinstitute.politics.ox.ac.uk/sites/default/files/Big Data For Media_0.pdf.

Stray, Jonathan. 2012. "Beyond the Crime Scene: We Need New and Better Models for Crime Reporting » Nieman Journalism Lab." *Nieman Journalism Lab*. http://www.niemanlab.org/2012/06/new-and-better-models-for-crime-reporting/.

Stray, Jonathan. 2016a. "What Do Journalists Do with Documents? Field Notes for Natural Language Processing Researchers." Paper presented at Computation + Journalism Symposium. Palo Alto, CA: Stanford University. https://journalism.stanford.edu/cj2016/files/What do journalists do with documents.pdf.

Stray, Jonathan. 2016b. "The Age of the Cyborg." *Columbia Journalism Review*. Accessed September 2016.

Stray, Jonathan. 2017. "Network Analysis in Journalism: Practices and Possibilities." Paper presented at Data Science + Journalism Workshop. Halifax: *ACM SIGKDD*. https://drive.google.com/file/d/0B8CcT_0LwJ8QMzFjTWxLSFVkVTg/view.

Teegardin, Carrie, Danny Robbins, Jeff Ernsthausen, and Ariel Hart. 2016. "License to Betray." *Atlanta-Journal Constitution*. Accessed July 5 2016. http://doctors.ajc.com/doctors_sex_abuse/.

Thurman, Neil, Steve Schifferes, Richard Fletcher, Nic Newman, Stephen Hunt, and Aljosha Karim Schapals. 2016. "Giving Computers a Nose for News: Exploring the Limits of Story Detection and Verification." *Digital Journalism* 4 (7): 838–848.

Vogel, Kenneth P., and Rachel Shorey. 2018. "Trump Groups Raised Millions, Then Paid It Out to Loyalists and a Trump Hotel – The New York Times." *The New York Times*. Accessed January 24 2018. https://www.nytimes.com/2018/01/24/us/politics/pro-trump-fundraising-trump-hotel.html.

Wu, Sen, Luke Hsiao, Xiao Cheng, Braden Hancock, Theodoros Rekatsinas, Philip Levis Schapals. and Christopher Ré 2018. "Fonduer: Knowledge base construction from richly formatted data" In Proceedings of the 2018 International Conference on Management of Data, Houston, 1301–1316. ACM.

Human Still in the Loop

Editors Reconsider the Ideals of Professional Journalism
Through Automation

Marko Milosavljević and Igor Vobič

ABSTRACT
The study investigates how automation novelties in the newsroom both challenge and maintain the core values of journalism's professional ideology. Building on semi-structured interviews with editors of legacy news institutions in the United Kingdom and Germany, the study reveals the rationales behind the changing journalism–technology relationship and the dynamics of the re-articulation of the core ideals of journalism. In discussing automation with respect to strategic newsroom development, the interviewees see journalism's professional ideology as being in a state of flux. They identify contradictions between automation and some of journalism's core ideals (public service, autonomy, and objectivity) and acknowledge both the potential and limits of technology with regard to others (timeliness and ethics). Despite the growing relevance of automation for news production, human journalists are still regarded as the dominant agents in news production and its continuous reinvention. This human-still-in-the-loop perspective highlights the idea that journalism is undergoing a profound yet long transformation where new technologies are not simply appearing and changing everything, but are innovations developed and embedded in established relations of the news production process. This perspective both reiterates and challenges the prevailing meanings of journalism.

Introduction

Throughout modern history, the introduction of new technologies in journalism has raised questions about control over the processes by which knowledge is legitimated, the representation of social reality and how the norms of participation are defined (Hardt 1998). Alongside the materiality of news production, technological innovations have always involved discursive processes that have rearticulated journalism's internal and external boundaries (Carlson 2016) and reconsolidated a consensual professional ideology among journalists (Deuze 2005). These issues remain in place despite recent steps to further automate news production, with algorithmic processes now being utilised to gather and assemble data, create news narratives, figures and graphics, and/or publish and distribute news items with different levels of human involvement beyond the programming of rule-based processes. The precept of "what can be automated will be automated" (cf. van Dalen 2012, 651) implies changes in the role of humans in journalism.

The increasing complexities of the human–machine divide (Lewis and Westlund 2016) not only call for continuous monitoring of the boundaries of journalism–automation connections, but for a reconsideration of the fundamental questions: *what* is journalism, *how* is it done, and *why*? In this regard, this study's main goal is to investigate how recent automated developments both challenge and maintain the core values of journalism's professional ideology in legacy news institutions. More precisely, understanding automation as a technique that ensures the partial or full substitution of humans with technology in production operations, as well as controlling their outputs and beyond, allows us to study the reciprocity between technological innovations and re-negotiations of journalists' professional ideology via the prism of strategic newsroom decision-making. While technological innovations in the newsroom have historically been embedded in the struggles between economic and social interests in defining journalism and its purpose (e.g. Hardt 1998; Örnebring 2010), recent human-automation modes of journalism have reignited these processes and discussions about them – from discourses acknowledging augmentation potentials of automation (e.g. Anderson 2013; Coddington 2015; Splendore 2016) to critical elaborations of its pauperising prospects for journalism (e.g. Cohen 2015; Splichal and Dahlgren 2016).

Our exploration sits at the intersection of contemporary debates on the boundaries of professional journalism and their discursive maintenance (Carlson and Lewis 2015; Peters and Broersma 2013, 2017), recent investigations of the manifold epistemological implications of automation for journalism (Anderson 2013; Carlson 2017; Coddington 2015; Splendore 2016) and studies dealing with professional reasoning for the emerging human–automation modes of journalism (Bucher 2017; Linden 2017; Thurman, Dörr, and Kunert 2017; Young and Hermida 2015). While the main academic concerns with automation have involved recent uses of new technologies in the newsroom and the broader social implications, it appears that researchers have not primarily explored the contingencies and contradictions in journalists' belief system in the context of the strategic development of newsroom practices and principles. By trying to address this research gap, we consider automation as a "cumulative transformation" (Boczkowski 2004, 52) whereby innovations in news creation and delivery unfold gradually and are shaped not only by a context-bound variety of material conditions but also by the continuous ideologisation of journalism and the discourses binding it. Therefore, we aim to interrogate the 'new' rationales for technological innovations given by those responsible for strategic development and bringing automation into the newsroom by tackling 'old' issues of professional journalism. How does journalism's belief system define appropriate practices and ideals? How are internal and external boundaries being preserved? How is journalism's authority self-legitimised?

This study expands on theoretical reasoning concerning journalism's changing perspectives on technology's role in news production, from the historical centrality of human agency to the growing prospects of the 'human-out-of-the-loop' approach, which implies that "the same technology that extends the intellectual power of humans can displace them as well" (Markoff 2016, 22). The study adds to empirical knowledge by exploring new aspects of automation in journalism not as effects but as re-articulations of journalism's professional ideology in specific political, economic and cultural contexts. The first part of the study discusses the 'old' contingencies of the journalism–technology relationship in the context of the 'new' connections between the core ideals of journalism and growing automation in news production. The second part explores how automation both questions and leaves intact the professional ideology in journalist work spaces at legacy news institutions in the United Kingdom and Germany. Historically and contemporarily, in newsrooms the key actors in the strategic decision-making have been the editors (e.g. Gans 2004; Morrison and Tumber 1995; Snider 1995), who also often act as authorities in the processes of introducing and justifying technological innovations (Fink 1996, 212; Wicks et al. 2004, 99). Therefore, we discuss commonalities and particularities in re-negotiations of journalist ideals via automation on the basis of qualitative interviews with editors of digital news departments and/or heads of newsroom innovation teams or projects. Building on this, we consider the larger dynamics between continuities and discontinuities in the professional ideology of journalists where technological innovations have historically been shaped in a strategic maintenance of the tensions between the public (cl)aims of journalism and the corporate interests of management.

Automation and Journalism's Professional Ideology – Reconsidered

As an innovation that promises and ensures the partial or complete replacement of humans with technology to produce and handle their outputs, automation has been on the agenda for decades. More than half a century ago, Pollock (1957, 247–253) saw the public debate on the implications of automation as polarised, with automation seen as a "curse" for those about to be displaced by machines in the factory or the office or as a "blessing" due to automation's emancipatory and transformative potential for human labour. This duality is also reflected in recent journalism research on human–automation modes which finds that the affordances of automation provide opportunities to save labour and augment the moral purpose of news (Anderson 2013; Coddington 2015; Splendore 2016), while simultaneously noting tendencies in the industry to make journalism more productive and efficient at the expense of its public substance (Cohen 2015; Splichal and Dahlgren 2016). Turning this discussion on its head, Linden (2017) asks "Why are there still so many jobs in journalism after decades of newsroom automation?", arguing that "journalism as ideology" has moderated the technological innovations, adapting them to the complex and contradictory set of social influences found both within and outside journalism.

New technologies have always had to fit in with existing social patterns, which in turn are shaped by a long process whereby the dominance of technology over journalism has been naturalised (Örnebring 2010, 69). Accompanied by claims about their journalistic nature, the affordances of new technologies have emerged as grounds for "technologically specific forms of work" (Powers 2012). While disturbances may be seen in the institutionalisation of certain forms – such as data, computational and automated journalism – the technological specificity of journalism is being transformed as the levels of technological dependence grow (Lewis and Westlund 2016). Automation *denotes* algorithmic processes with limited to no human intervention beyond the initial programming that are aimed at converting structured data into narrative texts, as in 'automated journalism' (Carlson 2015), gather, verify and assemble information and data (Bucher 2017) and engage in editorial decision-making in news delivery (Napoli 2014). It also *connotes* a specific interplay between the dominant social relations, professional ideals and institutional locales in which meaning is created within a variety of human–automation modes of journalism.

Historically, technological innovations have formed an integral part of the "professionalization project" as a kind of "brokered settlement" among journalists, news media owners and managers, and the public (Nerone 2013, 452). Together with the promise of autonomy and a special social status, professionalisation brought a set of occupational norms to routinise journalism and ensure stable production, serve as sources of journalistic self-legitimisation, and re-build the boundaries between journalists and the public as well as among journalists (Hardt 1998, 203–204). Although journalism has had various manifestations depending on specific social and technological contexts, the "hegemonic model" (Nerone 2013), which had taken on quite distinct forms in different countries since the late 19th century, gradually developed an "international existence" (447). With journalists imagined as autonomous and public-spirited verifiers of factual information and renderers of social realities on a timely basis, this model has been continuously re-established over a century of technological innovations, while gaining global prominence through local disruptions. A consensus on what is understood as a shared professional ideology among journalists has been constructed incrementally both through internal struggles for control within journalism and external struggles for legitimacy in social life (Russial, Laufer, and Wasko 2015, 303). This consensus seems to be disrupted in the "ongoing turn to the digital" (Young and Hermida 2015, 381), as the boundaries of professional journalism – not without opposition and controversy – have been re-established and its place in social communication disputed (Carlson and Lewis 2015; Peters and Broersma 2013; Zelizer 2009). The development and use of automation call for further reconsideration of contradictions with the dominant belief system, as journalism is increasingly being "defined by, embedded in, and understood through the particular structural and socio-cultural characteristics of technology" (Lewis and Westlund 2016, 342).

Drawing on the work of Mark Deuze (2005), we reconsider the complexities and contradictions of journalism's professional ideology and discuss its core ideals (public service, objectivity, autonomy, timeliness and ethics) with respect to the emerging human–automation modes of journalism and their implications for what Nerone (2013, 453) calls the "fantasy" of the hegemonic model.

Public Service: Problems of Personalisation

The public service ideal relates to journalism's particular connection with people and is rooted in what has emerged as the high-modern paradigm based on a belief in linear progress, absolute truth and human emancipation (Hallin 1994, 160). In this context, Nerone (2015, 2) writes that journalists believe "they should and do make" democracy work by providing information to the people, who then discuss it, reflect on it, make their minds up and participate in public life. In other words, by "doing it for the public" (Deuze 2005, 447), journalists aim for a heterogeneous citizenry with a shared public culture and serve as an "integrative force" for public debate (Dahlgren 2009, 147). Although high-modern journalism has been waning for some time now (ibid.), the public-service ideal continues to help journalists claim social responsibility in the face of commercial and political pressures (Coddington 2015, 73), but also to reinforce the *status quo* in journalism (and beyond) while endorsing a more responsive attitude to the people (Deuze 2005, 448).

While the wave of human–automation modes of journalism, foremost data and computational journalism, contribute to the public-service ideal with their potential to strengthen journalism's capacity to make social institutions more understandable to the public (Coddington 2015, 332), some ways of bringing automation into news creation and delivery weaken that ideal by striving for "pluralized personalisation" (Carlson 2017, 231). For instance, automated journalism promises the "horizontal expansion" of numbers of news items and the creation of "multiple – even personalised – versions of any story" (ibid.). Discussions on automation point to the problems inherent in personalising an individual's engagement with journalism (Thurman and Schifferes 2012), as well as point to the traditional debates on fragmentation of the public sphere and journalism's role in these processes.

Objectivity: The Promise of Algorithms

The ideal of objectivity relates to the detached way journalists approach and depict social realities (Maras 2013, 7–11) and is historically rooted in the broader cultural "scientific naturalism" movement of the early 20th century, which stresses the relevance of methods in giving evidence of facts (Splichal 2015, 858). Although objectivity has a problematic status in modern thinking on the "impossibility of value-neutrality", and is being revisited through concepts like fairness, detachment and impartiality (Deuze 2005, 448), these reconsiderations do not affect its ambiguous structural and discursive implications. While the promise of objectivity remains alive in journalism's professional ideology, it has always been characterised by a paradox (Splichal 1999, 299–300): as journalists attempt to provide impartial renderings of the world, they become partial through their reproductions of the existing social order.

Human–automation modes of journalism see the ideal of objectivity and the reconsiderations of that ideal meeting a bigger discourse that contrasts "inherent human subjectivity with the unthinking automated objectivity of computer programs" (Carlson 2018, 1764), although the journalistic search for sources and information through algorithmic systems is filtered in a specific way (Thurman et al. 2016). The "promise of algorithmic objectivity" is a "carefully crafted fiction" (Gillespie 2014, 179) by the dominant corporate players developing search engines, online social networks and other platforms, who are contributing to the image of algorithms as hands-off even though they are actually constructed by a particular knowledge logic (168). Unlike the objectivity of journalists, which relies on institutionalised norms and trained expertise, the objectivity of algorithms is based more on a "technologically inflected promise of mechanical neutrality" (181). Carlson (2018, 1768) asserts that "belief in computational objectivity further conceals journalistic judgment as avoidable through the intervention of algorithms or it perpetuates a crisis of journalistic authority by foreclosing on the value of human subjectivity for journalistic accounts". Both journalistic and algorithmic judgements are entangled in objectivity discourses revolving around automated journalism (10), which emerges as a site of struggles for authority maintenance in truth building and knowledge production.

Autonomy – with Algorithmic Power

The ideal of autonomy, reflecting the normative assumptions of classical liberalism, has been central to journalism's professionalisation project in the last century (Waisbord 2013, 43–72). The underlying premise that journalists require autonomy from power to contribute to democratic life has served their struggle to detach from and counter business, politics and publishers, though journalists have been criticized for maintaining a proximity to the elites in their everyday reporting, despite their proclaimed autonomy. (ibid.). The news media nurture their "rationalized" disconnection to politics at the same time as privileging official voices in the news (Schudson 2005, 216), and reproduce the "fiction" of the news–business divide at the same time as facing the contemporary issues of native advertising and entrepreneurial journalism (Coddington 2015, 68–69).

The ideal of autonomy with respect to automation can be reconsidered in the context of what Splendore (2016, 348) calls "the increasing intervention of machines" – both when informed by human agencies and when they work autonomously. The intrinsic crux of "algorithmic power" is "autonomous decision-making", in which rules may either be defined by programmers or be dynamic, based on machine-learning data (Diakopoulos 2015, 400). These power dynamics are novel and relate to the autonomy ideal at the level of an individual's news creation, where – as in multimedia journalism – journalists will have to "at least learn to share autonomy" (Deuze 2005, 456) with other (human and non-human) agents. Changes can also be observed from a broader perspective, as a new knowledge logic is being enforced via algorithms that exist as "socially constructed and institutionally managed mechanisms for assuring public acumen" (Gillespie 2014, 192).

Timeliness: Faster and Anticipatory

The ideal of timeliness reflects the historical salience of time in the creation and distribution of news, where time has primarily been understood as mechanical rather than as socially constructed (Rantanen 2009, 1–3). Professional journalism builds its vitality through the construction of "the news of the day" (Nerone 2013, 453–454), while the digitalisation of journalism has re-enforced the 24-hour news cycle introduced by satellite and cable television in the 1990s, privileging immediacy over more traditional forms of reflection, and naturalising the "instantaneous present" (Phillips 2012, 81–98). While the ideal has recently been problematised in research, most notably by the "slow journalism" movement (Le Masurier 2015), the contemporary notion of speed can be approached by professional journalists "as both an essentialized value and a problematized side effect of newswork" (Deuze 2005, 449).

The development and application of automation touches on the notion of time because it promises faster journalistic creation as well as the contextualisation of news events. Namely, algorithms save time in news production as they can scan and structure large amounts of data, enabling journalists to focus on analytic or investigative work (Anderson 2013). In addition, automated journalistic practices provide finished products or parts thereof, such as narratives, figures, charts and graphics, "faster than is humanly possible" or at "lightning speed" (Cohen 2015, 110–111), and at least partly increase workplace productivity (Splichal and Dahlgren 2016, 10). Concurrently, and at the present quite hypothetically, "algorithmic timing" entails prediction, interruption and anchoring, with algorithms being used "to suggest when an event is likely to happen, the time frames, the memories to recall" (Ananny 2016, 107). Similarly, Linden (2017, 133) writes about "anticipatory journalism" that is more focused on predictive than reactive routines and, as such, saves time and effort, making news production more efficient and relevant.

Ethics: A Shift of Responsibility

Groping for a common set of journalism ethics has lain at the heart of the profession-alisation process over the last century (Deuze 2005, 449). While discussions about a universal code of conduct continue, ethical diversity describes the situation facing global journalism better than unity and consensus (Waisbord 2013, 188). Also central to the ideal of ethical conduct in journalism is what McManus (1997, 5) critically calls "fantasy" rather than "fact": the idea that journalists alone control what becomes news. Placing this responsibility on the shoulders of individual journalists deflects criticism for ethical violations from systemic problems to individual violators, isolating that criticism and preserving the public image and authority of professional journalism (Coddington 2015, 71–72).

The issues of the moral purpose and ethics of journalism are pivotal in discussions of human–automation modes, because algorithms are composed of both "human intentionality and material obduracy" (Anderson 2013, 1016) and are gaining greater prominence in the "prioritization, classification, association and filtering" of information (Diakopoulos 2015, 400). Dörr and Hollbuchner (2017, 11) identify a "shift of responsibility" in journalism. Namely, the individual human journalist is no longer the prime moral agent, as numerous other actors (journalistic and non-journalistic) are involved in news production, such as algorithms with delegated agency, in-house and outsourced programmers, data collectors and data miners (ibid.). The consequential rise in the importance of news institutions as moral agents calls for a re-consideration of the meaning of ethical conduct in journalism, particularly with regard to "algorithmic transparency" (Diakopoulos and Koliska 2017) and "algorithmic accountability" (Diakopoulos 2015).

Research Question and Method

Automation does not mean that the contradictions within the core ideals of professional journalism have lessened, but that they have become more complex.

Table 1. Interviewees.

Editorial position, news institution	Date	Time and type	In-text reference
Associate editor and management editor, *Financial Times*	20/09/2016	47 min, Skype	(intFT1)
Head of interactive news, *Financial Times*	18/07/2016	69 min, in-person	(intFT2)
Technology editor, *Guardian News & Media*	19/07/2016	37 min, in-person	(intGuardian1)
Executive editor of digital, *Guardian News & Media*	19/07/2016	37 min, in-person	(intGuardian2)
Editor-in-charge, *Reuters.co.uk*	20/07/2017	38 min, in-person	(intReuters)
Mobile and new formats editor, *BBC News Online*	13/06/2017	28 min, Skype	(intBBC)
Editor-in-chief of digital media, *Frankfurter Allgemeine Zeitung*	05/05/2017	43 min, Skype	(intFAZ)
Head of innovation projects and new media, *Deutsche Welle*	30/03/2017	32 min, Skype	(intDW)
Head of *Bayerischer Rundfunk* data team, *ARD*	15/05/2017	37 min, Skype	(intARD)
Head of *Taz.de, Tages Zeitung Berlin*	25/04/2017	23 min, Skype	(intTAZ)
Head of data journalism, *Spiegel Online*	21/04/2017	31 min, Skype	(intSpiegel)
Editor-in-chief of *SZ.de, Süddeutsche Zeitung*	10/04/2017	Email	(intSZ)

The various human–automation modes hold implications for how journalism is done and how it relates to people as well as how journalism is understood and how this ties in with its dominant belief system. Studying both the material and discursive aspects of introducing automation into news production "can help to illuminate how these technologies reproduce, embody, or alter" professional ideology (Young and Hermida 2015, 384). We set the main research question:

RQ1: *How are the core ideals of professional journalism rearticulated by automation novelties in legacy news institutions?*

Exploring the relationship between professional ideology and automation requires a study of the inner logics and cultural patterns of technological innovation in news-rooms. Because socially specific connections between technology and journalism can be established, broken and re-constructed in particular circumstances defined by certain social interactions, we aim to study not merely how automation impacts news production and perceptions of journalism, but the rationale behind technological innovations at legacy news institutions. Within the dominant hierarchal structure of news institutions, there is a space between the business and editorial offices that is occupied by a particular 'breed' of editors; these professionals are usually found at the top of newsroom hierarchy, but below the managerial pyramid of news institutions' organisational structures. As a consequence, they manoeuvre between the ideals of professional journalism and the corporate interests of media management (Underwood 1995, 10). Although often removed from on-the-ground work, they would seem to be an ideal population for our research purpose as they are responsible for shaping, executing and communicating innovation that goes beyond the traditional news–business divide. In addition, editors are often described as key examples of the gatekeeper concept, which means these individuals are "likely to have personal views, attitudes and idiosyncrasies" which can help explain the decisions they make (Boyd-Barrett 1995, 271). Moreover, the role of such editors as gatekeepers not only involves influence over the selection of news and how it is covered, but also encompasses the use of technologies and production procedures, as acknowledged by the seminal journalism studies which confirm the notion that editors are key agents within news institutions, particularly their newsrooms (e.g. Gans 2004; Morrison and Tumber 1995; Snider 1995).

For these reasons, we decided to conduct qualitative interviews with editorial actors who head digital news departments and/or lead newsroom innovation teams or projects (Table 1) in order to obtain information on how automation is finding its way into news production and analyse novelties produced by automation with respect to the core ideals of professional journalism.

We purposively "stratified" the sample of interviewees according to the following categories (cf. Robinson 2014, 32): the socio-geographic spheres of influence of news institutions, the diversity of scope and functions of news institutions, and the specificity of editors' roles in news production and technological innovation. The rationale for employing this purposive strategy was to develop a sample that meaningfully relates to the main research question, provides a diversity of perspective on the subject matter, and strengthens the international relevance of the study. More precisely, when sampling we concentrated on news institutions from British and German news institutions due to the influence of media from these two countries on the wider evolution within Anglo-Saxon and Continental-European journalism. Then, to ensure diversity among the interviewees, we identified relevant editorial actors at news institutions with different scopes and functions, from news agencies and public broadcasters to commercial general and specialised news outlets with regional, national and/or international reach, including daily print outlets, weekly print outlets, broadcasters and online newsrooms of these legacy media. The 12 interviewees in the sample were senior figures in terms of their journalistic and/or editorial experience, with an average of just under 20 years' experience in professional journalism (minimum: 10; maximum: 40); almost all the interviewees have an educational background in the social sciences, arts and humanities (with the exceptions of intSpiegel, who also has a background in the natural sciences, and intDW, who graduated in the applied sciences) and have thus gained technical expertise with respect to journalism mostly in the workplace. The interviewees did not ask for anonymity, but stressed their opinions were personal and not the official positions of the news institutions for which they work.

The conversations were conducted in person (in London, in offices and newsrooms) or via Skype as semi-structured interviews. One of the authors (Marko Milosavljević) performed the role of interviewer with a "written list of questions" that was based on reconsiderations of the core ideals of professional journalism drawn from Deuze (2005) and placed in the automation novelty context as elaborated in the previous section. However, the interview guide was applied flexibly, allowing adaptation of the conversation dynamics to more profoundly tackle the main research question. Supplementary conversations, as well as off-the-record discussions, also took place with the interviewees to develop a fuller understanding of the subject matter. Although we were aware of the weaknesses and ethical issues of "internet interviews" (James and Busher 2012), in one case we opted for an email exchange due to timetable clashes and financial constraints. The mode of the email interview is a specific exchange, not having the flexibility of the semi-structured interview and not providing the depth of in-person conversation due to its asynchronous dynamics, but nevertheless allowing the researcher to gather meaningful considerations of the respondent beyond the initial set of questions.

The interviews were conducted in English, voice-recorded, transcribed in full, and analysed. In our interviews, we worked 'down' from theoretical reconsiderations of journalist professional ideology in the automation age, rather than conducting and analysing them with a grounded theory approach. We followed the multistep analysis

Table 2. Automation in news production according to interviewees.

News production phase	Function of automation
Gathering and assembling	Automatically "monitoring" and "prioritising" content on news agencies and social media (*Taz.de*)
	Using "automated bots" to send thousands of emails to a certain group of actors in order to gather a large number of responses (*ARD*)
	Developing automated online verification tools (*Deutsche Welle*)
	Using Google Refine to make cleaning and transforming large datasets "much easier" (*Guardian*)
Creating	Using automated prediction and text generation tools before the US presidential elections in 2016 (*Deutsche Welle*)
	Adopting automated visualisations on the basis of official data streams of football matches in order to enhance analyses (*Spiegel*)
	Automating highly repetitive tasks in chart and graphics creation to speed up production (*Taz.de, Financial Times*)
Publishing and distributing	Using algorithms to personalise the news experience on the basis of online user behaviour (*BBC, Frankfurter Allgemeine Zeitung, Financial Times*)
	Making editorial decisions on the basis of timely traffic metrics and related topics metadata (*Guardian, Reuters.co.uk*)
	Making recommendations on the basis of automated tagging of "meta keywords" in stories (*Deutsche Welle*)
	Automatically adapting produced content for delivery on different platforms (websites or social media) with human interference (*Guardian, Reuters.co.uk*)

outlined by Kvale (1996). First, we carefully read each conversation to get a sense of its depth and comprehensiveness, noting topics contained within. Meaning units were then determined, followed by a thematisation of the statements with respect to specific issues in the interviewees' viewpoints and positions. Finally, we interrogated the meaning units within each interview and across them all. The procedures of theory construction were applied during analysis of the interviews as we were sensitive to the dynamics that might exist between and within the ideals of professional journalism, and between those ideals and empirical material about the editors, their newsrooms, strategies and actions. This allowed us to identify what was common and what was distinct in the use of automation novelties in the newsrooms and the ways in which the ideals of professional journalism were re-negotiated among the editors.

Results

"Automation lite" (intARD), "early stage", "experimental stage" (intDW), and "fairly minimal" (intGuardian2) are expressions some interviewees used to describe the automation novelties adopted. At the outset, we note that the interview analysis shows automation is being implemented in all phases of news production, but differently across the interviewees' newsrooms (Table 2). According to the data, all but one news institution has introduced automation to news production in some manner, or experimented with it, with *Süddeutsche Zeitung* being the only exception – at least for now. The interviewed editors provided complex reconsiderations of technology, reflecting understandings of innovation as a non-linear process bounded by particular professional and institutional contexts. What is common in the interviews is that actual instances of automation in news institutions, and hypothetical instances are regarded as ways to enhance – or "augment" (intGuardian2; intFT2) – certain phases of news production, while keeping human journalists as the central actors.

Below, we analyse and discuss the editors' re-articulations of professional journalism ideals by exploring the relationships between their perceptions and practices of automation in news production. Although the interviews focused on the news production of the respective outlets, they were not limited to those outlets and went beyond the walls of their newsrooms. Therefore, the results section considers how the editors articulated the ideals with respect to their first-hand experience of automation, and also their knowledge of adaptations outside their newsrooms.

Public Service: Both Stronger and Weaker with Automation

Across the interviews, public service was commonly seen as a central constituent of journalism, to be continuously re-evaluated and re-affirmed to moderate the effects of corporate interests on the public value and moral purpose of news. However, three streams of thought among interviewees concerned their elaborations on public service with respect to automation.

First, some saw automation as a set of tools enabling the newsroom to provide more news faster and generate audience attention, while also being a potential disruption to the public relevance of journalism (intReuters, intSpiegel; intTAZ). For instance, at *Reuters.co.uk* they use a tool for editorial decision-making that shows "what is clicking in real time".

> [W]e cannot flip away from something which isn't a major story, of major significance just because it's not proving that popular with the consumer audience. So we do still have to have that sort of judgement about what is in our judgement in the public interest. *(intReuters)*

While the technology editor at the *Guardian* described public service as "tricky", the executive editor of digital drew a clear line between humans and algorithms in this context, arguing that technology alone cannot create a project such as the *Panama Papers,* which has made personal financial information about the powerful around the world public.

> [A] human being when he's writing for other human beings, you know, it might not be the biggest, it might not be the most powerful, it might be something relatively small but because it's happening, it's important, right, it's a story. There's an element of journalism, that's just not capturable algorithmically. *(intGuardian2)*

Second, some editors juxtaposed the public-service ideal with personalisation, but not necessarily in the sense of opposition. Using the "filter bubble" argument, some stressed that the rise of automated personalisation in news creation and delivery might weaken public service in the long run (intBBC; intFAZ). In this context, a "tricky balance" (intFT2) between public purpose and personalised appeal was identified by the head of interactive news at the Financial Times (FT), with a tension existing across the news–business divide. With the *myFT* feature, an initial step to personalise the FT reader website has been made, providing everyone with "a slightly different version" (intFT1) to suit their interests.

I mean of course in an extreme case you might end up with just the news that everyone deserves and that would then be a constant feedback loop of stories scraped from Twitter or Facebook, being written by algorithms and given a sexy headline and pushed out. [...] I think there is a danger that you end up in that sort of loop of the most popular stories being the most trivial stories. (intFT1)

Third, it was argued – particularly by the head of the data team at the public *Bayerischer Rundfunk* – that automation can strengthen the public-service ideal, not only in terms of saving time for journalists to do analytical or investigative journalism, but also by enabling them to gather large masses of data or analyse public datasets more easily. For instance, they used "automated bots" to send e-mails to thousands in order to retrieve relevant big data.

Our coders programmed bots that ask for apartments in the whole [of] Germany, in the biggest cities in Germany, and we get back the answers and we put, categorise them. [...] What we are trying to do with that is to look if there is discrimination on the German rental market [...] I think you can use this as part of your toolset as a journalist, and [as] with any other tool you can use it either to enhance public interest and to help to find out things about the public you don't know – public spending, public tax fraud, whatever – [or not]. (intARD)

Objectivity: Algorithms Are Not Objective

All interviewees moved beyond naïve conceptualisations of objectivity by stressing that the corresponding value-neutrality of journalism is not achievable and arguing that knowledge creation through technology is embedded in particular social, cultural and political contexts. In this setting, some interviewees stressed human dominance, saying, for instance, that "you can easily manipulate a robot" (intFAZ), "it's not the algorithm that's biased" (intGuardian2), algorithms "can only work if they are fed by people and if they are used by people" (intTAZ), and such journalism "depends mostly on the goals and techniques of its creator" (intSZ).

[T]here are so many decisions that are lying in the background of these algorithms. [...] When we decide which parts of articles are ... which parts of the datasets we use for automated news, we also draw decisions that are not objective at all and the data itself also is not objective. (intSpiegel)

Throughout the interview data, algorithms are described as "a set of encoded human choices" (intFT2), "written by humans" (intBBC), "initially programmed by humans" (intGuardian1), and "not objective at all" (intSpiegel). The head of innovation projects and new media at *Deutsche Welle* described a "public experiment" before the 2016 US presidential elections that their newsroom conducted with the *Ludwig-Maximilians-University* from Munich and the company *AX Semantics*. They employed automated prediction and text-generation tools: "That was, in a way, a nice little loop of auto-mated production process. [...] Okay, disclaimer, we got it wrong like everybody" (intDW). However, he argued that algorithms can develop meaningful multi-perspectiv-ity in news production that corresponds with the complexities of social reality. "[A piece of] software could of course compile different sources and different angles and different viewpoints on one specific topic", but if humans strive for a certain perspective, "a Republican text production bot will write different texts than a Democratic one" (intDW).

Autonomy: Automation Affecting Decision-Making

The interviewed editors discussed autonomy predominantly in relation to journalism's struggles with commercial pressures, with some describing those struggles as being in a state of "balance" (intDW) or resembling a state of "limbo" (intTAZ). Most editors contended, in recalling the existing audience metrics tools and emerging content management systems driven by algorithms, that their autonomy had not been eroded. A telling example of this position was given by the *Reuters.co.uk* editor, who was using testing tools to gauge "what is going to perform". She argued that she did not see her editorial autonomy as jeopardised.

> I think if my traffic started to drop off or didn't perform as well as, for instance, the US traffic or somewhere else's traffic, then my boss would come to me and say: 'Are you not using those tools well enough?' Because the tools are there to help me in my decisions but no, there is no overall 'you must move this around according to what is clicking'. (intReuters)

The editor-in-chief of online at *Süddeutsche Zeitung*, where they are reluctant in their implementing of automation, similarly described algorithms as providing "support" in the decision-making process.

> My experience is that algorithms can surely support editorial decision by pointing in interesting directions, but leaving the decision to the editor. That's a data-informed vs. a data-driven approach. Machines only can do it data-driven, and I think that that's not good enough, as data is never good enough to replace editors' choices. (intSZ)

At the same time, distinct positions stand out. On the one hand, the editor-in-chief of digital media at *Frankfurter Allgemeine Zeitung* argued that "inspiring and surprising reading experience" is not achievable without on-site "editorial thinking". "No robot tells me about the results, what to expect. I mean, you can have pretty good analysis, of course, but... I wouldn't, at the moment, I wouldn't use it" (intFAZ). On the other hand, editors from the *Financial Times*, where they (aim to) nurture personalisation, argued that we are witnessing a "slow process" that involves a "shift evermore to that algorithmic side" (intFT2) and that editorial autonomy "has possibly already eroded to a certain degree" (intFT1). This may represent a deepening of an old problem.

> [I]t's a kind of turbo-charged version of that original question of how you weigh up newspaper sales versus news value. I think that the autonomy of the editor has always depended on the type of publication, it has always been somewhat in play depending on that. [...] The danger of that seems to be that as you're making more data-based decisions, people get too wooed by the data and forget that over the long-term people might not want the same story again and again. (intFT1)

Timeliness: Automation "Freeing up" Journalists

The interviewees placed the concept of time at the centre of their understanding of professional journalism, with some of them working for news institutions that particularly prided themselves on timely news production (intSpiegel; intFAZ; intTAZ) and one discussing the importance of timeliness in relation to individual stories. (intARD). The interviewees more or less agreed that the automated creation of news is currently unrealistic given the scopes of their newsrooms, with some calling it "over-blown" (intGuardian2) and a "kind of a hype topic" (intDW). For instance, the executive editor at the *Guardian* stressed the reasonably constrained application: "To go from algorithm to story online? Yeah, I think it's actually fairly limited. I think the much more interesting bit is the augmentation piece that maybe an external user, viewer, reader wouldn't necessarily see in its raw form".

According to the interview data, a common position held by the editors was that automation has the potential to make some of the tasks facing journalists "easier" (intGuardian2) and "quicker" (intGuardian2), eventually "freeing them up" for more complex analytical, creative and investigative work (intBBC; intDW; intFT2).

> Can we do that so we can get those things produced faster and free up specialists' time to do more advanced work that will actually help our readers more in the longer run? That's certainly how I think about it, I think that's how everybody currently thinks about it. (intFT2)

The head of interactive news at the *Financial Times* said that in the last 5 years they had gone from a system where every graphics item was "drawn almost by hand" to a process that was "highly automated". Although interviewees gave similar rationalisations for the use of automation, actual applications of automation designed to save time and labour in news production, primarily assembling data and information and creating news, differed due to the specifics of newsrooms. At the news agency *Reuters,* they introduced automation to help their journalists with speed-reading press releases; at the *Guardian* they started using tools such as *Google Refine* to clean and transform large datasets faster; and at *Tages Zeitung Berlin* they automated highly repetitive tasks in chart and graphics creation to speed up production.

Ethics: Between Control and Transparency

Although, as the editor-in-chief of *SZ.de* stresses, we cannot yet fully grasp the extent and complexity of the ethical implications for journalism of automation, a common belief among the interviewees can be identified – that control over algorithms must be maintained in order to retain the ethical foundation of journalism and the moral purpose of news.

As grounds for their arguments, the editors cited recent ethically questionable automated decision-making in professional journalism and social media with respect to the distribution of fake stories, advertising placements, and the selection and display of photos. In this context, the executive editor of digital at the *Guardian* recalled problems with the automatic displaying of advertisements (Google Ads) alongside news stories, for instance where ski resorts were promoted next to a story about a snowstorm. "[A] human being would look at that and go 'Oh my God, how could you put a ski resort right there?' but a computer would look at that and say it's completely appropriate. [...] Yeah, it happens all the time. But, that's a monkey paw situation, right" (intGuardian2).

Some interviewees from news institutions with distinct profiles (intFAZ; intFT2; intSZ; intDW) all drew a sharp line between algorithmic and human logics. While, for instance, *SZ.de's* editor-in-chief stated that he believed in the "evolution of automation" rather than in "automation revolution", and stressed the need for "an editor next to the machine controlling it" (intSZ), the head of interactive news at the *Financial Times* expanded the argument to the very nature of news engagement.

> The assumption with news is that obviously it is mainly humans who are reading it, clearly in some cases in financial news, even that's not the case, because there will be some algorithms that will deliberately be talking to algorithms about the earnings report. […] But in most cases, if you've still got a human at the other end, you still have to please them in a way that makes it different than 'I just want the raw data'. (intFT2)

Some, in addition, emphasised the importance of "clarity of purpose" (intBBC) and transparency (intSpiegel; intARD) while developing and implementing automation in journalism. The head of the data team at the public *Bayerischer Rundfunk* was particularly articulate in this regard, drawing from data journalism ethics.

> [U]sing algorithms and data with those algorithms means that you have to control the way the data is collected, you have to understand those algorithms collecting this data, you have to build a context around the data when you publish it and you have to be transparent about your sources and you have to show how you work with the data and perhaps also you have to make transparent the decisions that lie behind those algorithms. (intARD)

Discussion and Conclusion

This article extends scholarship on automation in newsrooms and on professional rationales behind it. Uniquely, by drawing on interviewees from some of the leading British and German news institutions, where they occupy a space between business and editorial decision-making, the study analyses re-articulations of the hegemonic belief system in journalism in the presence of automation. As the study shows, for some tasks in news production, automation not only promises the partial or full substitution of humans with technology, but has brought it about, adding to tensions around the impact that technological innovation has on what journalism is, how it is done, and why.

Although the integration of technology into day-to-day work has, throughout history, fed technological reductionism in journalism's discourses about itself (Örnebring 2010), this study indicates that rationales behind strategic newsroom development retain the wider social, institutional and professional considerations while departing from either euphoric or dystopic perspectives on automation. The interviewees saw journalism's professional ideology as being in a state of flux, emphasising conflicts around certain core ideals (most notably public service, autonomy, and objectivity) and acknowledging the potential and limits of technology with regard to others (especially timeliness and ethics). However, their reconsiderations of journalistic professional ideology were not identical, particularly in discussions of how the public-service ideal may be both strengthened and weakened by automation or of how ethical dilemmas call for control and transparency. Their differences were less pronounced when it came to the ideals of objectivity, autonomy and timeliness.

This study's findings also come with some limitations. When a study bases its findings on interviews alone, there is a danger of a disconnection between how editors and journalists talk about their work and how they actually perform their jobs. In addition, the study is based on interviews conducted in relatively large media companies where the use and the perceptions of new automation tools might be different than at smaller companies and smaller newsroom. The study focuses on two larger European countries; the research in other, smaller European countries might show different approaches and issues. In addition, these are European countries and economically strong countries, and the inclusion of countries from other regions and/or with different economic strength and potential to implement new technologies might also lead to other conclusions. By documenting and analysing the interviews, the study contributes to larger discourses about technological innovations in journalism and beyond, but the quite narrow scope of the subset of editors does not allow generalising to a broader population of on-the-ground journalists with possibly different experiences of, and views on, automation.

Beyond the main findings and its limitations, the study's key contribution lies in identifying the salient common 'human-still-in-the-loop' perspective that sits between the 'old' (ideals of professional ideology) and 'new' (automation novelties) in the rationales of strategic newsroom development. As previous studies similarly suggest (e.g. Linden 2017; Thurman, Dörr, and Kunert 2017), it is no surprise that a common element of editors' sense-making was the centrality of human agency in technological innovation. While presenting a variety of human–automation modes in their newsrooms, the interviews highlight that human journalists are not only in the loop, but are regarded as the dominant agents in news production and its ongoing re-invention. This human-still-in-the-loop perspective highlights the idea that journalism is undergoing a profound yet long transformation where new technologies are not simply appearing and changing everything, but are innovations developed and embedded in established relations of the news production process. This perspective both reiterates and challenges the prevailing meanings of journalism.

The human-still-in-the-loop perspective rests on the belief that the emerging human–automation interactions – some interviewees even speak of "augmented" journalism (intGuardian2; intFT2) – are defined by the combination of (commanding) human agencies and (supporting) automated systems. This largely protective and unsurprising perspective, which insists on the persistence and relevance of human journalists in automation processes, might be described as self-serving. The data support analyses that see the affordances of automation as saving labour, speeding up news production, and strengthening the moral purpose of news (cf. Anderson 2013; Coddington 2015; Splendore 2016), but they may be at odds with the business imperatives, management tendencies, and institutional realities of the news industry (cf. Cohen 2015; Splichal & Dahlgren 2016). By deflating fears of automation in newsrooms, the human-still-in-the-loop perspective seems to help contain tensions between the public (cl)aims of journalism and the corporate interests of management, and thus to creating an accommodation between the material conditions and discursive underpinnings of journalism.

With the rise of social networks and platforms such as Facebook and Google, journalism seems not to have proper answers to the issues of "prismatic truth" (Dahlgren 2009); most notably, 'fake news', and journalism's crisis of viability, not exclusively financial, threatens the resources and existence of legacy news institutions (Blumler 2010). The identified human-still-in-the-loop perspective seems to enhance the perception of humans being central in human–automation modes of journalism without considering the larger struggles for control over the legitimation of knowledge or the representation of social realities. At best it seeks to ease the main problems of journalism and contributes to larger discussions about "journalism's crisis of hegemony" (Nerone 2015), which has accompanied the media infrastructure's transformation since the late 20th century. This crisis seems to be deepening, with automation being central for innovation in journalism and, more importantly, beyond its boundaries.

The study's limitations discussed above indicate that much more needs to be done to better understand the transformations taking shape – not only by expanding the scope of interviews (e.g. journalists, media managers, 'new' newsroom staffers) and also by concentrating on smaller newsrooms, but also by employing other methods from qualitative (e.g. observations and focus groups) and quantitative traditions (e.g. surveys). Moreover, it is crucial to historicise the journalism–technology relationship and diversify the theoretical perspectives on technological innovation to ensure a comprehensive and continual exploration of the difficult connection between journalism and automation. As history teaches us, journalism's internal and external struggles of today will affect how journalistic hegemonies are shaped tomorrow by those who control the "big pipes" (Nerone 2015, 326). As the ideals of professional journalism are already in a state of flux while journalism tries to overcome its political and business crises, the further re-articulation of those ideals could forestall more aggressive actions and self-justifications – not only in large legacy news institutions, but also in smaller news production settings that often without reservation go beyond the traditional news–business boundary. Allowing for the possibility of hybrids between human journalists and automated systems, many of which have yet to be invented, it is not hard to imagine the "posthuman future" of journalism (Carlson 2017, 226) – not as an unrealistic dystopia, but as a realistic promise of a "hybrid state" in which both machine and human fingerprints will appear all over what is now understood as professional journalism – defining both its production and ideologisation.

Funding

This research was partly supported by the Slovenian Research Agency, ARRS; Javna Agencija za Raziskovalno Dejavnost RS.

References

Ananny, Mike. 2016. "Toward an Ethics of Algorithms." *Science, Technology & Human Values* 41 (1): 93–117.
Anderson, C. W. 2013. "Towards a Sociology of Computational and Algorithmic Journalism." *New Media & Society* 15 (7): 1005–1021.
Blumler, Jay. 2010. "Foreword: The Two-legged Crisis of Journalism". *Journalism Studies* 11 (4): 439–441.
Boyd-Barrett, Oliver. 1995. "The Analysis of Media Occupations and Professionals." In *Approaches to Media*, edited by Boyd-Barrett, Oliver and Chris Newbold, 270–276. London: Arnold.
Bucher, Tina. 2017. "'Machines Don't Have Instincts'." *New Media and Society* 19 (6): 918–933.

Carlson, Matt. 2015. "The Robotic Reporter." *Digital Journalism* 3(3): 416–431.

Carlson, Matt. 2016. "Metajournalistic Discourse and the Meanings of Journalism." *Communication Theory* 26(4): 349–368.

Carlson, Matt. 2017. "Automated Journalism." In *The Routledge Companion to Digital Journalism Studies*, edited by Bob Franklin and Scott A. Eldridge II, 226–234. London: Routledge.

Carlson, Matt. 2018. "Automating Judgement?" *New Media & Society* 20 (5): 1755–1772.

Carlson, Matt and Seth C. Lewis (Eds.). 2015. *Boundaries of Journalism*. London: Routledge.

Coddington, Mark. 2015. "Clarifying Journalism's Quantitative Turn." *Digital Journalism* 3 (3): 331–348.

Cohen, Nicole S. 2015. "From Pink Slips to Pink Slime." *The Communication Review* 18 (2): 98–122.

Dahlgren, Peter. 2009. "The Troubling Evolution of Journalism." In *The Changing Faces of Journalism*, edited by Barbie Zelizer, 146–161. London: Routledge.

Deuze, Mark. 2005. "What is Journalism?" *Journalism* 6 (4): 442–464.

Diakopoulos, Nicholas. 2015. "Algorithmic Accountability." *Digital Journalism* 3 (3): 398–415.

Diakopoulos, Nicholas and Michael Koliska. 2017. "Algorithmic Transparency in the News Media." *Digital Journalism* 5 (7): 809–828.

Dörr, Konstantin Nicholas. 2016. "Mapping the Field of Algorithmic Journalism." *Digital Journalism* 4 (6): 700–722.

Dörr, Konstantin Nicholas and Katharina Hollbuchner. 2017. "Ethical Challenges of Algorithmic Journalism." *Digital Journalism* 5 (4): 404–419.

Fink, Conrad C. 1996. *Strategic Newspaper Management*. Boston, MA: Allyn and Bacon.

Gans, Herbert J. 1979/2004. *Deciding What's News*. Evantson: Northwestern University Press.

Gillespie, Tarleton. 2014. "The Relevance of Algorithms." In *Media Technologies*, edited by Tarleton Gillespie, Pablo J. Boczkowski and Kristen A. Foot, 167–194. Cambridge: MIT Press.

Hallin, Daniel. 1994. *We Keep America on Top of the World*. London: Routledge.

Hardt, Hanno. 1998. *Interactions: Critical Studies in Communication, Media, and Journalism*. Oxford: Rowman & Littlefield.

James, Nalita, and Hugh Busher. 2012. "Internet Interviewing." In *The Sage Handbook of Interview Research*, edited by Jaber F. Gubrium, James A. Holstein, Amir B. Marvasti and Karyn D. MyKinney, 177–192. London: Sage.

Kvale, Steinar. 1996. *Interviews*. London: Sage.

Le Masurier, Megan. 2015. "What is Slow Journalism?" *Journalism Practice* 9 (2): 138–152.

Lewis, Seth C. 2015. "Journalism in an Era of Big Data." *Digital Journalism* 3 (3): 321–330.

Lewis, Seth C., and Oscar Westlund. 2016. "Mapping the Human-Machine Divide." In *The Sage Handbook of Digital Journalism*, edited by Tamara Witschge, C. W. Anderson, David Domingo and Alfred Hermida, 354–369. London: Sage.

Linden, Carl-Gustav. 2017. "Decades of Automation in the Newsroom." *Digital Journalism*, 5 (2): 123–140.

Maras, Steven. 2013. *Objectivity in Journalism*. Cambridge: Polity.

Markoff, John. 2016. *Machines of Loving Grace*. London: Ecco.

Morrison, David E. and Howard Tumber (1995). "Journalists at War (Introduction)". In *Approaches to Media*, edited by Boyd-Barrett, Oliver and Chris Newbold, 313–318. London: Arnold.

Nerone, John. 2013. "The Historical Roots of the Normative Model of Journalism." *Journalism* 14 (4): 446–458.

Nerone, John. 2015. "Journalism's Crisis of Hegemony." *Javnost–The Public* 22 (4): 313–327.

Napoli, Philip M. 2014. "On Automation in Media Industries." *Media Industries Journal* 1 (1): 33–38.

Örnebring, Henrik. 2010. "Technology and Journalism-as-Labour." *Journalism* 11 (1): 57–74.

Peters, Chris and Marcel Broersma, Eds. 2013. *Rethinking Journalism*. London: Routledge.

Phillips, Angela. 2012. Faster and Shallower. In *Changing Journalism*, edited by Peter Lee-Wright, Angela Phillips and Tamara Witschge, 81–98. London: Routledge.

Rantanen, Tehri. 2009. *When News Was New*. Malden, MA: Wiley-Blackwell.

Robinson, Oliver C. 2014. "Sampling in Interview-Based Qualitative Research." *Qualitative Research in Psychology* 11(1): 25–41.

Russial, John, Peter Laufer, and Janet Wasko. 2015. "Journalism in Crisis?" *Javnost–The Public* 22 (4): 299–312.

Schudson, Michael. 2005. "Autonomy from What?" In *Bourdieu and the Journalistic Field*, edited by Rodney Benson, Erik Neuveu, 214–224. Cambridge, MA: Polity.

Snider, Paul B. 1995. "'Mr Gates' revisited". In *Approaches to Media*, edited by Boyd-Barrett, Oliver and Chris Newbold, 283–286. London: Arnold.

Splendore, Sergio. 2016. "Quantitatively Oriented Forms of Journalism and Their Epistemology." *Sociology Compass* 10 (5): 343–352.

Splichal, Slavko. 1999. *Public Opinion*. New York: Rowman and Littlefield.

Splichal, Slavko. 2015. "Journalism and journalists." In *International Encyclopedia of the Social & Behavioral Sciences*, edited by James Wright, 857–861. Amsterdam: Elsevier.

Splichal, Slavko, and Peter Dahlgren. 2016. "Journalism between De-professionalisation and Democratisation." *European Journal of Communication* 31 (1): 5–18.

Thurman, Neil, Konstantin Dörr, and Jessica Kunert. 2017. "When Reporters Get Hands-on with Robo-Writing." *Digital Journalism* 5 (10): 1240–1259.

Thurman, Neil and Steve Schifferes. 2012. "The Future of Personalization at News Websites." *Journalism Studies* 13 (5–6): 775–790.

Thurman, Neil, Steve Schifferes, Richard Fletcher, Nic Newman, Stephen Hunt and Aljosha Karim Schapals. 2016. "Giving Computers a Nose for News." *Digital Journalism* 4 (7): 838–848.

Underwood, Doug. 1995. *When MBAs Rule the Newsroom*. New York: Columbia University Press.

van Dalen, Arjen. 2012. "The Algorithms behind the Headlines." *Journalism Practice* 6 (5/6): 648–658.

Waisbord, Silvio. 2013. *Reinventing Professionalism*. Cambridge: Polity.

Wicks, Jan Leblanc, George Sylvie, Ann C. Hollifield, Stephen Lacy, and Ardyth Broadrick Sohn. 2004. *Media Management*. Mahwah, NJ: Lawrence Erlbaum Associates.

Young, Mary Lynn and Alfred Hermida. 2015. "From Mr. and Mrs. Outliner to Central Tendencies." *Digital Journalism* 3 (3): 381–397.

Zelizer, Barbie, Ed. 2009. *The Changing Faces of Journalism*. London: Routledge.

News Algorithms, Photojournalism and the Assumption of Mechanical Objectivity in Journalism

Matt Carlson

ABSTRACT

This article interrogates the relationship between epistemic authority and journalistic technology through the perspective of mechanical objectivity—a belief in technological systems capable of rendering a particular output in a manner that overcomes the limits of human subjectivity. By treating journalistic objectivity not as a stable referent, but as a contextual one prone to shifts in practices and understandings over time, it foregrounds how changing technologies of recording, creating, and distributing news content affect how journalistic objectivity is understood. Following this perspective, two technological practices are examined: photojournalism and algorithms. The development of photojournalism led to the prizing of news images as objective representations produced by the camera to the diminishment of human judgment. Similarly, the various outputs produced by news algorithms are accompanied by an orientation toward computational objectivity in contrast to human subjectivity. Exploring these dynamics sheds light on the ongoing relationship between news technologies and discourses of journalistic objectivity in the face of digital innovations in the production and circulation of news.

Introduction

As a mediated form of knowledge work, journalism cannot be separated from the technologies that make news possible. What news looks like and how it is created and shared relies as much on the vast technical infrastructure of journalism as it does on norms and practices. Following this perspective, new journalistic technologies warrant attention for their epistemic consequences concerning what counts as valid journalistic knowledge and how such knowledge can be attained (Lewis and Westlund 2015). Just as new technologies – and the possibilities and constraints they introduce – complicate ongoing understandings of news, journalistic norms affect how technologies are used. This reciprocity implicates both the material and the discursive, with a central concern over the shape of journalistic authority and public expectations of news

(Carlson 2017). Exploring these dynamics sheds light on the relationship between news technologies and journalism's legitimating discourses in the face of digital innovations in the production and circulation of news.

This article adopts a pragmatic perspective of the epistemology of news (see Ekström 2002) in order to examine issues involving journalistic objectivity (Maras 2013). It treats journalistic objectivity not as a stable referent, but as a contextual one prone to shifts in practices and understandings over time. Rather than the typical attention to professional norms or role conceptions, this perspective foregrounds how changing technologies of recording, creating, and distributing news content affect how journalistic objectivity is understood and practiced.

The relationship between objectivity and the epistemic authority of journalism is examined through two sets of technological practices: photography and algorithms. Each will be related to what Daston and Galison (2007) refer to as "mechanical objectivity" to describe how knowledge producers emphasize technological systems to legitimate their output. In adapting the concept to journalism, mechanical objectivity is defined in this article as the assumption of the epistemic utility of mechanical operations, whether overtly expressed or implicitly embedded in practice. With regard to overt assumptions, the introduction of the photographic image into everyday journalism presented journalists with an alluring technology for their aspirations to mirror the world (Raetzsch 2015). At a moment in the early twentieth century when objectivity was an ascendant norm, journalists endowed the camera with special powers to record and reproduce the world. The more recent rise of algorithmic practices and automated systems throughout the news-making process means this technology plays an increasingly central role in what audiences see (Zamith 2019). These technologies are often embedded in what Gillespie (2014) calls the promise of "algorithmic objectivity" through implicit assumptions that relate to discourses of mechanical objectivity. Mechanical objectivity provides a useful perspective for bringing to light epistemic assumptions surrounding sociotechnological aspects of journalistic practices, as well as concerns over the prominence and power of algorithms in journalism.

The sections that follow begin with an examination of objectivity's place in journalism before shifting to the concept of mechanical objectivity as a specific perspective for conceptualizing the role of technology in knowledge producing practices. Mechanical objectivity is then applied to photojournalism and algorithms. Because journalistic norms and practices are not uniform, the present study will largely focus on the perspective of US journalism, with some reference to other national contexts. This is not an effort to universalize the US experience, but rather to demonstrate the close correspondence between context and journalistic norms.

Objectivity and Journalism

Objectivity bedevils journalism. As a normative goal, objectivity provides a legitimating discourse that serves the democratic aspirations of journalism. As an ideal, objectivity entails the collection and dissemination of verifiable facts delivered in a detached manner, generating the raw material news audiences need to fashion their own judgments regarding public affairs. It shapes both the epistemic practices of journalists and the expectations of news audiences. But objectivity has well-known shortcomings. The foundational epistemological objection is that journalistic facts cannot be communicated independently of journalistic agents or the context in which they arise. News comes from somewhere, and the particular values and experiences journalists bring to their work have to be acknowledged. Despite such core objections to a strict reading of journalistic objectivity, arguments for journalistic authority often rely on an understanding of objectivity, even if such understandings vary (Hanitzsch 2007). It continues to influence news norms and practices (Maras 2013, Schudson 2001). Deuze (2005) argues that an ongoing cycle of defense and disparagement of objectivity keeps it poised as "an ideological cornerstone of journalism" (448).

The lexical slipperiness of objectivity is apparent in efforts to define its specific meaning, but Hanitzsch (2007) captures its essential claims in his definition of objectivity as "the view that one can and should separate facts from values" (376). This statement nicely encapsulates journalistic objectivity's dual nature of being at once normative and practical. It is a way of thinking and doing, and these two sides cannot be meaningfully separated from one another. Journalism is not a philosophical experiment but an institutionalized means of producing widely circulated texts often under strict time pressures. Nor can practice alone be examined; journalistic work is not haphazard or accidental but formulated to be accepted as a legitimate mode of producing accounts of the world.

Journalistic objectivity has no clear origin. Its antecedents coincide with the earliest forms of organized news or proto-news (Ward 2004). In the US context, scholars connect it to the rise of the Penny Press (Schiller 1981) or the turn to professionalism in the early twentieth century (Schudson 2001). Objectivity allows journalists to borrow the notion of detached observation and pre-existing reality from scientific authority, but it also has to be connected to the economic incentives of newspapers wanting to appeal to the broadest possible audience in response to newly achievable circulation scales made possible by improved printing technologies (Hamilton 2004). Around the world, objectivity became connected to public service broadcasting with the rise of radio and later television. In the UK, objectivity has been closely connected to the BBC and Reuters, even if it is less prominent with newspapers (Hampton 2008). In general, objectivity became an expectation solidified in the consciousness of journalists and their audiences in the later half of the twentieth century. This is not to discount its history of detractors, of which there have been many, but to establish that objectivity has multiple origins and needs to be understood in practice (Boudana 2011).

Over the past decades, journalistic objectivity has been subject to much public skepticism and critique (for an overview, see Maras 2013). Concerns about journalistic objectivity are rooted in the longer running tensions recounted above, and they surface as fresh complaints continue to make shortcomings clear. In the United States, objectivity has been linked to specific moments of press failure, such as McCarthyism in the 1950s (Zelizer 1993) or the faulty intelligence leading to the 2003 Iraq War (Bennett, Lawrence, and Livingston 2008). Further consternation surrounding objectivity involves questions about the limits of journalism's professional stance (Craft 2017). Objectivity presented not as naïve empiricism but as a learned position has its roots in professionalism. Claims of professionalism as a strategy for journalistic authority rest on twinning a shared epistemic orientation institutionalized through professionalism with an argument for the necessity of journalistic autonomy (Waisbord 2013). The professional, once having learned how to act as a professional and display professional judgment, is then expected to operate unmolested by external forces. This is surely an idealized position, but its resilience underscores how objectivity remains bound up in journalistic claims to professionalism. The journalistic position is one of practiced distance. This position does not discount judgment (Carlson 2018a), but rather locates judgment within institutionalized discernment made possible through learned reporting procedures. These critiques indicate how objectivity has been tarnished at the level of practice but also how it has lost power as a particular totem deployed symbolically by journalists to protect their work, as Tuchman (1972) asserted in another era. But its resilience, particularly in the US, also speaks to its complexity.

One means of assessing the continuation of objectivity as a journalistic norm is to give greater emphasis to the role that news technologies play in shaping news practices and the idealization of journalism. Doing so pushes the literature on journalistic objectivity forward by accentuating its contextual nature. The next section provides one possible conceptual lens linking technology and the legitimation of knowledge through the idea of "mechanical objectivity."

Mechanical Objectivity

Useful conceptual tools for diving further into the relationship between objectivity, epistemic authority, and technology can be found by moving outside of journalism to science. Scientific inquiry presupposes a separation from the knower and the known in its claims that the natural world can be discovered, observed, and represented accurately for further inquiry. Rather than dwell on the philosophical qualities of such claims (and their critiques), this section instead asks about their pragmatic implementation through the mediation of technology. Scientific progress proceeds from the continual improvement of its technologies of inquiry. New technologies of measuring and recording make new forms of evidence available, which leads to reconsiderations—if not rejections—of previous theories. This is a Whig history of science that is tied to deeply ingrained cultural notions of progress and improvement—a recognizable discourse since the Enlightenment. But it remains a driving force in scientific and technological development.

Going against the grain of scientific objectivism, scholars working in the science and technology studies tradition have continually challenged pat understandings of scientific objectivity, and in particular the separation between the knower and the known. Inquiries into the making of science reveal the complicated institutional, organizational, and interpersonal dynamics involved in the generation of scientific knowledge. Shapin and Schaffer (2011, 14), in their seminal history of the introduction of experimental methods, treat objectivity and the concepts of truth and adequacy "as accomplishments, as historical products, as actors' judgments and categories." The acceptance of scientific inquiry as an objective knowledge-making practice—one in which knowledge revealed itself to the scientist—was an accomplishment procured through struggle. Robert Boyle's advocacy of experimental methods was not abstract, but closely tied to technology in the form of his air-pump. The materiality of the device and its mobility provided both scientific evidence and a means of supporting such evidence.

Scholars embedding themselves among scientists highlight the sociality of scientific work as well as materiality when tracking the production of scientific claims (see Sismondo 2004). In the realm of philosophy, scientific objectivity has been further challenged by various iterations of standpoint theories that emphasize the connection between the production of knowledge and the knower (Haraway 1988). By challenging simplistic conceptions of the scientific observer as detached from what is observed, these perspectives direct attention to the networks, infrastructures, and legitimation strategies underlying various technological means of producing scientific observations.

In the realm of scientific observation and recording, Daston and Galison (2007) specify a nineteenth century shift from "truth-to-nature" representations in which objectivity was understood as the creation of idealized images to the desire for "mechanical objectivity," that is, "the insistent drive to repress the willful intervention of the artist-author, and to put in its stead a set of procedures that would, as it were, move nature to the page through a strict protocol, if not automatically" (121). They further identify "mechanical" as entailing both the production of images without human intervention and the subsequent mass reproduction of identical copies (135). The quest for mechanical objectivity acknowledges the difficulties of scientific observation and the recording of scientific data by human agents. It accentuates the mechanical as non-human, creating a machine–human dichotomy such that support for the machine doubles as a critique of the human observer. As stated in the introduction above, this article applies the concept of mechanical objectivity in a wider sense as the assumption of the epistemic utility of mechanical operations, whether overtly expressed or implicitly embedded in practice.

The invention of photography and its subsequent utilization in scientific inquiry well illustrates the ideology of mechanical objectivity in its scientific usage. Early on, the photograph was heralded for its distance from human recording practices. Daston and Galison note, "The automatism of the photographic process promised images free of human interpretation – *objective* images, as they came to be called" (130–131, original emphasis). Such a statement is understandable considering that picture-making practices had always involved human-made marks and therefore problems of skill differential or subjective interpretation. And while it elides the human practices that go into photography, it demonstrates well the continued hope for unbiased and untouched representations.

Ultimately the output of mechanical objectivity proved to be insufficient for the scientific atlases that Daston and Galison studied, leading scientists to adopt the position of "trained judgment" that combined professional discernment with mechanical reproduction. This hybrid approach to knowledge creation weds the mechanical with expert interpretation to produce representations that provide the most utility to scientists fashioning representations to be shared with others. It makes room for interpretation while retaining from mechanical objectivity a conceptual lens that shifts discussions of objectivity from abstract epistemology to technological practices of knowledge-making. In a meta-sense, both mechanical objectivity and trained judgment are ways of seeing ways of seeing. But the legacy of mechanical objectivity is a desire for techno-logical improvement to better capture nature. In science, it has manifested itself differently in different eras, and the constancy of the hope for pure observations it engenders along with the plasticity of the term makes it useful for thinking about journalistic objectivity.

Photojournalism and Objectivity

The shift in the recording of scientific observations via hand-drawn images to photographs has its parallel in journalism. Like science, journalism has relied on textual description abetted by images. Similarly, the acceptance of images as providing an objective representation of reality is cultural and technological. Raetzsch's (2015) history of journalistic image practices demonstrates the contingency of modes of mechanical objectivity. Because journalism is predicated on mass production, the technology to reproduce photographic images at scale lagged well behind the proliferation of photographic images outside of journalism. Journalists responded in the late 19th and early twentieth centuries with the use of more easily reproduced woodcuts derived from photographs. The existence of the photograph provided an argument for the objectivity of the image depicted by the woodcut, even if woodcut artists injected their own interpretive renderings in their work. The invention of half-tone printing led to a pivot away from the woodcut to the inclusion of photographs in news, but not immediately. News audiences accustomed to the artistry embedded in woodcuts confronted the reduced quality of half-tone photographs with suspicion before photographs came to replace engravings all together. This turnover demonstrates the need to pay close attention to the modes of legitimation within image practices. Raetzsch writes, "Each graphic style had distinct aesthetic, material and cultural qualities that impeded an equation of photographic objectivity with reproductions. Yet all of these images were in particular ways 'real' enough to offer added value to journalistic news" (306). As with Daston and Galison above, this argument locates mechanical objectivity as an important goal for legitimating knowledge claims, albeit a culturally specific one in which practices need to be understood within particular times and places. Finally, Raetzsch locates the shift from engravings to photographs within the larger historical developments surrounding the ascension of objectivity as a core norm for journalism. Journalists seeking to dispose of subjectivity in favor of faithful transmissions found photography to be a practice well suited to strong notions of journalistic objectivity as a mirror to the world. Barnhurst and Nerone (2001, 176) attribute the source of photographic authority to "the conviction that nothing intervenes between a reader and a scene." Schwartz (1999) quotes a writer explaining how when mass produced news photographs emerged in the 1920s, many readers suspicious of tabloid newspaper stories treated news photographs as a particularly credible form of evidence: "seeing was still believing" and a news photograph "was accepted as proof of a story's accuracy" (168).

The history of photojournalism is marked by the tension between images as a depiction of something that happened out there and as the product of professional activity (Brennen 2009). For Newton (2001), visual images are considered to be "at once mediated and true" (12). This position of being a representation and not the thing itself raises ontological questions about realist representation (Schwartz, 1999). Moreover, even as visual literacy discourses began to insert the suggestion of subjectivity into photojournalism, Schwartz notes a persistent assumption that the equipment continued to be objective (178). The use of news photographs also strays from arguments that their fidelity to what they capture is paramount. Griffin (1999) shows that iconic war photographs resonate not because of the specific depictions – i.e., their facticity – but because they demonstrate symbolic qualities that speak to the general nature of the horrors of war. This shift from specificity to generality is underscored by subsequent revelations that many famous images are suspicious if not entirely fabricated (see Carlson 2009).

The tension between the autonomy of the mechanically derived image and the subjective work of the photographer to produce the image has resulted in the downplaying of the professional status of the photojournalist. The lauding of the camera as an objective instrument hampers efforts by photojournalists to establish their place among their peers (Schwartz 1999, 173–4). The early days of scalable photojournalism made possible with the Associated Press's wirephoto technology met with backlash from print journalists in ways that heightened claims about the objectivity of news images by accentuating the machinery instead of its operator (Zelizer 1995, 84–87). Visual journalists still complain of feeling inferior in comparison to other journalists (Lowrey 2002), and visual journalists are marked as less important (Bock, Lough, and Fadnis 2017). Such examples in which journalists strategically expunge the humans on which visual practices depend indicates how the ideal of mechanical objectivity persists into the present. The epistemic authority of news image pushes aside the many layers of human judgment through which such images travel. Meanwhile, photojournalists continue to argue for their value in what may be closer to Daston and Galison's (2007) notion of "trained judgment" as both technically proficient operators of technology and skilled interpreters with a particular form of visual journalistic expertise. This positioning is clearly evident in the US-based National Press Photographers Association's Code of Ethics, with its emphasis on the conditions under which visual images are taken and subsequently edited (https://nppa.org/nppa-code-ethics).

More recently, photojournalism finds itself in a precarious place given the dual impact of declining resources at traditional news organizations and the flourishing of digital images with attendant questions concerning their accuracy (Solaroli 2015). The confusion caused by the proliferation of images secures the importance of the expertise of visual editors (Nilsson 2017) while simultaneously budget cuts threaten their employment. Photojournalists are struggling to adapt to this environment in which image-making and image-sharing are democratized and widespread (Mäenpää 2014). Again, the persistence of mechanical objectivity devalues the human role of image making by instilling cameras with the assumption that anyone with the technology can produce a news image – an old claim made as early as the 1940s (Zelizer 1995). At the same time, more recent developments point to the arrival of fabricated video in which real people can convincingly be made to look as if they saying things that they did not (Foer 2018)—a practice sure to further dampen claims to mechanical objectivity.

Although visual scholars confound claims of the mechanical objectivity of photojournalism, the desire for improved replication is a strong one forming a thread that runs through the present with the application of new visual technologies to journalism. Aitamurto (2018) tracks how proponents of omnidirectional immersive video technology – 360° journalism – argue for the greater accuracy and objectivity of these videos. They are lauded for providing the audience with a sense of being there instead of relying on the journalist as mediator. As one journalist remarked, "It's very much taking the journalist out of that storytelling process and allowing your audience to see for themselves what's happening" (9). As a new technology with developing norms and practices, disagreements arise regarding the degree of allowable manipulation – such as removing the camera or photojournalist from the image. Aitamurto labeled this a tension between faithful "as is" and manipulated "as if" accounts (16). Regardless of the debate, the journalists she interviewed expressed enthusiasm that virtual and augmented reality would present viewers with a more realistic representation than what has been previously possible with news images.

Ultimately, the camera provides a mode of representation different from either written accounts or even a drawn image (Zelizer 2005). Fixing on the ontology of photographic images, journalists have long turned to the camera as a technology that moves them closer to improved replication of the world. Cameras provide visual evidence and collapse the distance between event and viewer. Even as their ability to represent reality comes under fire, images retain a prominent place in the epistemology of news.

The Epistemic Authority of Algorithms

The rise of digital media has been accompanied by the increased prominence of computer algorithms as decision-making tools. As computer code that renders single or multiple inputs into an output, the utilization of algorithms across multiple domains of everyday life shapes knowledge practices. We rely on search engines to find knowledge, navigate across texts via recommendation engine suggestions, and even interact with algorithmically generated texts. This section examines the broader discourse around algorithmic decision-making—along with its critiques—before turning to the specific case of journalism in the next section.

In assessing the epistemic conditions and consequences of algorithms, an important starting point is the recognition that algorithms do not possess inherent epistemic authority. Instead, human agents produce an argument that "certifies [an algorithm] as a reliable sociotechnical actor," in Gillespie's words (2014, 179). Because algorithms vary in their opacity—with the most complex ones obscured by proprietary claims— the rendering of their unseen processes into valid forms of knowledge rests on a set of encompassing discourses that their creators use to tout the technology. Speed, scale, and customizability are certainly attributes that are celebrated, but Gillespie goes further to locate algorithmic legitimization in the "technologically inflected promise of mechanical neutrality" (181). Beer (2017, 11) labels this attribute "calculative objectivity," noting the symbolic character of algorithms as "shorthand for the power and potential of calculative systems that can think more quickly, more

comprehensively and more accurately than humans." Such an argument for legitimization rests on what Sundar (2008) calls the "machine heuristic" – the assumption of a
lack of bias in computer selection practices. When isolated, an algorithm is reduced to
a set of instructions programmed into code, which can be contrasted with human
interpretation and subjective judgment.

The reliance of algorithmic processes crosses many domains. For example, studies
of "automation bias" (Skitka, Mosier, and Burdick 1999) show how professionals in
such fields as aviation and clinical care come to rely on automated systems for guidance. These systems become imbricated into professional practices as trusted actors,
even when their decisions go against training protocols. Meanwhile, in the realm of
policy, attributing decision-making to seemingly neutral algorithmic outputs rather
than human judgment is an epistemic strategy that defends policy makers against
criticism (Rieder and Simon 2016).

The epistemic consequences of algorithms are visible in the recent phenomenon
known popularly as "big data." The lauding of big data rests on an assumption that
extensive data sets can be meaningfully analyzed through computing techniques that
far surpass the capacity of human judgment. This argument was put forth in *Wired*
magazine by editor-in-chief Chris Anderson (2008), who argued:

> [M]assive amounts of data and applied mathematics replace every other tool that might
> be brought to bear. Out with every theory of human behavior, from linguistics to
> sociology. Forget taxonomy, ontology, and psychology. Who knows why people do what
> they do? The point is they do it, and we can track and measure it with unprecedented
> fidelity. With enough data, the numbers speak for themselves

The numbers, of course, speak through computerized data analytics software capable of sifting through enormous data sets to identify patterns. Anderson goes on to
target science as the knowledge practice most susceptible to big data upheaval via
the replacement of modeling and hypothesizing with data analysis:

> We can throw the numbers into the biggest computing clusters the world has ever seen
> and let statistical algorithms find patterns where science cannot.

This last statement juxtaposes the human-driven scientific process with algorithmic
processes capable of exceeding the limits of human cognition. Notably, Anderson's
argument is forward-looking, with the promise of discoveries tied to future innovations in data gathering, storage, and analysis. This argument not only implies the per-
ceptual limits of humans, but also the problem of subjectivity.

The emphasis on algorithms as automated and unthinking resonates with the ten-
ets of mechanical objectivity. Although algorithmic output is not the same as the outputs of visual technologies described above, the mechanical nature of algorithmic
processes explains their deployment in many sites in which the removal of human
judgment is a prized goal. A key example of this is prison sentencing. At a time when
the US prison population outpaces most other nations, patterned discrepancies in sentencing according to race or ethnicity are a clear problem (Alexander 2012). For officials responsible for sentencing pursuing the normative goal of impartiality, algorithms
provide an enticing alternative to human judgment. In a 2013 TED talk espousing the
virtues of algorithmic judgment former New Jersey attorney general Anne Milgram
made this argument explicit, stating of judges: "They're being subjective, and we

know what happens with subjective decision making, which is that we are often wrong. What we need in this space are strong data and analytics" (quoted in Christin 2017, 6). Distilled down, the hope is that the mechanical objectivity of algorithms can replace human bias. In practice, the use of algorithms for sentencing has been more complex, often relying on inputs that reproduce inequality (O'Neil 2016, pp. 24–27) as well as differences in how they are put into practice (Christin 2017). The aura of algorithmic objectivity makes exposing biased assumptions written into code more difficult. The appeal of automated decision-making is strong when humans are viewed as already deficient.

As algorithmic decision-making becomes more widespread across different domains, experimental studies show algorithmic decisions to be considered less biased than human decisions. A *Harvard Business Review* article summed up the literature on algorithmic decision-making positively: "the existing studies on this topic all have a remarkably similar conclusion: Algorithms are less biased and more accurate than the humans they are replacing" (Miller 2018). For example, Logg, Minson, and Moore (2018) found that people preferred algorithmic advice over the advice of humans in exercises when they asked to make estimates or forecasts. Only experts seemed to eschew algorithmic advice, even when their own judgment was less accurate. In somewhat of a contrast, Lee (2018) found an equal appreciation of algorithmic and human judgment with regard to mechanical tasks, but a preference for humans for evaluations of hiring and job performance.

Discussions of the epistemic assumptions surrounding algorithmic decision-making harken back to the earlier example of photography. Discourse surrounding both regularly separate out the technology as mechanical and unthinking from the subjectivity of human actors. The camera lens converts an external image into a representation; the algorithm converts a series of inputs into a specific output. Also, like photography, this perspective depends upon eliding human involvement. The photojournalist struggles for professional status in the face of assumptions about images while the agents behind various algorithmic practices often fade into the background. Even though this view of algorithms versus humans treats algorithms as unduly discrete, this imputed division dominates discourse around the technology (Bucher 2018). In this way, the concept of mechanical objectivity again provides a way of conceptualizing the legitimatization of algorithmic knowledge around a) the partitioning of human from algorithmic processes, and b) the ascription of decisions to detached automated processes.

Although a great deal of hope surrounds the epistemic utility of algorithmic decision-making, a growing body of critique questions its benefits. The nascent field of critical algorithm studies has quickly amassed a body of work interrogating diverse aspects of algorithms and their social consequences.[1] These works universally reject both the claims of neutrality and separation from human actors associated with mechanical objectivity in favor of a socially situated perspective examining the production, implementation, and use of algorithms across domains of public and private life. Algorithms have become targets for questions concerning the creation, sorting, and transmission of information (Gillespie 2014; Kitchin 2017) and have spurred the development of algorithmic ethics (Ananny 2016; Mittelstadt et al 2016) and calls for new accountability systems (Diakopoulos 2015). More broadly, assumptions of algorithmic neutrality have come under scrutiny within public discourse challenging the inherent neutrality of algorithmic practices in a string of notable books (Eubanks 2018, Noble 2018, O'Neil 2016, Pasquale 2015) – with more sure to follow. These works and others spur public consciousness by challenging implicit notions of the mechanical objectivity of algorithms. It is in this tumult of supporters and detractors that journalists and their organizations find themselves as they turn to algorithms at various points in the news process.

News Algorithms and Journalistic Epistemology

Algorithms have entered into news processes at many different levels (Zamith 2019). Increasingly, computer code can drive news selection (Weber and Kosterich 2018), make items visible or invisible (Bucher 2012), and enable the personalization of news in ways that were not previously possible (Thurman 2011). Algorithms can be used to analyze data (Parasie 2015), write stories (Dörr 2016), or provide newsrooms with metrics (Christin 2017). As algorithms serve up news stories, crunch data, make recommendations, write stories, and so forth, the notion of mechanical objectivity provides an analytical tool for assessing how it is that algorithms come to be legitimated as a part of journalism's knowledge apparatus (Christin 2016). The concept helps attune us to the often-passive assumptions that surround and add legitimacy to the uptake of algorithmic practices across news.

As with any news technology, journalistic algorithms are built and executed within a context of preexisting conventions. The previous section reviewed both the enthusiasm and concern surrounding algorithms that stem from their automaticity. Fitting these discussions into journalism requires acknowledgment of journalism's existing cultural apparatuses of legitimacy (Carlson 2017; Zelizer 1993), including a tension between active interpretation and detached neutrality. Journalism is a peculiar type of knowledge-producing field, given its mandate to continuously produce timely-yet-accurate news stories mediated through a variety of mass communication channels. The unceasing demand for more news content requires the regimentation of news work, including systems for collecting information, the replication of story forms, and shared normative commitments. As argued above, objectivity – even with its critiques – continues to act as a legitimizing norm and a guide for news practices (Maras 2013). It is an idea bound up in what it means to provide factual information at a mass scale.

Even as journalistic algorithms are made to fit existing models of news, they simultaneously alter how news can be imagined. In this sense, assumptions surrounding the neutrality of algorithms discussed above – i.e., the "machine heuristic" (Sundar 2008) – are imported into news. As Bucher (2017) argues: "The computational is as much about what can and what cannot be calculated, as it is an organising framework and discursive order for thinking and talking about journalism in the digital age" (930). The existence of journalistic algorithms shape what is possible, simultaneously extending new practices while being constrained by preexisting norms and practices. It is not just about adding new tools to existing news epistemologies, but how algorithmic tools alter how knowledge is produced, thought about, and legitimated (Parasie 2015). This push and pull between residual and emerging practices is not unique to algorithms, but a persistent tension accompanying the introduction of new technologies, including photojournalism as discussed above or the early implementation of computers in newsrooms (Powers 2012). Anderson (2018, 134) argues that the growing use of computers for data analysis in the early days of computer-assisted-reporting applications was not about establishing new types of objectivity, but more efficiently executing existing modes of data-oriented investigative reporting. As such, examining the relationship of algorithms to the ideas and practices of journalism exposes how cultural values are embedded in technologies as well as how the materiality of the technology affects how news values are expressed.

Automated journalism presents itself as one of the most advanced applications of algorithms to journalism (Carlson 2015, Napoli 2014, van Dalen 2012). The software mimics conventional newswriting by analyzing data and using natural language generation software to craft fully automated, unique stories (Dörr 2016). This extends news coverage into sites that would not generate enough traffic to warrant the investment of human labor, such as quarterly earnings reports for publicly traded companies or college sporting events. It does not disrupt as much as augment existing news structures, as research reveals how difficult it can be for audiences to differentiate what is human-authored from what is written by an algorithm (Clerwall 2014; Graefe et al. 2018). Studies are mixed as to whether audiences prefer algorithmic authorship (Wölker and Powell 2018) or not (Waddell 2018). Liu and Wei (2018) found higher perceptions of the objectivity of automated journalism stories, but not their expertise. Automated journalism also raises a host of new questions, such as whether algorithms have the agency to commit libel (Lewis, Sanders, and Carmody 2018). Yet few seem to question the underlying technology and its legitimacy as a creator of news content.

Empirical research regarding algorithmic news selection has shown largely positive assessments of algorithmic decision-making, albeit with some caveats. In an experiment conducted nearly two decades ago to measure source trust for news information, Sundar and Nass (2001) found that people trust news attributed to the computer more than human news editors. More recently, a study of over 50,000 participants across 26 countries by Thurman, Moeller, Helberger, and Trilling (2018) shows support for "algorithmic appreciation." Given different options, respondents overall had a greater preference for algorithmically selected news based on past news behavior – that is, personalized news – than news selected by human editors (although, algorithmically selected news based on peer news behaviors was less preferred than either). The study found that those with a lower degree of trust in journalism were more likely to support algorithmic news: "users are, to an extent, divorcing the operation of automated news personalization from the operation of news organizations, believing the technology has a degree of immunity from contamination by a politically compromised or untrustworthy news media" (14). Although, as the authors point out, this statement is complicated by the separation of news content providers from different platforms for news content, like Facebook. Meanwhile, Fletcher and Nielsen (2018), combining a portion of the same survey data with focus groups, found younger news users tended to show a preference for algorithmically personalized news content. However, they also identified "generalized scepticism" to news selection of any kind on social media and no "naïve confidence" in algorithms per se (8). These results point to larger issues of declining trust in news at a time when shifts in distribution technologies and advertising revenues have eroded revenues at news organizations, particularly in the largely for-profit newsrooms of the United States.

Algorithms also appear in the backend of journalism with the rise of digital news audience metrics (Zamith 2018). Metrics have an uncertain place in newsrooms, as they are both touted as a means of bringing the news more in alignment with audience demands while also resisted for fear of their interference with human decision-making. Although there are debates about which metrics are most adequate for capturing the audience's interests, the metrics themselves enter into the newsroom as objects that journalists then have to respond to – even if they ignore them (Anderson 2011; Christin 2017). Journalists are not disputing data analytics systems as reliable agents, but rather are more divided on what the numbers mean and how they fit with their working practices (Carlson 2018b).

What mechanical objectivity provides to journalism studies is a perspective for examining how algorithms are made to work as an epistemic actor within news. The usefulness of algorithms stems from a mix of factors surrounding the digitalization of news production and distribution. How they are legitimated as tools has received some attention, but they certainly deserve more focused research connecting their use to presumptions of their automaticity and separation from human judgment. In particular, mechanical objectivity can be perceived through implicit assumptions about the value of mechanized practices. Yet equally important are challenges to notions of journalism's mechanical objectivity. In their study of scientific atlases, Daston and Galison (2007) discuss the transition from mechanical objectivity to "trained judgment" where the learned expertise of the investigator augments the objective renderings of visual technologies. Journalists too have pushed back against the overreliance on algorithms as deficient compared to "shoe-leather epistemologies" (Lewis and Waters 2018), have found ways to subvert algorithmic systems (Christin 2017), or display some mixture of curiosity and skepticism (Thurman, Dörr, and Kunert 2017). The perspective of trained judgment allows for a mix of a reliance on algorithms while also finding support for human interpretation and judgment.

Conclusion

The capabilities and limitations of journalistic technologies shape the means for producing and distributing news as well as ways of imagining what news practices ought to look like. Adapting the idea of "mechanical objectivity" (Daston and Galison 2007) to journalism provides a conceptual framework for examining assumptions of epistemic utility connected to the adoption of new technologies. Doing so highlights the epistemic role of technology in journalism. The two sets of journalism practices examined, photojournalism and news algorithms, are both forms of technological intervention that transform an input – data or the image in a lens – into an output. Mechanical objectivity provides a way to conceptualize the epistemic work taking place in this transformation, and how it connects to discourses of journalistic legitimacy.

Visual modes of journalism pre-exist both the camera and viable high-speed photographic reproduction technologies through illustrations that operated according to particular epistemic conventions. News audiences took these illustrations not as interpretations but as accurate depictions (Raetzsch 2015). With the rise of the camera as a mechanical intermediary, visual modes came to support a notion of mechanical objectivity by asserting the elimination of the distance between a representation and what is represented via technological transmission (Newton 2001; Schwartz 1999). This is a powerful idea even in the face of questions surrounding the intentions of the photojournalists, the limited context of any image, and the authenticity of digital images in an era of easy manipulation.

The notion of mechanical objectivity also helps situate the symbolic power of algorithmic practices. In many domains, supporters of algorithms tout their coded procedures as neutral and a means for avoiding human biases (Gillespie 2014; Kitchin 2017). The danger in such thinking is the dehumanization of the epistemic assumptions built into the creation and implementation of algorithms. As algorithms become increasingly embedded in news production and distribution, the lure of algorithmic neutrality spills over into journalism. Future research should examine how a desire to implement technological solutions to overcome the limits of human subjectivity relates to the resiliency of objectivity as a journalistic norm. Given that debates about photography have arisen for well over a century, the comparatively recent arrival of algorithmic practices in journalism is likely to spark similar debates for years to come.

Disclosure statement

No potential conflict of interest was reported by the author.

Note

1. For a reading list of scholarship, see https://socialmediacollective.org/reading-lists/critical-algorithm-studies/.

References

Aitamurto, Tanja. 2018. "Normative Paradoxes in 360° Journalism: Contested Accuracy and Objectivity." *New Media & Society* 21 (1): 3–19.

Alexander, Michelle. 2012. *The New Jim Crow*. New York: The New Press.

Ananny, Mike. 2016. "Toward an Ethics of Algorithms: Convening, Observation, Probability, and Timeliness. *Science, Technology and Human Values* 41 (1): 93–117.

Anderson, Chris. 2008. "The End of Theory: The Data Deluge Makes the Scientific Method Obsolete." *Wired*, 23 June. https://www.wired.com/2008/06/pb-theory

Anderson, CW. 2011. "Between Creative and Quantified Audiences: Web Metrics and Changing Patterns of Newswork in Local US Newsrooms." *Journalism* 12 (5): 550–566.

Anderson, CW. 2018. *Apostles of Certainty*. New York: Oxford.

Barnhurst, Kevin G. and John Nerone. 2001. *The Form of News*. New York: Guilford.

Beer, David. 2017. "The Social Power of Algorithms." *Information, Communication & Society* 20 (1): 1–13.

Bennett, W. Lance, Regina G. Lawrence, and Steven Livingston. 2018. *When the Press Fails: Political Power and the News Media from Iraq to Katrina*. Chicago: University of Chicago Press.

Bock, Mary Angela, Kyser Lough, and Deepa Fadnis. 2017. "'Her' Photographer: The Roanoke Live-Shot Murders and Visual Communication's Place in the Newsroom." *Visual Communication Quarterly* 24 (3): 162–173.

Boudana, Sandrine. 2011. "A Definition of Journalistic Objectivity as a Performance." *Media, Culture and Society* 33 (3): 385–398.

Brennen, Bonnie. 2009. "Photojournalism: Historical Dimensions to Contemporary Debates." In *The Routledge Companion to News and Journalism*, edited by Stuart Allan, 115–125. London: Routledge.

Bucher, Taina. 2012. "Want to Be on the Top? Algorithmic Power and the Threat of Invisibility on Facebook." *New Media and Society* 14 (7): 1164–1180.

Bucher, Taina. 2017. "'Machines Don't Have Instincts': Articulating the Computational in Journalism." *New Media and Society* 19 (6), 918–933.

Bucher, Taina. 2018. *If … Then: Algorithmic Power and Politics*. Oxford: Oxford University Press.

Carlson, Matt. 2009. "The Reality of a Fake Image: News Norms, Photojournalistic Craft, and Brian Walski's Fabricated Photo." *Journalism Practice* 3 (2): 125–139.

Carlson, Matt. 2015. "The Robotic Reporter: Automated Journalism and the Redefinition of Labor, Compositional Forms, and Journalistic Authority." *Digital Journalism* 3 (3): 416–431.

Carlson, Matt. 2017. *Journalistic Authority: Legitimating News in the Digital Era*. New York: Columbia University Press.

Carlson, Matt. 2018a. "Automating Judgment? Algorithmic Judgment, News Knowledge, and Journalistic Professionalism." *New Media & Society* 20 (5): 1755–1772.

Carlson, Matt. 2018b. "Confronting Measurable Journalism." *Digital Journalism* 6 (4): 406–417.

Christin, Angèle. 2016. "From Daguerreotypes to Algorithms: Machines, Expertise, and Three Forms of Objectivity." *ACM SIGCAS Computers and Society* 46 (1): 27–32.

Christin, Angèle. 2017. "Algorithms in Practice: Comparing Web Journalism and Criminal Justice. *Big Data & Society* 4 (2). doi:10.1177/2053951717718855

Clerwall, Christer. 2014. "Enter the Robot Journalist: Users' Perceptions of Automated Content." *Journalism Practice* 8 (5): 519–531.

Craft, Stephanie. 2017. "Distinguishing Features: Reconsidering the Link Between Journalism's Professional Status and Ethics." *Journalism and Communication Monographs* 19 (4): 260–301.

Daston, Lorraine and Peter Galison. 2007. *Objectivity*. New York: Zone Books.

Deuze, Mark. 2005. "What is Journalism? Professional Identity and Ideology of Journalists Reconsidered." *Journalism* 6 (4): 442–464.

Diakopoulos, Nicholas. 2015. "Algorithmic Accountability." *Digital Journalism* 3 (3): 398–415.

Dörr, Konstantin Nicholas (2016). "Mapping the Field of Algorithmic Journalism." *Digital Journalism* 4 (6): 700–722.

Ekström, Mats. 2002. "Epistemologies of TV Journalism: A Theoretical Framework." *Journalism* 3 (3): 259–282.

Eubank, Virginia. 2018. *Automating Inequality: How High-Tech Tools Profile, Police, and Punish the Poor*. New York: St. Martin's Press.

Fletcher, Richard and Rasmus Kleis Nielsen. 2018. "Generalised scepticism: how people navigate news on social media." *Information, Communication & Society*. doi:10.1080/1369118X.2018.1450887

Foer, Franklin (2018). "The Era of Fake Video Begins." *The Atlantic*. https://www.theatlantic.com/magazine/archive/2018/05/realitys-end/556877/

Gillespie, Tarleton. 2014. "The Relevance of Algorithms." In *Media Technologies*, edited by Tarleton Gillespie, Pablo Boczkowski, and Kristen Foot, 167–194. Cambridge, MA: MIT Press.

Graefe, Andreas, Mario Haim, Bastian Haarmann, and Hans-Bernd Brosius. 2018. "Readers' Perception of Computer-Generated News: Credibility, Expertise, and Readability." *Journalism* 19 (5): 595–610.

Griffin, Michael. 1999. "The Great War Photographs: Constructing Myths of History and Journalism." In *Picturing the Past*, edited by Bonnie Brennen and Hanno Hardt, 122–157. Urbana: University of Illinois Press.

Hamilton, James T. 2004. *All the News That's Fit to Sell*. Princeton, NJ: Princeton University Press.

Hampton, Mark. 2008. "The 'Objectivity' Ideal and Its Limitations in 20th-century British Journalism." *Journalism Studies* 9 (4): 477–493.

Hanitzsch, Thomas. 2007. "Deconstructing Journalism Culture: Toward a Universal Theory. *Communication Theory* 17 (4): 367–385.

Haraway, Donna. 1988. "Situated Knowledges: The Science Question in Feminism and the Privilege of Partial Perspective." *Feminist Studies* 14 (3): 575–599.

Kitchin, Rob. 2017. "Thinking Critically about and Researching Algorithms." *Information, Communication and Society* 20 (1): 14–29.

Lee, Min Kyung. 2018. "Understanding Perception of Algorithmic Decisions: Fairness, Trust, and Emotion in Response to Algorithmic Management." *Big Data & Society* 5 (1): 1–16.

Lewis, Norman P., and Stephenson Waters. 2018. "Data Journalism and the Challenge of Shoe-Leather Epistemologies." *Digital Journalism* 6 (6): 719–736.

Lewis, Seth. C., Amy K. Sanders, and Casey Carmody. 2018. "Libel by Algorithm? Automated Journalism and the Threat of Legal Liability." *Journalism and Mass Communication Quarterly*. doi:10.1177/1077699018755983

Lewis, Seth C. and Oscar Westlund. 2015. "Actors, Actants, Audiences, and Activities in Cross-Media News Work: A Matrix and a Research Agenda." *Digital Journalism* 3 (1): 19–37.

Liu, Bingjie and Lewen Wei. 2018. "Machine Authorship In Situ." *Digital Journalism.* doi:10.1080/21670811.2018.1510740

Logg, Jennifer M., Julia A. Minson, and Don A. Moore. 2018. "Algorithm Appreciation: People Prefer Algorithmic to Human Judgment." Harvard Business School Working Paper, No. 17-086, March 2017.

Lowrey, Wilson. 2002. "Word people vs. Picture People: Normative Differences and Strategies for Control over Work among Newsroom Subgroups." *Mass Communication & Society* 5 (4): 411–432.

Mäenpää, Jenni. 2014. "Rethinking Photojournalism: The Changing Work Practices and Professionalism of Photojournalists in the Digital Age." *Nordicom Review* 35 (2): 91–104.

Maras, Steven. 2013. *Objectivity in Journalism*. Cambridge, UK: Polity.

Miller, Alex P. 2018. "Want Less-Biased Decisions? Use Algorithms. *Harvard Business Review*, 26 July. https://hbr.org/2018/07/want-less-biased-decisions-use-algorithms

Mittelstadt, Brent Daniel, Patrick Allo, Mariarosaria Taddeo, Sandra Wachter, and Luciano Floridi. 2016. "The Ethics of Algorithms: Mapping the Debate." *Big Data & Society* 3 (2): 1–21.

Napoli, Philip. M. 2014. "Automated Media: An Institutional Theory Perspective on Algorithmic Media Production and Consumption." *Communication Theory* 24 (3): 340–360.

Newton, Julianne. 2001. *The Burden of Visual Truth: The Role of Photojournalism in Mediating Reality*. Mahwah, NJ: LEA.

Nilsson, Maria. 2017. "A Faster Kind of Photojournalism?" *Nordicom Review* 38 (2): 41–55.

Noble, Safiya U. 2018. *Algorithms of Oppression: How Search Engines Reinforce Racism*. New York: NYU Press.

O'Neil, Cathy. 2016. *Weapons of Math Destruction: How Big Data Increases Inequality and Threatens Democracy*. New York: Crown Books.

Parasie, Sylvain. 2015. "Data-Driven Revelation? Epistemological Tensions in Investigative Journalism in the Age of 'Big Data'." *Digital Journalism* 3 (3): 364–380.

Pasquale, Frank. 2015. *The Black Box Society: The Secret Algorithms that Control Money and Information*. Cambridge, MA: Harvard University Press

Powers, Matthew. 2012. "'In Forms That are Familiar and Yet-to-be Invented': American Journalism and the Discourse of Technologically Specific Work." *Journal of Communication Inquiry* 36 (1): 24–43.

Raetzsch, Christoph. 2015. "'Real Pictures of Current Events:' The Photographic Legacy of Journalistic Objectivity." *Media History* 21 (3): 294–312.

Rieder, Gernot and Judith Simon. 2016. "Datatrust: Or, the Political Quest for Numerical Evidence and the Epistemologies of Big Data." *Big Data and Society* 3 (1): 1–6.

Schiller, Dan. 1981. *Objectivity and the News: The Public and the Rise of Commercial Journalism*. Philadelphia, PA: University of Pennsylvania Press.

Schudson, Michael. 2001. "The Objectivity Norm in American Journalism." *Journalism* 2 (2): 149–170.

Schwartz, Dona. 1999. "Objective Representation: Photographs as Facts." In *Picturing the Past*, edited by Bonnie Brennen and Hanno Hardt, 158–181. Urbana: University of Illinois Press.

Shapin, Steven, and Simon Schaffer. 2011. *Leviathan and the Air-Pump*. Princeton, NJ: Princeton University Press.

Sismondo, Sergio. 2004. *An Introduction to Science and Technology Studies*. Malden, MA: Blackwell.

Skitka, Linda J., Kathleen L. Mosier, and Mark Burdick. (1999). "Does automation bias decision-making?" *International Journal of Human-Computer Studies* 51 (5): 991–1006.

Solaroli, Marco. 2015. "Toward a New Visual Culture of the News: Professional Photojournalism, Digital Post-Production, and the Symbolic Struggle for Distinction." *Digital Journalism* 3 (4): 513–532.

Sundar, S. Shyam and Clifford Nass. 2001. "Conceptualizing Sources in Online News." *Journal of Communication* 51 (1): 52–72.

Sundar, S. Shyam. 2008. "The MAIN Model: A Heuristic Approach to Understanding Technology Effects on Credibility." In *Digital Media, Youth, and Credibility*, edited by Miriam J. Metzger and Andrew J. Flanagin, 73–100. Cambridge: The MIT Press.

Thurman, Neil. 2011. "Making 'The Daily Me': Technology, Economics and Habit in the Mainstream Assimilation of Personalized News." *Journalism* 12 (4): 395–415.

Thurman, Neil, Konstantin Dörr, and Jessica Kunert. 2017. "When Reporters Get Hands-on with Robo-Writing: Professionals Consider Automated Journalism's Capabilities and Consequences." *Digital Journalism* 5 (10): 1240–1259.

Thurman, Neil, Judith Moeller, Natali Helberger, and Damian Trilling. 2018. "My Friends, Editors, Algorithms, and I: Examining Audience Attitudes to News Selection." *Digital Journalism*. doi: 10.1080/21670811.2018.1493936

Tuchman, Gaye. 1972. "Objectivity as Strategic Ritual: An Examination of Newsmen's Notions of Objectivity." *American Journal of Sociology* 77 (4): 660–679.

Van Dalen, Arjen. 2012. "The Algorithms Behind the Headlines: How Machine-written News Redefines the Core Skills of Human Journalists." *Journalism Practice* 6 (5–6): 648–658.

Waddell, T. Franklin. 2018. "A Robot Wrote This?" *Digital Journalism* 6 (2): 236–255.

Waisbord, Silvio. 2013. *Reinventing Professionalism*. Cambridge: Polity.

Ward, Stephen J. A. 2004. *The Invention of Journalism Ethics: The Path to Objectivity and Beyond*. Montreal: McGill-Queen's Press.

Weber, Matthew S., and Allie Kosterich. 2018. "Coding the News: The Role of Computer Code in Filtering and Distributing News." *Digital Journalism* 6 (3): 310–329.

Wölker, Anja, and Thomas E. Powell. 2018. "Algorithms in the Newsroom? News Readers' Perceived Credibility and Selection of Automated Journalism." *Journalism*. doi:10.1177/1464884918757072

Zamith, Rodrigo. 2018. "Quantified Audiences in News Production: A Synthesis and Research Agenda." *Digital Journalism* 6 (4): 418–435.

Zamith, Rodrigo. 2019. "Algorithms and Journalism." In *Oxford Encyclopedia of Journalism Studies*, edited by Henrik Örnebring. Oxford, UK: Oxford University Press, forthcoming.

Zelizer, Barbie. 1993. "Journalists as Interpretive Communities." *Critical Studies in Media Communication* 10 (3): 219–237.

Zelizer, Barbie. 1995. "Journalism's 'Last' Stand: Wirephoto and the Discourse of Resistance." *Journal of Communication* 45 (2): 78–92.

Zelizer, Barbie. 2005. "Journalism through the Camera's Eye." In *Journalism: Critical Issues*, edited by Stuart Allan, 167–176. New York: Open University Press.

Structured Journalism and the Semantic Units of News

David Caswell

ABSTRACT
The growing influence of computation on news has intensified the need for an analytical framework that describes the common foundations of different computational approaches to journalism. This article proposes such a framework, founded on the concept of units of journalistic knowledge smaller than the article, expressed partially or completely as structured data and positioned along a continuum of news artifacts. The emerging practice of structured journalism and its use of "atomized" news is described and is presented as an embodiment of the framework. Different approaches to the use of computation within journalism are then positioned as specific instances of that practice. This conception, analogous to "semantic unit" paradigms currently emerging in other information-centric domains, is then used to reinterpret several of journalism's urgent problems. A research agenda for developing computational journalism as an editorial activity within an increasingly data-centric communication environment is proposed, and several implications of the conception are discussed.

Introduction

The influence of computation on journalism is not immediately apparent to consumers or observers of news. In 2019, news is still overwhelmingly gathered by human reporters, who record it in writing for publication as text articles or as scripted videos. Although these news artifacts are now conveniently distributed over digital networks, they generally look much the same as articles printed with ink on the pages of newspapers, or video segments broadcast as analog signals from transmission towers. A cursory analysis of the present digital news ecosystem might therefore conclude that, while the distribution of news has clearly been revolutionized by computation, the essential form of journalism and its artifacts have not.

Computational journalism is important beyond its present influence, however, because it may portend a second digital revolution for journalism—this time changing the nature of news artifacts rather than merely the means of their distribution (Anderson 2017b). Data journalism, automated journalism, sensor journalism, news bots, and other variants of computational journalism represent a change in the conception of the foundations of news, because they each maintain their essential journalistic knowledge as data rather than solely as writing or speech—as "records" rather than as "reports" (Anderson 2015, 2018). This re-conception is not abstract or speculative. Software and workflows that interpret journalism computationally (i.e., as carefully structured data, wholly accessible to computation) have been in daily operation in major newsrooms for years, albeit still in a very limited capacity (Dörr 2016; Graefe 2016). Furthermore, there is widespread expectation that the use of such methods will expand in scale and scope, driven by economic necessity, by technical advances, by new consumer expectations and by the increasing authority of data as an alternative to individual or collective human judgment (Hansen et al. 2017; Marconi 2017; Harari 2016). Journalism is likely to become more computational.

   Despite the increasing possibility of a significant role in journalism, comprehensive descriptions of what Anderson has called "the shaggy, emerging beast" of computational journalism have remained elusive (Anderson 2013). Computational approaches to news have largely developed *ad hoc*, as opportunistic adoption of technical innovations originating in other fields, and the academic study of computational journalism has similarly developed *ad hoc*, often as case-by-case responses to specific technologies applied to journalism. This emergent origin has enabled early deployment of computational methods in journalism and useful analysis of those methods by scholars, but it has left the status of computational journalism as a discrete and coherent field somewhat ambiguous. Many practitioners and some scholars define the field as nothing more than the use of computing tools or algorithms to facilitate traditional journalism (Hamilton 2016; Diakopoulos 2016), while others have sought to understand the field as a naturalistic phenomena, employing observational methods and emphasizing description, definitions and taxonometric categorization (Coddington 2014; Anderson 2013; Lewis 2015; Dörr 2016). The journalism and communications literature lacks comprehensive descriptions of computational journalism as a digitally native system of knowledge, and there have been few attempts to develop comprehensive explanatory theories from first principles (Ausserhofer et al. 2017).

   The lack of an integrated framework for understanding computational journalism has left the field ill-equipped to proactively influence the adaption of journalism to a technologically mediated future. Journalism is currently in crisis on multiple fronts, largely as a result of externally imposed technological disruption (Anderson et al. 2012; Posetti 2018). The news industry suffers the economic consequences of democratized news distribution, while news consumers experience the declining relevance of news and the collapse of shared narratives amid overwhelming volumes of text and video artifacts (Wu 2017; Peters and Broersma 2016; Swift 2016). The technological drivers of these changes are accelerating, requiring journalism to find new ways to serve societies in which data-driven and artificially intelligent communications systems may be increasingly common (Anderson et al. 2012; Roca-Sales 2017). Conceptions of computational journalism rooted solely in practice, observation, description, and categorization are, essentially, historical perspectives that do not empower journalists or news organizations to participate fully in ongoing technological change. Proactive participation requires a predictive perspective—an interpretation of computational journalism that remains consistent and useful regardless of changing technological fashions.

This article proposes a starting point for such an interpretation—an analytical framework for computational journalism founded on the concept of fundamental units of journalistic knowledge. After first providing a specific definition of computational journalism I develop the theoretical basis of a complete framework by applying principles from knowledge engineering and computational semantics (Brachman and Levesque 2004) to journalistic knowledge. I then examine an emerging form of computational journalism, known as "structured journalism", that incorporates the notion of "units", or "atoms", of journalistic knowledge expressed as data (Jones and Jones 2018). I describe specific examples of structured journalism in terms of their semantic units, and use those examples to construct a generalized description. Assuming my definition, I then argue that this generalized description is synonymous with an analytical framework that encompasses *all* forms of computational journalism—an equivalence between "structured" and "computational" that is common in computer science and is now beginning to appear in journalism scholarship (see Anderson 2018a, 138). After using this structured perspective of computational journalism to re-interpret several of journalism's intractable problems, I then propose a research agenda for computational journalism that anticipates and accommodates unpredictable technological change. I conclude the article by reviewing some long-term implications of a structured conception of news.

Journalistic Knowledge and Its Carriers

Journalism is not generally conceived of as a formal body of knowledge, but as a language-centered craft characterized by nuance, style and an inextricable dependence on individual human authorship—a conception that appears impervious to formal description. Computer science is sometimes also conceived of as a craft, but unlike journalism both the theory and the practice of computation are built upon precisely described elementary components and their formal relationships to each other. From the perspective of computation the defining characteristic of journalism is its dependence on natural language, sometimes referred to by programmers as "unstructured data". From the perspective of journalism the defining characteristic of computation is its requirement of extreme precision (Meyer 2002; Anderson 2016). Neither the language of journalism nor the precision of computation are, however, ends in themselves. They are both merely mechanisms for referencing, reasoning with and communicating semantic information, variously referred to as entities, concepts, topics, stories, events, facts or even data. Data and language are carriers of semantic information.

In the context of journalism it is useful to interpret this underlying semantic information as "journalistic knowledge", which I define as *externally represented knowledge that is under human editorial control in the service of journalistic values*. In this definition the distinction between traditional language-centered journalism and the various computational interpretations of journalism is merely in the means by which journalistic knowledge is represented externally. This distinction leads to a clear definition of computational journalism as *a practice in which journalistic knowledge is represented computationally, as structured data, during reporting, analysis, distribution or consumption*. This is in contrast to traditional journalism, in which journalistic knowledge is reported, analyzed, distributed, and consumed as natural language text or speech, whether in analog or digital media. In this view, therefore, computational journalism is fundamentally an interpretation of the nature of journalistic knowledge and its representation.

The need for this relatively constrained definition of computational journalism, and for its constituent definition of journalistic knowledge, arises from an effort to base my analysis as much as possible on clearly specified first principles rather than solely on prior work in the field (Lewis 2019; Caswell and Anderson 2019). Note that these definitions may not be required for, or even be relevant to, other interpretations of journalism, such as literary interpretations or interpretations rooted in social or cultural criticism. Furthermore, these definitions are more compatible with journalism as "news" or even "hard news", rather than with journalism as literary style, opinion or taste, and are also more focused on the products of journalism rather than on its processes or workflows. Nonetheless they provide useful starting points for a broadly applicable interpretation of computational journalism.

This data-centric definition of computational journalism will be assumed throughout this article and offers an alternative to definitions founded on algorithms (Hamilton 2016), tool use (Diakopoulos 2016) or artificial intelligence. Algorithms have no obvious analog in the essentially artisanal practice of language-centered journalism, which makes them an obvious feature with which to distinguish computational journalism. This same characteristic, however, may also present a barrier to the transfer of concepts and workflows from language-centered journalism into computational journalism. Alternative definitions of computational journalism as the application of computing tools to journalism are, essentially, tautological, and are therefore useful primarily for categorization and description (Cohen et al. 2011). Expectations, often by technologists, that a comprehensive theory of computational journalism will somehow emerge from statistical machine learning, such as natural language processing using deep learning techniques, may not fully consider the central role of deterministic explanation in journalism, and may not be compatible with definitions of journalism centered on human editorial control. These perspectives are not incorrect, but they have not yet demonstrated utility in addressing the fundamental relationships between journalism, natural language, and data. They may therefore be unable to explain computational journalism in a way that provides meaningful influence over its development, use and criticism.

Interpreting knowledge about the world as structured data is an old idea, dating to Aristotle (Halliwell 1998), and was a particular ambition for prominent figures of the enlightenment (Descartes 1629). More recently structured knowledge has fallen out of favor, due to the practical challenges in defining and maintaining useful ontologies and to the favoring of computing paradigms centered on probability and correlation (particularly machine learning), rather than on structure and deterministic processes (Hiltzik 2002). Structured knowledge has, however, enjoyed a quiet resurgence in the form of knowledge graphs—collections of interconnected entities and concepts constructed by Google, Facebook, Microsoft, and others (Paulheim 2017). These immense repositories of structured knowledge are now the foundational infrastructure behind online search, and the scale and scope of their influence is expanding, enabled by new methods for constructing ontologies. Knowledge engineering is a growing field and its application to journalistic knowledge is already in its infancy, as evidenced by a growing number of academic workshops focused on analytical and engineering interpretations of news (see list at http://eventstory.news).

Defining journalistic knowledge as structured data appears at first to be a quixotic ambition. In addition to its tradition as a language-centered craft, journalism also has at least three characteristics that render it exceptionally impervious to structure. First, journalism is inherently editorial. It is not an information filter, or an act of information retrieval, but an explicit interpretation of reality defined by the editorial choices of humans. Second, the central focus of journalism is events, not entities. Furthermore, journalism is concerned not merely with events in isolation, but with the contextualization of events in relation to each other and also in relation to entities (Harcup and O'Neill 2001). The representation of events and their contextualization remains an advanced research problem for knowledge engineering. Third, the consumers of journalism are human beings whose primary mechanism for interacting with semantic information is natural language, and for whom data is an alien form of communication (Anderson 2017a, 2017b). Furthermore, the flexibility and semantic granularity available from natural language are vastly greater than that of any data schema presently conceivable. These barriers ensure that data will not displace language as the primary means of representing and consuming journalistic knowledge.

But data need not fully displace language as a carrier of journalistic knowledge in order to have a profound impact on how that knowledge is produced, distributed, analyzed and consumed. Rich annotation (or "tagging") with data can clearly enhance the utility of text artifacts. This has been demonstrated by personalized news distribution using named entity recognition, topic modeling, and similar tools, although its potential in developing novel news artifacts and products remains mostly unexplored. Alternatively, even coarse representations of journalistic knowledge as fully structured data can clearly enable novel news artifacts. This has been demonstrated in limited form by numerous interactive data journalism products developed for stand-alone projects, although its potential for more routine and systematic use remains mostly unexplored. Framing the relationship between language and data as mutually exclusive, or even adversarial, is therefore unjustified by experience. Data can work symbiotically with text, enabling hybrid new artifacts that combine detail and precision with nuance and complexity (Rule et al. 2018). If journalism becomes increasingly computational, journalists will likely be required to re-conceive of at least some journalistic knowledge as structured data. This, in turn, will require recognizing the limits of data with respect to language and, perhaps more importantly, the limits of language with respect to data.

Units of Journalistic Knowledge

Any system for representing semantic knowledge, whether based on natural language or on data, must be constructed from a canonical set of symbols whose meanings are

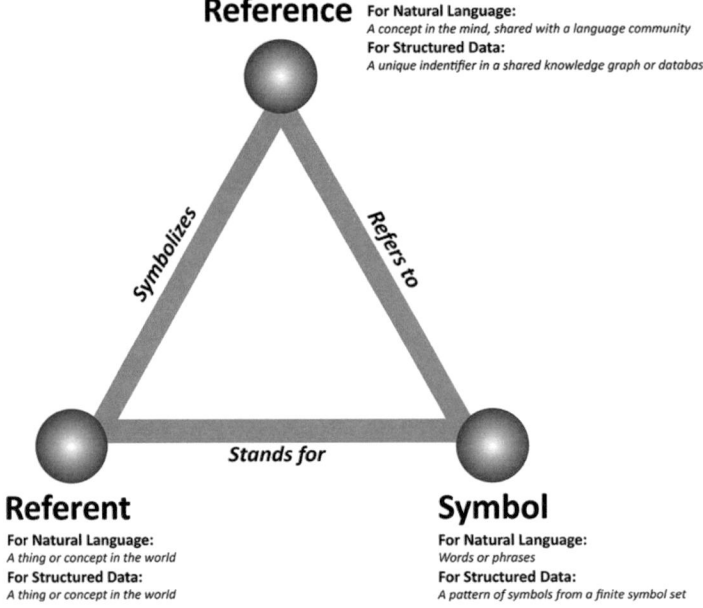

Figure 1. The Ogden & Richards semantic triangle, labeled for language and data.

shared among users of that system—a concept known as "semantic grounding" or "symbol grounding" (Liu and Yu 2004). This three-way relationship between symbols, shared semantic references, and things or concepts is illustrated by the famous Ogden and Richards "semantic" or "semiotic" triangle (Ogden and Richards 1927), shown in Figure 1 as modified to include interpretations for both language and data.

This foundational perspective can be applied to any semantic system, including computational systems that seek to represent journalistic knowledge as data. There are two fundamental requirements of such systems: A set of symbols with which to represent journalistic knowledge; and a system of shared references that can semantically "ground" those symbols to real-world things and concepts. A foundational analysis of any system of computational journalism can therefore begin with the identification of these symbols and references within that system.

Consider, for example, a system that annotates ("tags") text articles with metadata identifying specific people, places, and things mentioned in that text—perhaps extracted automatically using named entity recognition or classification software. In such a system, the semantic symbols are the list of named entities or classes available for recognition, and semantic grounding of those named entities is provided by unique references in an internal or external knowledge base. Although such metadata is not used to communicate journalistic knowledge directly—the text articles do that—it nonetheless has a substantial journalistic impact because it determines the semantic granularity with which text articles can be routed within the distribution system. The algorithm of a hypothetical news distribution platform cannot explicitly recommend articles using the category "populism", for example, if "populism" is not available as a symbol or as a reference within its semantic systems.

Consider a second example, in which a data journalist obtains a SQL database from a city government about hiring practices in the city's fire department, then analyses that data and writes a text article using that analysis. In this example, the journalistic knowledge upon which the analysis and article are based originates from a "found database" that has been designed and constructed using a particular schema. That schema is an arrangement of tables, fields, keys, and allowable categories that determine what data can be sensibly stored within that database. Although database schemas are not usually interpreted in semantic terms, they implicitly establish a set of allowable and bounded categories, text records and numbers (symbols) and a set of defined fields and keys by which those symbols can be grounded within the database (references). As in the previous example, these symbols and their references are not used to communicate journalistic knowledge directly—the resulting text article does that—but they nonetheless have a substantial journalistic impact because they determine what is or is not accessible to the analysis that produces the article. The resulting article cannot include an analysis of hiring practices by, for example, country of origin, if country of origin is not an allowable category or field in the database.

These examples describe practical applications of computation to journalism that are now common and unremarkable. The usefulness of describing them in terms of their semantic basis becomes apparent, however, if one considers them as point examples on a continuum of computational journalistic artifacts.

The labeling of text with metadata in order to make some of its semantic meaning accessible to computation can be applied, for example, to units of text smaller than the article—to paragraphs, or even to sentences. Such labeling is awkward if applied to paragraphs or sentences within an existing text article, but much less awkward if applied to paragraphs or sentences intentionally written and annotated for specific purposes. These sub-article text artifacts, known as "textemes" and "micro-textemes", are the subject matter of the field of text linguistics (de Beugrande 1997) and have practical applications outside of journalism, including in translation, technical documentation, and typesetting (Haralambous and Bella 2005). Textemes are also used widely within digital journalism, in the form of headlines, ledes, summaries, image captions, and the like. A system of journalism that extends the use of textemes beyond these traditional cases would, in effect, be extending the scope of journalistic knowledge accessible to computation by changing the units of journalistic knowledge from the article to the texteme. Computational access to journalistic knowledge within the texteme would still be limited to that which could be manually or automatically annotated, but the contextual and editorial functions of their texts would now also be accessible. Extending this text deconstruction approach to its ultimate conclusion results in journalistic artifacts that contain no text, but which remain semantically coherent. Such post-text artifacts, which I will call "structured statements", are constructed solely from data. The journalistic knowledge they contain is, inevitably, much sparser than that available from text, however it is also entirely accessible to computation. This continuum, from annotated article, to annotated texteme, to structured statement is useful for organizing artifacts that carry computationally accessible journalistic knowledge. It orders the units of computational journalism Figure 2.

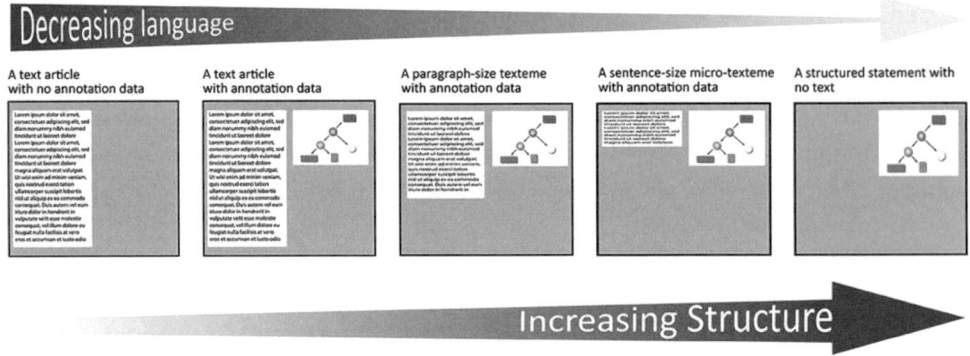

Figure 2. Artifacts of computational journalism as an ordered continuum.

The emerging practice of data journalism is tightly constrained by the design schema of the databases it employs, whether "found databases" or databases created "*de novo*" by data journalists. These databases are essentially repositories of fully structured journalistic knowledge, and their individual records are, essentially, structured statements. If individual records in these databases are labeled with short text descriptions (e.g., summaries of police shootings—see Bedi and Humburg 2017), then those text labels are, essentially, annotated textemes. A text description of the full database, or a data journalism article based on a computational analysis of the database, can loosely be considered as an annotated article (e.g., an analysis of government unemployment data—see Wolfe 2018). This rough interpretation of journalistic databases—from fully structured statement to annotated texteme to annotated article—recalls the continuum described above. As with the earlier examples of semantic grounding of computable journalistic knowledge, this continuum of computational artifacts can be developed either from language towards data, or from data towards language.

Applying this view of computational journalism in practice requires overcoming several challenges related to knowledge infrastructure. Consumers of journalistic knowledge, whether in data or language, must have access to the semantic symbols and references with which that knowledge has been encoded in order to interpret it. Access by computers to journalistic knowledge encoded as data therefore requires a shared semantic grounding system that is computational accessible. Such a system must be capable of semantically expressing knowledge of a kind and granularity that is broadly useful, and it must also be broadly adopted in order to function as a computational "*lingua franca*". The recent appearance of large entity knowledge graphs such as WikiData, GeoNames, Satori, and others has at least partially addressed this need for semantic grounding (Paulheim 2017). Application of this knowledge infrastructure to journalism is being explored in academic work (see Shiralkar et al. 2017), and in experimentation by practitioners (e.g., the WikiData track at the European Centre for Press and Media Freedoms 2017 "Wikipedia Edit-a-thon").

Existing knowledge infrastructure is, however, limited in a particular way of special importance to computational journalism. These resources focus almost entirely on "noun knowledge"—named entities, concepts, locations, topics, categories, measurements and other static knowledge. Journalism, however, consists primarily of "verb knowledge", in the form of news events that describe the actions and interactions of entities, and of news stories that contextualize those events (Caswell and Dörr 2017). Computationally accessible references that can describe news events are enabled by the concept of "frame semantics" (Fillmore 1976), which conceives of comprehensive units of activity ("frames") in which specific entities play specific "semantic roles". The use of semantic frames as grounding references for news events, although still largely experimental, is facilitated by the existence of comprehensive catalogs of frames, particularly FrameNet (Baker 2008). These structured events, and their contextualization within larger structures, are explored and studied by computational semanticists and by the field of computational narrative (Zarri 2009; Mani 2013). All of the essential elements of journalistic knowledge can therefore be captured as computational representations, albeit at semantic granularities much sparser than possible using natural language.

Structured Journalism

Representing journalistic knowledge as semantically grounded structured data is more than an abstract or speculative conception. Over the past decade a particular form of computational journalism has emerged that conceives of journalistic knowledge entirely as structured "atoms" of news, smaller than text articles and natively computational. Known as "structured journalism", this approach is usually defined as the reporting of journalism directly into structured data (Gourarie 2015; Jones and Jones 2018). Examples of structured journalism have been demonstrated in various experimental and production news products, using units of journalistic knowledge that range from annotated articles and textemes to fully structured statements describing news events.

The most prominent examples of structured journalism products to date have been based on textemes manually annotated with editorial knowledge—typically categories or contextual links. These products usually originate with significant involvement from journalists, and their creation has usually been driven by specific and pragmatic journalistic goals. PolitiFact, which structures "fact checks" of statements by politicians, is the earliest and most successful example (Adair 2017; Anderson 2018). PolitiFact captures journalist knowledge as a set of named entities (people), editorial categories ("truth-o-meter" labels communicating degrees of truthfulness of statements) and manually annotated textemes (for example, "rulings" succinctly describing a fact check assessment), thereby enabling assembly of histories for politicians and navigation of political statements by their factuality. Another early example of structured journalism is D.C. Homicide Watch, which structured journalistic knowledge about homicides (Amico and Amico 2011). Like PolitiFact, Homicide Watch captured journalistic knowledge manually, as sets of named entities, editorial categories, and annotated textemes, enabling features such as categorization, maps and access to source documents. These early projects focused on narrow subject matter, but examples of generalized texteme-based structured journalism products quickly followed. Most prominent among these was Circa, a venture-financed commercial start-up which structured long-running news stories into a series of interconnected "points"—small annotated textemes, captioned images, and quotes each contributing a specific item of journalistic knowledge communicated via computationally-assembled and personalized story experience (Coddington 2015; Cohn 2014). Although Circa ceased operations in 2015, new products based on similar concepts appear periodically, including the Timeline App, the New York Times' "Editor" project, the BBC's "Atomized News" project (Jones and Jones 2018), and "Smarticles", a structured news product developed by the Guardian's mobile innovation lab (Sidahmed 2017). Despite the relatively simple and familiar nature of their structured units, each of these products delivered news consumption experiences that would not be possible without the computation enabled by their structure.

Examples of structured journalism based on fully structured statements are less common. These have been primarily experimental projects and usually originate from computer scientists, often in academic settings and often without significant involvement from journalists. Repositories of structured statements in these systems are assembled both automatically and manually (Caswell 2016). A prominent example of an automated system is the NewsReader project, a major multi-university research effort that assembled news storylines from structured events extracted automatically from corpora of text articles about financial and industrial topics (Rospocher et al. 2016). Similar systems are used commercially for business and government intelligence applications (Kwak 2016), and basic research into the underlying technologies is expanding on multiple fronts.

At least one experimental structured journalism project simultaneously demonstrates independence from natural language and full editorial control by journalists. Structured Stories, developed by the author, is a prototyped knowledge representation platform designed to enable journalists to manually capture general news events as structured data and assemble those events into networked narrative structures (Caswell 2015; Anderson 2016). These narrative structures can then be explored by news consumers using various computable news products, including interactive tools, flow charts, and automatically written articles (Caswell and Dörr 2017). The prototype was used to conduct a series of experiments in which journalism students and working journalists captured news from various domains as structured events within editorial workflows (Caswell et al. 2015). These experiments, while rudimentary and deeply unfamiliar to journalists, suggest that an editorially controlled journalism workflow based on fully structured journalistic knowledge is feasible (Russell et al. 2016). By empirically demonstrating the operation of such a workflow these experiments have sought to clarify explicit questions about the relationship between journalistic knowledge, language, and data, and about the role of abstraction and patterns in journalism (see Anderson 2016 and chapter 7 of Anderson 2018).

Structured journalism provides numerous tangible examples of entirely new journalistic artifacts that can, in some circumstances, supplement or replace text articles as units of news. Editorial variants of structured journalism, such as Polifact and Circa, have demonstrated that some journalists can readily work with annotated textemes as news artifacts, and that some consumers will consume them. Technical variants, such as NewsReader, have demonstrated that it is feasible to assemble vast quantities of fully structured journalistic knowledge computationally. Structured Stories, a hybrid variant, has demonstrated that it is possible for some journalists to work directly with structured statements, reporting and contextualizing news events and stories as data. Many of these experiments have not been successful or sustainable. Collectively, however, they have provided a body of practical experience in developing, creating and publishing new journalistic artifacts across the entire continuum of computational journalism. Structured journalism represents a persistent line of editorial and technical experimentation that, despite its failures, has not yet uncovered any clear argument against its core assertion—that journalistic knowledge can be represented as data and used to create an entirely new class of useful news products beyond what is possible from journalistic knowledge represented solely as language.

Computational Journalism as Structured Journalism

Structured journalism can be considered as more than just another emerging practice in the zoology of computational journalism. If the earlier data-centric definition of computational journalism is assumed, then the semantic unit paradigm provided by structured journalism can provide a framework for describing and orienting *all* forms of computational journalism. This framework can best be appreciated if one considers structured journalism as an end-to-end system, extending from reporting to consumption (see Figure 3). This system includes not merely the data models and databases with which journalistic knowledge is captured, but also the various sources of, and uses of, that structured data. In such a system any particular form of computational journalism can be described as a combination of four factors: a source of structured

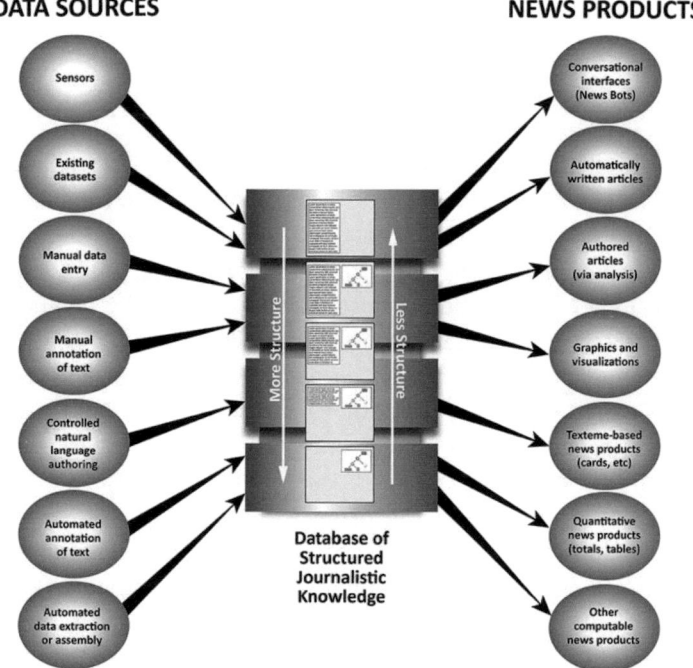

Figure 3. Computational journalism as variants of sources and uses of structured journalism.

journalistic knowledge; a semantically grounded data model; a set of journalistic arti-facts defined by that data model, and a specific manner in which that structured jour-nalistic knowledge is provided to news consumers. This interpretation can be applied across the complete continuum of computational journalism artifacts described earlier.

Consider data journalism (Anderson 2017a). The source of journalistic knowledge used in data journalism is a found or *de novo* data set, defined by a schema—its seman-tically grounded data model. This dataset may be subject to editing or refinement by the data journalist, and then put to various uses, such as analysis for the manual writing of text articles, or providing charts or interactive elements directly to news consumers.

Consider automated journalism (Caswell and Dörr 2017). The source of journalistic knowledge used by automated journalism is also a structured dataset, such as that produced by sports statisticians or financial data aggregation firms. This data, defined by a data model, is then applied to templates within an automated journalism system to generate text articles.

Consider sensor journalism (Waite 2013). The sources of journalistic knowledge are records collected from electronic sensors and stored in a dataset, defined by a data model. This dataset can then be used to provide various news products similar to those produced by data journalism or automated journalism.

Consider news bots—a nascent form of computational journalism delivered via chat or voice devices and providing conversational interactions with news in ways that resemble artificial intelligence. The source of journalistic knowledge for news bots is, essentially, annotated textemes produced by journalists and stored in a database. The annotation of these textemes, defined by a semantically grounded data model, facili-tates their selection and conversational recitation to news consumers using algorithms.

Consider automated story detection or automated fact checking, each of which uses structured data (perhaps as annotation of training data) to represent features identifying a potentially newsworthy story or a fact claim, and each of which is there-fore constrained by that data.

All examples of structured journalism can, by definition, also be described using this interpretation. The current digital news ecosystem, based on the algorithmic distri-bution of text articles annotated with metadata can also be described using this inter-pretation. The heart of all of these computational journalism variants is their semantically grounded data models, whose semantic units fully determine what jour-nalistic knowledge can, and cannot, be represented within that system.

This interpretation of computational journalism is analogous to similar "semantic unit" paradigms currently emerging in other information-intensive domains, including scientific publishing, government intelligence, enterprise knowledge management, technical writing, finance, law and others. Like journalism, these domains are experi-encing a digitally-driven exponential increase in the quantity of text and video docu-ments available within the domain, accompanied by a corresponding reduction in the utility and value of each individual document. Like news consumers, the consumers of the information products of these domains are overwhelmed by the volume of docu-ments, and are increasingly unable to contextualize and navigate the information con-tained within them. Like the experiments in structured journalism described earlier, each of these domains has pursued alternatives to the text document as the sole carrier of information, particularly alternatives founded on new semantics units that can convey and contextualize information about the domain in a computationally accessible form (Kuhn and Dumontier 2017).

In scientific publishing, for example, the Nanopublication movement seeks to deconstruct biomedical and other research down to the "smallest unit of publishable information", which can then be explored in aggregate with computational tools (Groth et al. 2010). In the government intelligence domain, the U.S. research agency DARPA is currently funding systems that map "knowledge elements" derived from news media sources into a common semantic representation (Onyshkevych 2017), as part of a broader structured intelligence paradigm known as "Activity-Based Intelligence" (Biltgen and Ryan 2016). In the technical writing domain, an entirely new form of content production founded on textemes has emerged, known as "structured authoring" and supported by a standardized data model for structuring the purpose of textemes (Eberlein et al. 2010). Similar approaches have emerged in financial technology start-ups (event-centric knowledge graphs, see Rospocher et al. 2016), in legal research departments (computable law, see Casanovas et al. 2008), in enterprise knowledge management and in other domains.

These parallel initiatives emphasize an important truth about computational journalism—that its emergence is driven by technological and societal factors that extend beyond journalism, and that it has originated from a paradigm of considerable cultural breadth and acceptance. This paradigm, sometimes called "computational thinking", prioritizes fundamental concepts over particular examples, and emphasizes abstractions or patterns over individual artifacts (Wing 2006). It is deeply compatible with a scientific and engineering worldview, centered on evidence, logic and first principles, and has increasingly influenced descriptions of human interaction with reality since the enlightenment (Gottlieb 2017). The appearance of computational journalism, and especially of a deconstructive interpretation of computational journalism based on semantic units, may therefore be seen as a consequence of the application of computational thinking to journalism (Anderson 2016). Computational thinking applied to the scholarship of journalism remains less common (Witschge et al. 2018).

The Utility of Computable News

Re-interpreting computational journalism as journalistic knowledge in the form of structured data provides an opportunity to also re-interpret the challenges that have accompanied journalism's digital transition. Previous experiences of media transitions suggest that the ongoing replacement of print by the internet as the primary medium for journalism should require an accompanying replacement or modification of the artifacts communicated via that medium (McLuhan 1964). The persistence of journalism's primary artifact of the pre-digital era—the text article—onto the internet should therefore be expected to create tensions between artifact and medium. The challenges currently facing journalism may therefore be interpreted as manifestations of a mismatch between the text article as a unit of journalism and the medium in which those units are now distributed—the ubiquitous hyperlinked internet.

Journalism's economic disruption, for example, is usually seen as a consequence of the unraveling of the media bundles by which news was distributed in the pre-digital media environment. But this disruption can also be seen as a failure by publishers to find new ways to bundle their information products amid large quantities of near-commodity text articles. In this environment text articles can only be differentiated by brand. In contrast, structured news artifacts can be linked together and accumulated in competitively defensible repositories that manifest network effects. Such networked news structures may be more resistant to commodification, less subject to wasteful duplication between producers, and more suited to re-bundling than text articles.

Journalism also faces a crises of trust and even of relevance (Peters and Broersma 2016). Faced with vast quantities of competing text articles, news consumers may place less value on the certification of news by publishers (Swift 2016). More generally, society is experiencing a reduction in the authority vested in individual human judgment, and an increase in the authority vested in data (Harari 2016). This loss of trust and authority may require publishers to certify their journalistic work in new ways, centered on evidence and demonstration rather than merely on authorship and branding. Such certification may be better facilitated by journalism available as linked units of structured data—for example as systematic records traceable to sources, documents, quotes or other evidence—than it is with journalism available only as text.

The economic and trust challenges faced by publishers are accompanied by a sense-making challenge facing news consumers. This is often referred to as "information overload" (Holton and Chyi 2012), and may be related to the breakdown of shared narratives and the susceptibility of news consumers to commercial or political manipulation (Wu 2017). As news is increasingly sourced from distribution platforms and as the branding power of news organizations diminishes (Kalogeropoulos and Newman 2017), digital news consumers are now expected to assemble coherent mental constructions of social reality from enormous quantities of stand-alone text articles, many of which carry duplicate journalistic knowledge. Each of these articles may be internally coherent, but assembling coherence *between* articles is now the sole responsibility of the consumer. Algorithms and search tools offer only crude grouping of text articles by topic cluster or named entity and are therefore not much help, and hyperlinking has been used more as a mechanism to encourage recirculation within news sites rather than a means of facilitating journalistic context (Larsson 2013). More efficient news consumption requires removing duplication and enabling navigation of journalistic structures larger than those containable within single text articles—functions served by distribution bundles in the pre-digital era. Sense-making products that might facilitate such efficiency are likely to require at least some structuring of journalistic knowledge, perhaps enabling the computational assembly of context-based or personalized experiences of news.

Computational journalism, interpreted as structured journalism, can therefore provide new strategies for addressing journalism's multiple crises. For these strategies to be feasible beyond niche uses, however, news consumers must be receptive to news in computable forms. This requires either that computable news products interact with consumers using natural language, or that consumers interact with news as structured artifacts.

Existing computational journalism products suggest that a primary modality by which news consumers interact with computational journalism is, in fact, natural language. The output of automated journalism, for example, is a text article or scripted video, even though the underlying units of knowledge are data, not text or speech. The interaction between news consumer and news bots is usually natural language, in text or speech, even though those interactions may be constructed from annotated textemes. Data journalism is almost entirely communicated via text articles, or by diagrams supplemented by text. The utility or feasibility of computational journalism products therefore do not necessarily depend on consumer adoption of entirely new data-centric modalities.

Nonetheless, news consumers are also exhibiting new behavior that is amenable to communicating news as structured artifacts, especially on mobile devices. The news consumption pattern known as "snacking" or "grazing", characterized by shorter but more frequent consumption sessions, is particularly suited to delivery of news as annotated textemes (Molyneux 2018). Publishers respond to this behavior by customizing and repurposing news as push alerts, updates, short posts and social media posts, all textemes suitable for richer annotation with structured data. Study of these new journalistic forms, and others such as listicles and bullet points, has tended to focus on description of their use by journalists rather than on their structure, consumption characteristics or potential as a new form (Rom and Reich 2017), however their extensive adoption suggests a willingness among at least some news consumers to engage with smaller units of journalism. More broadly, computable news artifacts are more suited to growing consumer expectations of personalized consumption and consumer choice than are one-size-fits-all text articles (Fenech and Perkins 2015).

A deeper understanding of the differences between consumer responses to news presented as traditional text articles and news presented as structured units of journalism will likely requires comparative surveys in which semantically identical news is presented in both forms. Such comparative surveys could provide not only an assessment of consumer reactions to each form, but also assessments of any differences in trust, knowledge retention and contextualization associated with each form. Several studies of this kind have already been applied to automated journalism, with useful results (e.g., Graefe et al. 2018).

A Research Agenda for Computational Journalism

The data-centric definition and conception of computational journalism described in this article implies a series of questions about the interface between journalism and data—questions that may be different from those posed by more descriptive or observational perspectives. These questions may also offer an agenda for research that is broad or even foundational, rather than specific to any particular variant of computational journalism, and that may therefore be useful in exploring entirely new opportunities for journalism within a computational media ecosystem. Some examples of such questions are

What are the recurring patterns in news events and storylines, and what abstractions can represent those patterns? Much of everyday journalism repeats patterns that are deeply familiar to experienced beat reporters but which remain essentially unexplored by scholars, while computational categorization of news has been limited to subjects derived from traditional newspaper sections (such as IPTC Codes—see Troncy 2008) or relatively coarse topic modeling. Systematic identification and categorization of patterns within news may yield journalistic grammars that could semantically ground computable news. Such grammars could extend the reach of data journalism beyond one-off investigative projects into more routine news, and could enable automated journalism techniques to improve the productivity of newsrooms.

What are the existing editorial micro-structures of news? The deconstruction of article-scale editorial structures, such as the inverted pyramid, is necessary for working with journalistic knowledge in smaller units of language. News is filled with fine-grained editorial structures (description, recitation of events, background, anecdote, direct and indirect quotation, etc.) that are essential components of the human craft of journalism but which remain relatively poorly documented, presenting a barrier to their computational representation.

What is journalistic context and how can it be precisely described? It is clear that articles provide significant context internally and also that journalistic structures larger than the article exist—storylines that develop over time as events unfold. A more specific understanding of the context-forming components of news—for example editorial micro-structures such as transitional phrases or ordering—may reveal patterns in context formation that can enable new opportunities for computer-aided sense-making. Similarly, a more rigorous understanding of the mechanisms that signal continuity between successive articles in a developing storyline—for example background summarization, standardization of terms and phrases, explicit reference, etc.—might aid in developing approaches for the computational assembly of context from structured journalistic artifacts.

What new forms of journalistic work are associated with computable news? Some earlier conceptions of computationally based journalistic work focused predominantly on "coding" (Doherty 2012; Weber and Kosterich 2018). Viewing computational journalism in terms of its data structures, however, suggests editorial workflows focused more on abstraction, information modeling and story architectures than hands-on tool-building (Coddington 2015; Caswell et al. 2015). This emerging "meta-journalism", its adoption by journalists and its intersection with journalistic values remains poorly understood, even though its practice has been emerging since the earliest examples of computer-assisted reporting (CAR) (Meyer 2002).

What editorial infrastructure is required by computable news? The inability of content management systems to accommodate structure is a significant barrier to deploying computable news products. Specifying a CMS capable of accommodating the full continuum of computable news artifacts may facilitate integration of computable news into existing newsrooms. This approach has been pioneered by the Washington Post's Arc CMS and the New York Times Oak system, which enable recursive management of annotated sub-article content items like textemes (Engel 2015; Ciocca 2018). New ways for journalists to interact editorially with structured news are also required. Emerging technologies like constrained natural language—essentially a computer-friendly version of VOA's "Special English"—may offer practical interfaces between journalists and structured journalistic knowledge (Schwitter 2010).

How can consumption of computable news be understood and evaluated? The pre-digital bundling of news may have negated the need to understand how news consumers use journalistic knowledge, because diverse uses were accommodated by a single news product. Journalism based on smaller units, however, must distinguish between informative, educational, entertainment, social and other uses of news, because those units must serve more specific functions. Tools such as functional neuroimaging or psycho-behavioral experimentation may offer fresh opportunities to understand the cognitive and even neurobiological underpinnings of news consumption in human beings. Mapping the uses of digital news, identifying uses suited to computational fulfillment, and designing ways to measure that suitability may help to better match computable news products with consumer needs.

What are the semantic boundaries of computation in journalism? Data structures are vastly sparser than natural language in their ability to represent journalistic knowledge, creating significant potential for explicit biases in the design of data structures, and implicit biases arising from their coarse semantic granularity. A clear understanding the limits of computational representation in journalism is therefore urgently needed.

A significant barrier to progress on these, and similar, foundational research questions is the absence of an obvious research community that might pursue them. This gap arises from multiple factors, including the historical interpretation of journalism as a craft without need of theoretical foundations, the extreme multidisciplinary nature of computational journalism and, ultimately, the deep gulf between humanistic and scientific perspectives (Snow 1959). A preference among funders of innovation in journalism for projects that support traditional forms rather than explore radical new forms may be an additional barrier (Posetti 2018). Nascent efforts to deeply integrate journalism with computational thinking, such as joint masters degree programs at a handful of universities and small research teams at major news organizations may likewise be too pragmatically focused to address foundational questions. An understanding of journalism's components and uses developed from questions like these may not necessarily increase the standing of traditional news organizations relative to other centers of cultural, social or commercial power, but it might enable society to better adapt the essential functions of journalism to a much more computational and data-driven information environment in coming decades.

Conclusion

The revolution in the distribution of news artifacts over the last two decades may be followed, sooner or later, by a revolution in the essential nature of those artifacts. This second revolution, should it occur, will likely be characterized by the representation of journalistic knowledge as structured data rather than as natural language, albeit often associated with natural language textemes and articles. Portents of this revolution have already emerged as various forms of computational journalism, especially as structured journalism, as well as in other information-centric domains. Conceiving of computational journalism in terms of its data structures rather than in terms of algorithms or as a toolkit can clarify the roles of data, abstraction and editorial oversight within an increasingly data-driven media environment. This conception can also provide new interpretations of journalism's urgent problems and a direction for future research.

The units of journalistic knowledge available to computational journalism can be viewed as existing on a continuum ranging from simple annotation of articles to annotated textemes to fully structured statements. They are constrained by the symbols that represent them and, especially, by the availably of a shared semantic grounding system with which those symbols can reference actual things, concepts or events in the world. Variants of computational journalism are differentiated by their various sources of, and uses of, structured journalistic knowledge. A theoretical basis for this conception is available from the fields of computational semantics, text linguistics, frame semantics and computational narrative, and a relevant body of practice is available from knowledge engineering. These sciences, technologies and practices can be used by journalism to imagine, design and build digitally native news artifacts that remain under human editorial control.

Computable news has implications beyond mere problem solving. Commercial and political power is investing heavily in computable media (Schmidt 2018), and journalism will increasingly need to compete with automated propaganda campaigns (Allenby and Garreau 2017). In this environment, data-driven computable news products that augment human sense-making may offer ways to rebuild authoritative shared narratives founded on new forms of objectivity rooted in transparency and evidence.

The longer-term implications are more startling. Structured journalism, and its analogs in other information-centric domains, may be precursors of a new kind of hybrid language capable of narrative representation in the same way that programming languages are capable of process representation. Unlike designed languages intended for human communication, such as Esperanto and Lojban, structured knowledge may be an emergent language—a pidgin resulting from the necessity of communication between humans and machines (Masterman and Kay 1960; Lewis et al. 2019). Even in rudimentary form, such a language could be transformative. Journalistic and other knowledge could be accumulated at immense scale, over decades, while remaining fully accessible to human sense-making via computational tools designed to support human cognitive processes. This accumulated knowledge would essentially be a new form of externalized understanding on a societal scale, error-correcting and open to continuous refinement over time. Other phenomena exhibiting this characteristic include software, DNA and science itself.

It is likely that the proportion and influence of computational news artifacts within the media ecosystem will increase, perhaps dramatically. As this occurs a key strategic objective for journalism as a profession should be to maintain editorial control over journalistic knowledge represented as data. To do this journalists, scholars and editorial technologists must reimagine journalism as activity and knowledge that transcends the manner in which it is expressed.

Acknowledgments

The author would like to thank the Donald W. Reynolds Journalism Institute at the Missouri School of Journalism for their early support of the author's work. This article is the result of independent research by the author and does not necessarily reflect the views of the BBC.

Disclosure Statement

No potential conflict of interest was reported by the author.

Funding

This work was not funded.

References

Adair, Bill. 2017. "Behind the Unlikely Success of PolitiFact and the Truth-O-Meter." *Columbia Journalism Review*, August 21. https://www.cjr.org/first_person/politifact-fact-checking-anniversary.php.

Allenby, Brad, and Joel Garreau. 2017. *Weaponized Narrative: The New Battlespace*. Phoenix: Center on the Future of War, Arizona State University.

Amico, Laura, and Chris Amico. 2011. "Homicide Watch D.C." http://homicidewatch.org/about/.

Anderson, C. W., Emily Bell, and Clay Shirky. 2012. *Post-Industrial Journalism: adapting to the Present*. New York: The Tow Center for Digital Journalism.

Anderson, C. W. 2013. "Towards a Sociological Analysis of Computational and Algorithmic Journalism." *New Media & Society* 15 (7): 1005–1021.

Anderson, C. W. 2015. "Between the Unique and the Pattern: Historical Tensions in Our Understanding of Quantitative Journalism." *Digital Journalism* 3 (3): 349–363.

Anderson, C. W. 2016. "Our Audience is a Machine": Structured Stories and the Computation of Journalistic Context." Paper presented at the 66th Annual Conference of the International Communication Association, Fukuoka, Japan, June 11.

Anderson, C. W. 2017a. "Where Data Journalism Comes From." Demystifying Media at the University of Oregon, May 15. https://soundcloud.com/demystifying-media/cw-anderson.

Anderson, C. W. 2018. *Apostles of Certainty*, 138. Oxford: Oxford University Press.

Anderson, Kevin. 2017b. *Beyond the Article, Frontiers of Editorial and Commercial Innovation*. Oxford: Reuters Institute.

Ausserhofer, Julian, Robert Gutounig, Michael Oppermann, Sarah Matiasek, and Eva Goldgruber. 2017. "The Datafication of Data Journalism Scholarship: Focal Points, Methods, and Research Propositions for the Investigation of Data-Intensive Newswork." *Journalism*. Advance online publication. doi: 10.1177/1464884917700667.

Brachman, Ronald, and Hector Levesque. 2004. *Knowledge Representation and Reasoning*. Burlington, USA: Morgan Kaufmann.

Baker, Colin. 2008. "FrameNet, Present and Future." Paper presented at the First International Conference on Global Interoperability for Language Resources, Hong Kong, January 9–11.

Bedi, Neil, and Connie Humburg. 2017. "If you're black", *Tampa Bay Times*, April 4, http://www.tampabay.com/projects/2017/investigations/florida-police-shootings/if-youre-black/.

Biltgen, Patrick, and Stephen Ryan. 2016. *Activity-Based Intelligence: Principles and Applications*. Boston: Artech House.

Casanovas, Pompeu, Giovanni Sartor, Núria Casellas, and Rossella Rubino, eds. 2008. *Computable Models of the Law*. Berlin: Springer-Verlag.

Caswell, David. 2015. "Structured Narratives as a Framework for Journalism". Paper presented at the Sixth International Workshop on Computational Models of Narrative, Atlanta, May 26–28.

Caswell, David, Frank Russell and Bill Adair. 2015. "Editorial Aspects of Reporting into Structured Narratives." Paper presented at the 2015 Computation + Journalism Symposium, New York, October 2–3.

Caswell, David. 2016. "Computable News Ecosystems: Roles for Humans and Machines." Paper presented at the Second Workshop on Computing News Storylines, Austin, November 5.

Caswell, David, and Konstantin Dörr. 2017. "Automated Journalism 2.0: Event-Driven Narratives." *Journalism Practice* 12 (4): 477–496. doi: 10.1080/17512786.2017.1320773.

Caswell, David, Frank M., Russell, Maggie Angst, Hellen Tian, Arthur C. Bremer, Hui-Hsien Tsai, and Esther Thorson. 2018. "Text or Data? A Survey of Consumer Responses to Structured Journalism". Work in progress.

Caswell, David, and C. W. Anderson. 2019. "Computational Journalism." In *The International Encyclopedia of Journalism Studies*, edited by Tim P. Vos and Folker Hanusch. London: John Wiley & Sons, Inc.

Ciocca, Sophia. 2018. "Building a Text Editor for a Digital-First Newsroom", Times Open, April 12. https://open.nytimes.com/building-a-text-editor-for-a-digital-first-newsroom-f1cb8367fc21.

Coddington, Mark. 2015. "Clarifying Journalism's Quantitative Turn: A Typology for Evaluating Data Journalism, Computational Journalism, and Computer-Assisted Reporting." *Digital Journalism* 3 (3): 331–348.

Coddington, Mark. 2015. "Telling Secondhand Stories: News Aggregation and the Production of Journalistic Knowledge". PhD diss., University of Texas at Austin.

Cohen, Sarah, James T. Hamilton, and Fred Turner. 2011. "Computational Journalism." *Communications of the ACM* 54 (10): 66–71. doi: 10.1145/2001269.2001288.

Cohn, David. 2014. "At Circa, it's not about 'chunkifying' news but adding structure". *The Poynter Institute blog*, February 7. https://www.poynter.org/news/circa-its-not-about-chunkifying-news-adding-structure.

de Beugrande, Robert. 1997. *New Foundations for a Science of Text and Discourse: Cognition, Communication, and the Freedom of Access to Knowledge and Society*. Westport, CT: Greenwood Publishing Group.

Descartes, René. 1629. In a letter to Mersenne, 20 November. Translated by J. Cottingham, R. Stoothoff, and D. Murdoch. Accessed in *The Philosophical Writing of Descartes*. Vol. 3, 13. Cambridge: Cambridge University Press.

Diakopoulos, Nicholas. 2016. "Computational journalism and the emergence of news platforms". In *The Routledge Companion to Digital Journalism Studies*, edited by Bob Franklin and Scott Eldridge. London: Routledge.

Doherty, Skye. 2012. "Will the Geeks Inherit the Newsroom? Reflections on Why Journalists Should Learn Computer Science." *International Journal of Technology, Knowledge and Society* 8 (2): 111–121.

Dörr, Konstantin. 2016. "Mapping the Field of Algorithmic Journalism." *Digital Journalism* 4 (6): 700–722.

Eberlein, Kristen James, Robert D. Anderson, and Gershon Joseph. 2010. *Darwin Information Typing Architecture (DITA), Version 1.2. Committee Draft 01*. Burlington, MA: OASIS.

Engel, Gregory. 2015. "Arc Native Specification schema" (XML data schema). GitHub repository. Accessed February 15, 2018. https://github.com/washingtonpost/ans-schema.

Fenech, Céline, and Ben Perkins. 2015. *Made-to-Order: The Rise of Mass Personalization. 11th Deloitte Consumer Review*. London: Deloitte.

Fillmore, Charles J. 1976. "Frame Semantics and the Nature of Language." *Annals of the New York Academy of Sciences* 280 (1 Origins and E): 20–32.

Gottlieb, Anthony. 2017. *The Dream of Enlightenment: The Rise of Modern Philosophy*. New York: Liveright.

Gourarie, Chava. 2015. "Structured Journalism' Offers Readers a Different Kind of Story Experience." *Columbia Journalism Review*, July 30. https://www.cjr.org/innovations/structured_journalism.php.

Graefe, Andreas. 2016. *Guide to Automated Journalism*. New York: The Tow Center for Digital Journalism.

Graefe, Andreas, Mario Haim, Bastian Haarmann, and Hans-Bernd Brosius. 2018. "Readers' Perception of Computer-Generated News: Credibility, Expertise, and Readability." *Journalism* 19 (5): 595–610.

Groth, Paul, Andrew Gibson, and Jan Veltero. 2010. "The Anatomy of a Nanopublication." *Information Services & Use* 30 (1–2): 51–56.

Haralambous, Yannis, and Gabor Bella. 2005. "Injecting Information into Atomic Units of Text." In *Proceedings of the 2005 ACM symposium on Document Engineering*, 134–142. Saarbrücken: Schloss Dagstuhl.

Halliwell, Stephen. 1998. *Aristotle's Poetics*. Chicago: University of Chicago Press.

Hamilton, James. 2016. "Accountability and Algorithms." Chap. 8 in *Democracy's Detectives—the Economics of Investigative Journalism*. Cambridge, MA: Harvard University Press.

Hamilton, James. 2017. "The Future of Computational Journalism." Panel discussion at Stanford University, December 13. https://www.youtube.com/watch?v=N9U6NyOw7qk.

Hansen, Mark, Meritxell Roca-Sales, Jonathan M. Keegan, and George King. 2017. *Artificial Intelligence: Practice and Implications for Journalism*. New York: The Tow Center for Digital Journalism. https://towcenter.org/research/artificial-intelligence-practice-and-implications-for-journalism/.

Harari, Yuval Noah. 2016. *Homo Deus*. London: Harvill Secker.

Harcup, Tony, and Deirdre O'Neill. 2001. "What Is News? Galtung and Ruge Revisited." *Journalism Studies* 2 (2): 261–280.

Hiltzik, Michael. 2002. "A.I. Reboots." *MIT Technology Review*, 105 (2): 46–55.

Holton, Avery E., and Hsiang Iris Chyi. 2012. "News and the Overloaded Consumer: Factors Influencing Information Overload among News Consumers." *Cyberpsychology, Behavior, and Social Networking* 15 (11): 619–624.

Jones, Rhianne, and Jones. Bronwyn 2018. "Atomising the News: The (In)Flexibility of Structured Journalism." Automation, Algorithms and News: An International Conference, Ludwig Maximilians Universität, Munich. May 2018.

Kalogeropoulos, Antonis, and Nic Newman. 2017. *'I Saw the News on Facebook' Brand Attribution When Accessing News from Distributed Environments*. Oxford: Reuters Institute for the Study of Journalism.

Kuhn, Tobias, and Michel Dumontier. 2017. "Genuine Semantic Publishing." *Data Science* 1 (1–2): 139–154.

Kwak, Haewoon, and Jisun An. 2016. "Comparison of widely used world news datasets: Gdelt and eventregistry." In *Proceedings of the 23rd International Conference on Web and Social Media*. New York: ACM Digital Library.

Larsson, Anders Olof. 2013. "Staying in or Going out? Assessing the Linking Practices of Swedish Online Newspapers." *Journalism Practice* 7 (6): 738–754.

Lewis, Seth C. 2015. "Journalism in an Era of Big Data: Cases, Concepts, and Critiques." *Digital Journalism* 3 (3): 321–330.

Lewis, Seth C. 2019. "Journalism." In *The International Encyclopedia of Journalism Studies*. London: John Wiley & Sons, Inc.

Lewis, Seth C., Andrea L. Guzman, and Thomas R. Schmidt. 2019. "Automation, Journalism, and Human-Machine Communication: Rethinking Roles and Relationships of Humans and Machines in News." *Digital Journalism* 7 (4): 409.

Liu, Ying, and Yu Jin. 2004. "Grounding Knowledge of Engineering Applications in Systematic Terms." *Proceedings of the First International Workshop on Philosophy and Informatics*. Saarbrücken: Schloss Dagstuhl.

McLuhan, Marshall. 1964. *Understanding Media: The Extensions of Man*. New York: McGraw-Hill.

Mani, Inderjeet. 2013. *Computational Modeling of Narrative*. San Rafael, CA: Morgan and Claypool.

Marconi, Francesco. 2017. *How Artificial Intelligence Will Impact Journalism*. New York: Associated Press Insights.

Masterman, Margaret, and Martin Kay. 1960. *Mechanical Pidgin Translation*. Cambridge: Cambridge Language Research Unit.

Meyer, Philip. 2002. *Precision Journalism: A Reporter's Introduction to Social Science Methods*, 4th ed. New York: Rowman & Littlefield.

Molyneux, Logan. 2018. "Mobile News Consumption—A Habit of Snacking, Digital Journalism." *Digital Journalism* 6 (5): 634–650.

Ogden, Charles Kay., and Ivor Armstrong Richards. 1927. *The Meaning of Meaning*. New York: Harcourt, Brace & Company.

Onyshkevych, Boyan. 2017. "DARPA program information for Active Interpretation of Disparate Alternatives – AIDA." https://www.darpa.mil/program/active-interpretation-of-disparate-alternatives.

Peters, Chris and Marcel Broersma, eds. 2016. *Rethinking Journalism Again: Societal Role and Public Relevance in a Digital Age*. London: Routledge.

Paulheim, Heiko. 2017. "Towards Profiling Knowledge Graphs." Paper presented at the 4th International Workshop on Dataset Profiling and Federated Search for Web Data (PROFILES 2017), Vienna, Austria, October 22.

Posetti, Julie. 2018. *Time to Step Away from the 'Bright, Shiny Things'? towards a Sustainable Model of Journalism Innovation in an Era of Perpetual Change*. Oxford: Reuters Institute for the Study of Journalism.

Roca-Sales, Meritxell. 2017. *Artificial Intelligence: Practice and Implications for Journalism*. New York.: The Tow Center for Digital Journalism.

Rom, Shelly, and Zev Reich. 2017. "Between the Technological Hare and the Journalistic Tortoise: Minimization of Knowledge Claims in Online News Flashes." *Journalism: Theory, Practice & Criticism*. Advance online publication. doi: 10.1177/1464884917740050.

Rospocher, Marco, Marieke van Erp, Piek Vossen, Antske Fokkens, Itziar Aldabe, German Rigau, Aitor Soroa, Thomas Ploeger, and Tessel Bogaard. 2016. "Building Event-Centric Knowledge Graphs from News." *Journal of Web Semantics* 37: 132–151.

Rule, Adam, Aurélien Tabard, and James Hollan. 2018. "Exploration and Explanation in Computational Notebooks." In *proceedings of the ACM CHI Conference on Human Factors in Computing Systems*, April 21–26, Montréal. New York: ACM Digital Library.

Russell, Frank M., David, Caswell, Maggie Angst, Hellen Tian, Arthur C. Bremer, Hui-Hsien Tsai, and Esther Thorson. 2016. "Structured Stories: Testing the Technical, Editorial, and Cultural Feasibility of a Computational Journalism Project." Paper presented at the 2016 Conference of the Association for Education in Journalism and Mass Communication, Minneapolis, August 4–7.

Schmidt, Christine. 2018. "China's news agency is reinventing itself with AI." *Nieman Lab blog*, January 10. http://www.niemanlab.org/2018/01/chinas-news-agency-is-reinventing-itself-with-ai/.

Schwitter, Rolf. 2010. "Controlled natural languages for knowledge representation." In The *Proceedings of the 23rd International Conference on Computational Linguistics*. Stroudsburg, PA: Association for Computational Linguistics.

Shiralkar, Prashant, Alessandro Flammini, Filippo Menczer, and Giovanni Luca Ciampaglia. 2017. "Finding Streams in Knowledge Graphs to Support Fact Checking." https://arxiv.org/abs/1708.07239.

Sidahmed, Mazin. 2017. "Introducing a New Format for Evolving Stories." *Blog of The Guardian Mobile Innovation Lab*, October 18. https://medium.com/the-guardian-mobile-innovation-lab/introducing-a-new-format-for-evolving-stories-281d2724b416.

Snow, Charles Percy. 1959. *The Two Cultures and the Scientific Revolution*. New York: Cambridge University Press.

Swift, Art. 2016. "Americans' Trust in Mass Media Sinks to New Low." In *Gallup Poll Social Series*, edited by Frank Newport. Washington: Gallup. http://news.gallup.com/poll/195542/americans-trust-mass-media-sinks-new-low.aspx.

Troncy, Raphaël. 2008. "Bringing the IPTC News Architecture into the Semantic Web." In Sheth A. eds. *The Semantic Web—ISWC 2008: Lecture Notes in Computer Science*. 5318. Berlin: Springer.

Waite, Matt. 2013. "How sensor journalism can help us create data, improve our storytelling." The Poynter Institute website. Accessed June 16, 2019. https://www.poynter.org/reporting-editing/2013/how-sensor-journalism-can-help-us-create-data-improve-our-storytelling/.

Weber, Matthew S., and Allie Kosterich. 2018. "Coding the News." *Digital Journalism* 6 (3): 310–329. doi: 10.1080/21670811.2017.1366865.

Wing, Jeannette. 2006. "Computational Thinking." *Communications of the ACM* 49 (3): 33–35.

Witschge, Tamara, C. W. Anderson, David Domingo, and Alfred Hermida. 2018. "Dealing with the Mess (we Made): Unraveling Hybridity, Normativity, and Complexity in Journalism Studies." *Journalism* 20 (5): 651–659. doi: 10.1177/1464884918760669.

Wolfe, Julia. 2018. "A Better Way To Think About August's Jobs Numbers." *FiveThirtyEight*, September 7, https://projects.fivethirtyeight.com/jobs-report-growth-unemployment/.

Wu, Tim. 2017. *Is the First Amendment Obsolete? A Report in the Emerging Threats Series*. New York: The Knight First Amendment Institute at Columbia University.

Zarri, Gian Piero. 2009. *Representation and Management of Narrative Information*. Berlin: Springer.

Atomising the News: The (In)Flexibility of Structured Journalism

Rhianne Jones ⓘD and Bronwyn Jones ⓘD

ABSTRACT
The field of data-driven news production and delivery is maturing, and public service media are among a wide range of news organisations innovating to exploit these advances. This article extends the literature on computational journalism by analysing two of the BBC's recent experiments in "atomizing" the news–an object-based approach, which seeks to make news more adaptable and scalable using media components that can be automatically and algorithmically combined in multiple ways. Findings suggest atomised news is viewed by the organisation as offering opportunities for greater efficiency and personalisation and sits within a broader turn towards "structured journalism." We highlight three characteristics of atomisation—recording, recombining and re-use—to illustrate how it breaks from traditional approaches. We find journalists are "writing for machines" by converting unstructured information into structured data to enable automated recombination and future re-use of content. This impacts editorial control by delegating responsibility to either the algorithm or the audience, in the name of choice. We propose a research agenda that maps the field of structured journalism, contextualises it in the politics of data and technology, and further considers the implications for public service journalism.

Introduction

Rapid advances in digital, networked and Internet-enabled technologies have led to vastly increased capacity for creating, capturing, storing, and distributing information as data. This expanded capacity has in turn fostered momentum behind innovation that exploits data. In journalism, a related area of experimentation that has been gradually gaining traction is the "atomisation" of news, in which a story is broken down into "atoms" of information, which are abstracted and represented as data. These many atoms (also sometimes called objects, units or components) can then be used multiple times in multiple ways to build and rebuild different hybrid stories. This is achieved using algorithms and automation as opposed to, or in conjunction with, human curation. The atoms live on within, and can continually build, databases of organised and structured information. Atomised news sits within a wider trend within computational journalism towards the increased use of structured data—a practice often referred to as "structured journalism." It has been described as moving away from the traditional "story-centric worldview" (Holovaty 2006) prevalent in newspaper and broadcast journalism, which sees the article or radio/television package as the primary unit. Instead, it refocuses attention on the individual bits and pieces of information that make up the news and the potential connections that can be made between them. Abstraction and automation are key to these approaches and to understanding the contribution of computational thinking to journalism norms and practices more generally (Coddington 2015). As journalism's traditional business models flounder in a fragmented online advertising market, and public service media (PSM) struggle to effectively serve all sections of society, news organisations view the algorithmic automation of atomised approaches as promising desirable time and money savings. Moreover, as the news industry pivots towards personalisation (EBU 2015, Helberger 2015), the potential for telling diverse stories via flexible manipulation of these atoms becomes an attractive proposition (Bucher 2018, Chua 2010). Caswell argues (2018) that such instances of structured journalism may portend a "second digital revolution" characterised by "the representation of journalistic knowledge as structured data rather than as natural language," albeit often associated with the latter. He suggests that this re-conceptualises the foundations of news and may not only help tackle journalism's urgent problems but, in the long term, develop a transformative "new kind of language" between humans and machines, which could build accumulated knowledge and augment human sense-making (see Anderson 2015). How this could impact public service journalism is, however, yet to be interrogated.

Modern-day newsrooms have become increasingly reliant on not only digital, networked and social media technologies but also data-driven, algorithmic, automated, (semi-)autonomous and artificially "intelligent" technologies. It is important to examine what impact these changes have on journalism, and a significant amount of recent research in journalism studies has tackled this (e.g., Diakopoulos 2015, Dörr 2015). However, the public service context is understudied, the process of trialling a news technology is rarely addressed, and the emerging field of "structured" or "atomised" journalism has faced little scrutiny (important exceptions include Caswell 2015; Caswell and Dörr 2017; Anderson and Caswell 2018). The resurgence of interest in materiality and the "objects of journalism" (Anderson 2015, Neff 2015) has helped refocus attention on how journalistic knowledge is produced in relation to such objects. We argue that the stage at which technology is developed is a crucial moment for investigation. This is because it enables interrogation of how, through an iterative process of mutual shaping, technologies influence, and are influenced by, journalists and journalism (Boczkowski 2004, Lievrouw and Livingstone 2006) as well as technologists and businesspeople (Westlund and Lewis 2015). It is this interplay between material and immaterial elements, both established and new, that is at the heart of the transformation of journalism. Professional journalists are subject to numerous enabling and constraining forces—economic, socio-cultural, political, professional, institutional/organisational and technical—which are interlinked and influence their actions. Journalists also help shape these forces and the socio-material infrastructures through which they play out. These infrastructures comprise assemblages of multiple human actors and technological actants brought together in the purposeful practice of news production, in a particular context. Even though they are complex, infrastructures are important for researching changes to journalism because they can be identified and explicated by analysing both the material and immaterial elements that constitute them, and the relationship between these elements. In this paper, we interrogate how the BBC is developing "atomised" approaches to news production and delivery by analysing trials of prototype technologies and the news products they have created. The paper discusses the practical, editorial and ethical opportunities and challenges these forms of atomising the news present in a public service context and the potential implications if these approaches were to be integrated into the newsroom. We assert that incremental changes to the socio-technical infrastructure underpinning BBC News are increasing the amount and importance of structured data for journalism and outline pertinent areas this is likely to impact that necessitate further research.

Related Literature

Computational and Structured Journalism

Journalism "is clearly among the most influential knowledge-producing institutions of our time" (Ekström 2002, 259), and, as a consequence, investigating how it is changing and with what impact on the nature of news and its public role is vital. Journalists' claims to authority and legitimacy rest on adherence to professional codes and sets of values that guide news production practice as well as recognition and respect of these professional frameworks by audiences. New technologies and capabilities brought about by socio-technical systems can disrupt established ways of working and create not only new opportunities but also novel challenges to maintaining standards. For example, Lewis and Westlund (2015b) find the applications of big data potentially have great meaning for journalism's epistemology (ways of knowing), expertise (ways of doing), economics (negotiation of value) and ethics (values). Disruption occurs when the core concepts, values, and practices that are fundamental to journalism come up against those on which computer science is premised, and it is particularly prominent when journalism's requirements for the interpretation, nuance and context that are characteristic of human-authored natural language-based news face computational requirements for precision, structure and abstraction. Studies of computational journalism have recognised the rising prevalence and importance of technical communities in journalism (e.g., Lewis and Usher 2013, 2014, 2016), which bring into the newsroom different ways of viewing the world through computational and algorithmic logics. They highlight how the nature of experimenting with computation for media production necessitates the translation to differing degrees of unstructured data (e.g., natural language assets) into structured data (i.e., highly organised information, which has attributes that are consistent across a domain). Thus, contemporary technology developers for news organisations are fundamentally focussed on making the world "machine-readable," driven by the prediction that this will enable new and hitherto impossible forms of journalism.

News producers have long been exploring how computational approaches can be incorporated into established cultures of news production in order to reap the benefits of digitisation and "datafication" (Kennedy 2018) whilst maintaining professional standards. The study of computation in journalism has a long history, spanning early research into computer-assisted reporting in the 1990s to later analysis of multiplying forms of data-driven journalism (Young and Hermida 2015) that exemplify a quantitative turn in the field (Coddington 2015). Research has grown and matured in recent years to encompass the role of big data (see the Digital Journalism special issue edited by Lewis in 2015), algorithms in news (Bucher 2018), content creation (Napoli 2014) and content delivery, prompting important debates with regard to algorithmic accountability (Diakopoulos 2015), judgement (Carlson 2018), authority (Carlson 2015), objectivity (Gillespie 2014) and transparency (McBride and Rosenstiel 2013). It has more recently turned to machine learning (ML) and artificial intelligence in news work (Broussard 2014) as well as structured journalism—an area that is growing in maturity and significance for the industry (Anderson 2018; Caswell 2018).

For Anderson, structured journalism represents the fullest extension of computational thinking into the journalistic process (2018, 13). Structured journalism is an umbrella term under which are grouped approaches that encode information into machine-readable forms, as data and metadata, allowing algorithmic systems to then do the work of storytelling, to differing degrees. Structured journalism is more than just tagging and annotating journalistic input and output—it creates potentially deep and rich datasets that feed atoms of journalistic information to algorithms that make connections and may create narratives. It involves rethinking how a story is gathered, organised and built, and what it looks like to audiences. Discussion of the ideas underpinning structured journalism began to appear in the late 2000s (see in particular Holovaty 2006; Chua 2010) followed closely by early forays into applying these ideas. These included: PolitiFact (2007)—a fact-checking website that rates the accuracy of claims by elected officials and others; Homicide Watch DC (2010–2015)—a site pulling diverse documents together to track homicide cases from crime to conviction; Reuters' Connected China project (2014)—an application to visualise links between Chinese leaders and political institutions; the Washington Post's Knowledge Map (2015)—a database of categorised text and graphics that provide context to complicated news topics; and Circa's atomised news (2012–2015, relaunched in 2016)—an app using granular chunks of news "cards" to distil complex news into a more accessible format; and more recently Structured Stories—an academic project begun in 2015. Bill Adair said PolitiFact, which he founded, is structured journalism, "because the articles contain fields of information that can be sorted and tallied. They provide readers with many ways to explore the content, both through individual articles and the data the articles create" (2014). Meanwhile, Structured Stories requires journalists to consider structure from the very beginning by entering "journalistic events and narratives into a 'story database that is not based on written text, but instead uses the semantics, or 'meaning', of journalistic events to represent news stories entirely as structured data" (Caswell and Dörr 2017, 4). The project is "evaluating the feasibility of computational narrative structures as the basis of new forms of journalism" (ibid.: 3). During this period, the BBC has also been experimenting with what it has at different times termed "Structured," "Elastic," (BBC R&D 2014a) "Snackable" (BBC R&D 2014b) and "Atomised" (BBC R&D n.d.) news, launching in 2015 a Manifesto for Structured

Journalism (BBC News Labs 2015). By March 2019, this work had led to the organisa-tions first live trial of "semi-automated" news production from structured data, which focussed on serving area-specific NHS performance stories to local audiences (BBC News Labs 2019).

Computational systems set particular rules and boundaries for what can be known and what can be done - shaped by the socio-material conditions in which they are developed and enacted. These systems are not neutral or an objective reflection of reality but are encoded with the subjective decisions of engineers/developers (and numerous others) in their design and development. The categorisation necessary for these systems to function—and fundamental to any instance of structured journal-ism—is "a powerful semantic and political intervention" (Gillespie 2014, 171). Increasing use of structured data in news prompts us to examine how the nature of professional journalistic work may be changing and what aspects of news production are being automated or algorithmically configured. A particularly important but chal-lenging task for researchers analysing such complex systems is locating agents of influence, power, and control over editorial content and any changes to these. The emerging domain of Human-Machine Communication (HMC) may offer a lens for inter-rogating such matters, as it foregrounds the creation of meaning among humans and machines and challenges the assumption "that humans are communicators and machines are mediators by asking what happens when a machine steps into this formerly human role" (Lewis, Guzman, and Thomas 2019). However, as Lewis and Westlund argue, in order to begin analysing how journalism is becoming "interconnected with technological tools, processes and ways of thinking," we must "account for the full array of actors, actants, audiences and activities in cross-media news work" (2015b, 33) and interrogate the ways in which they might intersect.

Public Service Journalism and Innovation

The value of public service news has traditionally been defined in terms of provision of a universal offering characterised by diversity of output and editorial independence from government and commercial interests (Hendy 2013), and situated in a normative conception of journalism as the "fourth estate," holding power to account. PSM are charged with providing impartial, balanced and high-quality news on issues of com-mon concern and representing diverse viewpoints. As publicly funded institutions, they have a duty to be transparent and accountable and are typically placed under great scrutiny. The expertise and judgement of their journalists is central to maintain-ing the trust of audiences on which their legitimacy rests. Though viewed as a useful counterweight to their commercial counterparts, PSM are, however, subject to many of the same pressures of today's competitive media environment. In a climate charac-terised by an explosion in news providers, on-demand content, and the rise of new media platform intermediaries (van Dijck and Poell 2015), which has given rise to an abundance of "choice"—a trademark of the marketisation of media (Bennet 2018)—and increasing audience fragmentation, PSM must strive to remain relevant, prominent and findable (EBU 2015). PSM have had to adapt to changing technologies in the past, making the transition from radio to television to digital, but there are increasing demands on them to innovate in response to an increasingly social and mobile news environment and changing audience practices. In Europe, newsrooms trying to bolster reach, particularly when it comes to younger audiences (Sehl, Cornia, and Nielsen 2016), have introduced teams to manage a panoply of social media such as Facebook, Twitter and Instagram, created new mobile applications and online formats (Sehl, Cornia, and Nielsen 2017), introduced new algorithmic tools and are increasingly capturing analytics and metrics in an effort to measure audiences' engagement across multiple devices (Sehl, Cornia, and Nielsen 2018).

Emerging technologies provide opportunities to reimagine and redefine public service journalism, but PSM face the challenges of balancing such transformation with maintaining, if not improving, standards and fulfilling their remit at a time when many are seeing declining funding. New tools supporting investigative and data journalism have clear potential for fulfilling PSM goals (Brehmer et al. 2014), while forms of "robo journalism" enable multiple customised versions of the same story, catering for specific interests (Carlson 2018). The turn to automated, algorithmic and personalised technologies in PSM (Helberger 2015, Van den Bulck and Moe 2017) promises to make content more individually "relevant" to members of a diverse public. However, to do this PSM must profile audiences (Baym 2013; Kennedy 2016), and an algorithmically enhanced media environment that increasingly sorts and filters content based on audience members' individual profiles is in stark contrast to earlier notions of broadcasting to "the public" (Sørensen and Hutchinson 2018; Van Es 2017). Moreover, PSM have had to increasingly integrate third-party sites and software into their operations (see Jones and Jones in this special issue). This has ignited debates about how PSM should adapt to wider technological changes, for example determining the right type and balance of personalisation (Helberger 2015) and applying and overseeing increased automation responsibly (Sørensen and Hutchinson 2018) to avoid undesirable or unintended consequences.

Given the important role of public service journalism in civic life, it is vital to reflect on the interplay between technology and the evolution of the PSM mission (Sørensen and Hutchinson 2018; EBU 2015; Freedman and Goblet 2018). It is important to consider how emerging technologies are being developed in PSM contexts and remits and examine their interaction with established notions of public service journalism and established ideas about journalistic expertise and practice. This study takes the opportunity to analyse experimentation with atomisation and structured journalism at its early stages in order to begin a conversation about the implications of this approach for public service news provision.

The BBC: Structure and Atomised News

The extent and success of on-the-ground innovation in PSM news have been linked to the existence of dedicated research and development (Sehl, Cornia, and Nielsen 2018). The BBC has a long and notable history in technological innovation from colour television to the digital switchover, and more recently video-on-demand services and new production technologies and standards. This role in the development and diffusion of media innovation in the UK is mandated by the Royal Charter, which requires collaboration with external organisations, such as academic institutions and other media labs. The BBC has a well-resourced R&D department with a specific team dedicated to news—BBC News Labs[1]—which is experimenting with linked data, voice technology, and ML and looking ahead to future trends such as connected devices and augmented reality. The BBC has for years been incrementally building its capacity for structured information stored in digital databases and archives, for example creating an open digital archive of historical and contemporary output. It has simultaneously been developing an increasingly sophisticated Linked Data Platform, which uses tagging of content with people, organisations, places, themes etc. to automatically populate and curate online services. In 2012, linked data automatically fed hundreds of web pages about particular athletes, sports and competitions for the London Olympics. It has since become central to the website's news and sport coverage and now underpins internal news content management systems such as Vivo (used primarily for live streams), as well as automated content curation systems (such as online Local Topic Pages). However, BBC News Labs has outlined its aim to go further in the case of journalism and create "a database of knowledge - which already exists in the collective knowledge of our newsroom staff … to provide context at scale across all our output" (BBC 2015). Launching a Manifesto for Structured Journalism in 2015, it said the approach uses the "wealth of knowledge created during the "gathering and assessing" phases of reporting that most publishing systems ignore" (ibid.). The public service value it sees in this "is a living resource of open knowledge for journalists and society at large," which they hope can empower journalists, improve the quality of reporting and "promote a greater public understanding of current affairs and issues—what the BBC's Royal Charter describes as 'sustaining citizenship and civil society'" (ibid.). The challenges of this lie in creating the necessary infrastructure (technological and social) for an atomised and structured future whilst protecting and ideally bolstering public service value. One way they have begun working towards these goals is through experimentation in "atomisation."

The earliest mention of "atoms" in relation to news appears in 2014, and references to "atoms," "atomised," "objects" and "object-based" have since become increasingly common. The BBC's work in atomised news and structured journalism builds on earlier work (outside of news) in Object-Based Media (OBM). OBM is based on "the idea that a piece of media lives together with its metadata and [the two elements] are manipulated as a single entity" (BBC R&D 2016). It sits within a bigger drive towards delivering programmes and content over the internet (the IP Studio project,[2] and R&D view it as key to facilitating further integration of media formats. This is important for the BBC because its output spans TV, radio, and online, so technical development often needs to scale across and between these domains. Although, in contrast to most PSM in Europe, the BBC has achieved high reach for news online and has been recognised for fostering "a pro-digital culture" (Sehl, Cornia, and Nielsen 2016, 5), it remains structured primarily around legacy broadcast media rather than digital media[3]. Given the investment of time and resources into OBM and linked data, and the stated aim to develop atomised approaches to news and structured journalism, this area looks likely to play an important role in the future direction of BBC innovation in news. Whilst trials exist as singular experiments rather than routine journalistic practice, they provide a critical and timely opportunity to consider what the implications might be for public service journalism. It is therefore important to consider the potential implications of these approaches for public service news.

Method

We aim to better understand the implications of structured and atomised approaches for news production and delivery in a public service context through evaluation of early trials. To do this, we employ a conceptual framework of mutual shaping that views technologies as complex socio-material phenomena (Gillespie, Boczkowski, and Foot 2014) that shape and are shaped by people, discursively and in practice. We build on a growing strand of socio-technical research in journalism studies that looks at "the distinct interplay of and tension between human and technology, or manual and computational modes of orientation and output" (Lewis and Westlund 2015a, 33). We consider the early experimentation stage to be an opportune moment at which to analyse the interplay between journalists, with their professional codes and established practices and prototype technologies, with their associated affordances and logics. Technologies tend to solidify as they mature, and interrogating early understandings of technology is important because it creates space for critical reflection and intervention. The trials offer an entry point into wider discussions about the role atomised and structured data could play in future news innovation at the BBC and the implications this may have for public service journalism. The authors come from an informed position and draw on their own knowledge and expertise in Research and Development and Journalism at the BBC during analysis[4].

In this research we ask:

- RQ1 - How is the BBC experimenting with atomised approaches to news?
- RQ2 - How is the BBC framing atomised technology for news?
- RQ3 - What are the distinctive characteristics of atomised approaches to news production at the BBC?
- RQ4 - What are the implications of this for public service journalism?

Inspired by methodological approaches to understanding the social construction of technologies, we answer these questions by examining documentation related to trials conducted at the BBC and interviewing key actors involved in their technical development. We analyse 22 publicly available documents, and 12 internal documents. To identify relevant source documents, we conducted a web search for publications that referenced and discussed either "structured journalism," "objects," "object-based," "atoms" or "atomization" alongside the terms "BBC" and "news"—key terms we identified as important through desk research and literature review. We collated 22 publications identified as a corpus of material focussed explicitly on atoms, objects and news/journalism[5]. This included eight BBC project pages, five BBC blog posts, four BBC online videos and five news or industry articles on BBC atomised work dated from

2014 to 2018. We collated and reviewed this sample of material to create an overview of BBC atomised projects, which could be split into two groups—audience-facing pilots and production tools. We then validated the overview with two people in BBC R&D working on atomisation and honed in on two example trials—Newsbeat Explains (audience-facing pilot) and Squeezebox (journalist-facing production tool). BBC R&D then provided access to further internal documentation about these prototypes and associated trials. Developers and journalists regularly and deliberately reflect on the work they are doing and what it means, or could mean, for the organisation and for journalism, which creates a record ripe for analysis. This material included two project proposals, six internal documents about the process of developing, prototyping, testing, researching, iterating and refining, two user guides, and two evaluations. We cross-referenced and supplemented this information with two unstructured open-ended interviews with the leading members of each of the teams developing the two example prototypes.

Our findings are presented in two parts. Firstly, we explain how the BBC is framing atomisation in news, identifying a broadly shared narrative by analysing how these projects were described in documentation—a key part of the social construction of atomisation. Researchers have employed framing as an analytical lens to interrogate how issues and artefacts are packaged in communicative texts through the use, placement, recurrence and contextualisation of key words and concepts, which emphasise and foreground certain aspects whilst de-prioritising or discounting others (de Vreese 2005). Drawing from two illustrative examples, we then explicate shared characteristics of atomised approaches and the affordances of their underpinning technologies that make them distinctive from existing news production technology. Secondly, we use these cases to discuss the impact of atomisation on journalistic practice and draw out significant (potential) implications under two emergent themes: writing for machines and (in)flexibility, choice and control. We highlight key points at which the approach and its underpinning technologies are being (re-)configured, contested and negotiated as they are brought into contact with existing journalistic workflows and established practices. Finally, we discuss how atomised approaches might impact on journalism in PSM, highlighting practical, editorial, and ethical challenges that emerge in a public service context. In particular, we discuss the interplay of such approaches with PSM journalists' ability to apply expertise and exercise editorial control, the better to assess how atomised news might impact claims to authority and legitimacy.

The analysis of these trials is not intended to be directly generalisable but rather to illuminate, through concrete examples, how one organisation that has a history of leading in technological innovation is crafting an emerging approach to news production that may have implications more widely.

Findings

Why Atomise? The BBC View

Though the terminology and definitions around atoms have yet to stabilise, we identify an emerging narrative of personalisation and efficiency that is being used to frame atomisation. These are both key factors motivating technological change

across the industry (Carlson 2018), and indeed across all information-centred industries. However, in this context they are being (re-)framed as directly beneficial for
public service news by the prioritising of two particular assumptions - that better
serving individuals will better serve society and that creating more content from less
human effort will fend off threats to PSM's position in society. It is yet to be seen
whether these assumptions are validated, and much will depend on how the "public
service" ethos is interpreted and encoded into the developing socio-technical
assemblages of atomisation.

In terms of its benefits with regard to personalisation, atomisation is described as
making news more appealing to audiences—particularly underserved and young audiences—in that such news can adapt to differing needs and desires (D-6, D-14). This
links to recent commitments made by Director General Tony Hall to provide a more
personalised BBC (2017). The value of structured data and atomised content is
described as the enabling of "truly personalised experiences with content adapting to
context, preferences and devices" (D-3, D-14). The ultimate goal is for "news to be tailored to the individual by being delivered in different formats depending on devices,
location, lifestyle, age and preferences by using object-based broadcasting
components" (D-1, D-8), with content for news stories written in ways that allow it to
be "re-used across platforms" (D-14). Prototypes are described in a similar fashion; for
example, one is a "mobile-first prototype aimed at young audiences using the concept
of object-based production and atomised news to make stories easier to understand
and access" (D-14).

This goal of personalisation at scale is tied to the concomitant objective of efficiency in both news production and consumption. Firstly, atomisation is presented as
a solution to increasingly demanding and complex journalistic workflows—with the
technology ideally doing the heavy lifting and freeing up journalists to concentrate
more on their craft. Automation is framed as doing the "repetitive tasks," freeing up
time and resources to allow the best possible content to be created (D-9). One prototype aims to "instantly produce edits" of a captioned video montage to "assist" journalists in situations "where rapid re-editing of content is required" (D-12). This
suggested daily efficiency is coupled with an aim of longer-term efficiency through
future re-use of the archived content, which is categorised in structured databases. As
D-15 explains, "the objective we share is to achieve better, more efficient storytelling
across proliferating device and syndication use cases." This efficiency extends to consumption of news by enabling options best suited to audience members' time and
depth preferences, with one prototype described as providing choice to "people who
want to skim stories and those who want to dig deeper" (D-14). Recognising a trade-
off in terms of time and resource investment, developers said they "hope to show that
there's a tipping point" at which authoring Squeezebox mark-up would become more
efficient than editing by hand (D-12).

Finally, it is notable that the inherent premise of atomisation - breaking down
media content into atoms or "segmenting stories into the constituent parts" (D-2) - is
presented only through the potential benefits it may bring. It is important to note
that none of the public documentation contains discussion of potential risks to, or
negative impacts on, editorial quality or journalistic authorship.

Table 1. Defining characteristics of atomisation as manifested in two prototypes

	Recording	Recombining	Re-use
Squeezebox	Instead of editing, journalists must add metadata - encoding structure to describe unstructured data	Instead of a journalist manually crafting multiple edits, the algorithm automates variable length video montages using different durations of shots, in real-time	The possibility of re-using atoms is designed into the system (though not activated during the trial)
Newsbeat Explains	Instead of constructing 'free text' linear articles, journalists must input atoms of media into a structured template	Instead of a journalist deciding how much information to display, the format enables customisation of amount of detail at the point of consumption, on demand	The possibility of re-using atoms is designed into the system (though not activated during the trial)

Breaking from Tradition? Recording, Recombining and Re-use

We identify three characteristics that illustrate how atomisation breaks from traditional approaches. These are:

1. Recording—an increasing requirement for journalists to record information in machine-readable forms, i.e., encode structure to represent unstructured data
2. Recombining—new automated or algorithmic intermediary processes that act on atomised content in order to create multiple versions or narratives
3. Re-use—the persistence in databases of categorised atoms which can be manipulated for continuing use

These characteristics were arrived at through expert analysis of two distinct cases of atomisation in news production and delivery—Newsbeat Explains (an audience-facing pilot) and Squeezebox (a journalist-facing production tool). Table 1 illustrates how the three characteristics manifest in the two prototypes.

Newsbeat Explains was a new format that presented a string of headline-like pieces of information, which could be expanded to give more information by clicking on them (see Figure 1). The trial (August–December 2016) consisted of 10 atomised stories on the BBC website. For journalists, it involved producing the stories using a new production routine in which they created self-contained modular units (atoms) of multimedia information and set rules about how those units should be linked together to tell what would otherwise be a linear story. Squeezebox was a production tool for the automation of variable-length video news montages (see Figure 2). It automatically analysed and segmented streams of video into individual shots, which a journalist would then rank in order of importance via manually entered metadata. It then used this metadata to algorithmically condense or extend a video to a desired timeframe.

These cases illustrate how structured data is playing an increasing role in news innovation at the BBC. We articulate the implications for journalists' working practices and the nature of the news produced through two emergent themes: writing for machines and (in)flexibility, choice and control.

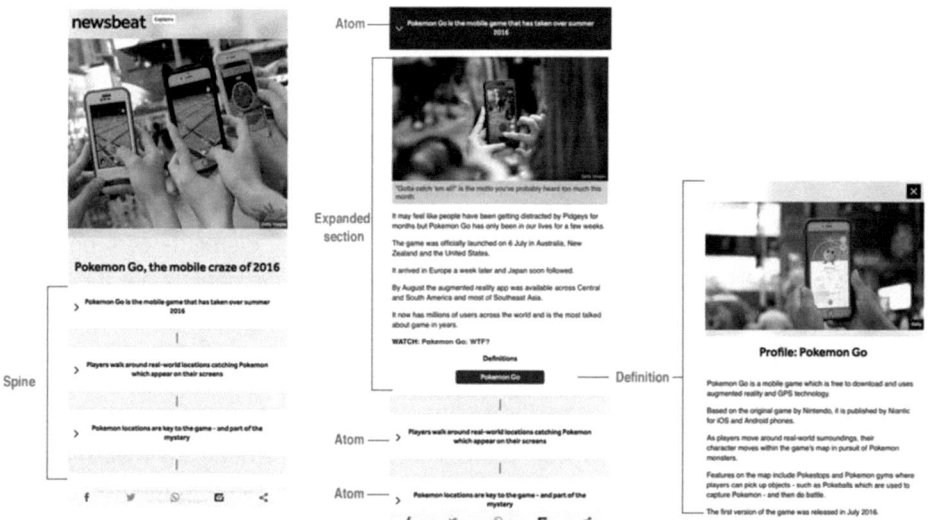

Figure 1. Annotated screenshot of the Newsbeat Explains audience interface, showing 'atoms' expanded and contracted. Source BBC R&D Blog.

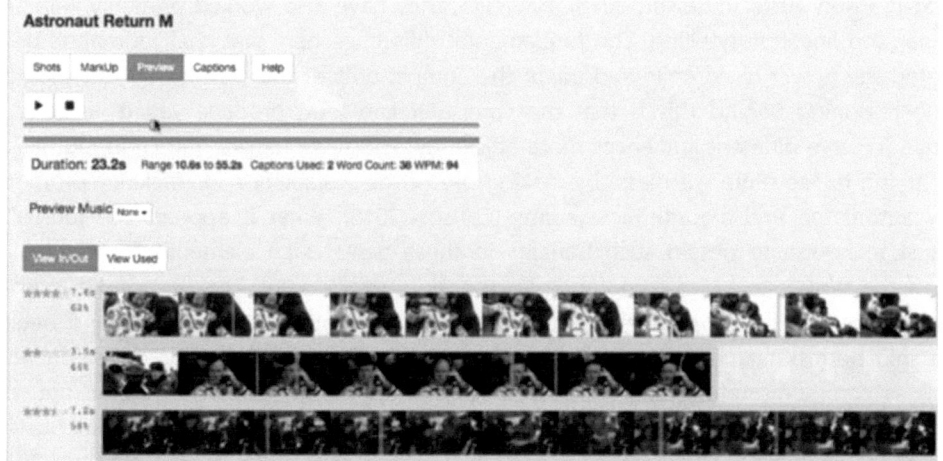

Figure 2. Journalist interface of Squeezebox, showing duration slider and shot ranking feature. Source BBC R&D Blog.

Encoding Structure: Writing for Machines

Journalists in these trials were increasingly required to "write for machines" in order to delegate future responsibility for (re-)composition to the computer. This was achieved by writing into increasingly structured templates or adding metadata to content to enable automated or algorithmic decision-making. Newsgathering for this was unchanged—what differentiated atomised processes from existing approaches was how the story narrative(s) was recorded and delivered. Constructing this narrative has always been the central role of the journalist—a core task in which their expertise and judgement are deployed most extensively and which is highly valued. Though journalists continued to set the rules for narrative creation via templates and meta-data, the actual assembly of news was delegated to the machine. Journalists therefore maintained a core but changed role in storytelling. In atomisation, the biggest opportunity and the biggest risk are thus one and the same—the computational system's ability to make manifold versions over which journalists cannot maintain oversight.

To meet the requirements of the atomised templates, journalists had to alter their working practices—an example of the materiality of these technologies shaping news production. For both Newsbeat Explains and Squeezebox, all elements of a news story had to be recorded in discrete, self-contained chunks. Core elements were identified as integral by manually added metadata and formed the necessary foundation of the narrative, whilst further optional chunks enabled various levels of depth dependent on user/producer requirements. Journalists remained authors of the now potentially multiple narratives, but the computational template and algorithms played an increasing part in story composition. In this way, professionals used to writing for their (imagined) audience had to first consider "writing for the machine" to ensure the multiple potential outputs it was designed to create would be editorially coherent and robust. Journalists have always worked with content management systems that have specific constraints to which they must conform, from newspapers' character-limited headlines, column format and typeface requirements to search engine optimised online headlines and hyperlinked text (Carlson 2018; Anderson 2018). However, they have also worked primarily with singular and linear storytelling. The fundamental difference here was that journalists delegated the power to compile and adapt the components of the story to the technology. The reasoning behind this is that the computer can then produce varied versions at scale to serve different audiences more efficiently. This fits a familiar refrain in journalism of trying to "do more with less" by making use of the scalability and efficiency promised by automated and algorithmic systems (Carlson 2018). What it appears the journalist must relinquish to obtain such benefits in these cases is an element of control over how the story is told and comprehensive oversight over output. This part of the journalistic process thus becomes increasingly prescribed by computational logics and begins to shift from human interaction through machines towards such technologies functioning as communicators (Lewis, Guzman, and Thomas 2019). As Carlson points out, the "production of news knowledge combines tacit elements of professional judgment with an acknowledgment of the importance of this judgment to journalistic authority" (2018: 1760). It is therefore important to ask if there is a risk that such tacit elements could be lost or transformed in unanticipated ways in the process of writing for machines, and what the impact might be on journalistic authority. This question is most pressing in public service newsrooms where authority is so closely tied to audience trust. Here, what may appear small mistakes from algorithmic decision-making can have disproportionately large impacts by undermining trust.

Writing for machines was an additional task, which necessitated the externalisation of journalistic judgement regarding which elements were important and how they should be ordered. This judgement had to be communicated to the technology through templates, rules and metadata, which required a reduction of complexity and elimination of ambiguity. For example, Squeezebox journalists ranked the importance of images through metadata mark-up in order for the machine to manipulate media atoms. In some ways, this proved beneficial. As Newsbeat's editor explained, the for-mat "made us more disciplined about story structure and simplicity" (Zambrini 2017). However, journalists said it also required extra work to make sure that "each segment worked in isolation as well as part of the whole" (ibid.). Practically, reordering chunks of text/atoms was described as "fiddly." This was a new requirement for journalists: to learn and think about the forms of computational logic needed to craft a story that would have different possible journeys through it. For Newsbeat Explains this meant constructing a "spine" of integral information and deciding how this should connect to additional information such as explainer text and definitions. The journalists described these new production processes as being more time-intensive. For instance, a Newsbeat Explains journalist said: "Aside from the journalism, building Atomised News stories took at least twice as long as a normal article. Average articles take one to two hours to put together" (Technical Document 5). Similarly, "writing descriptions for tags" was seen as "useful for the audience," but it "would be very time-consuming to build and maintain a decent library of these." Similarly, Squeezebox journalists pri-oritised shots using a star-based system to indicate which were necessary and which could be stripped out and in what order. However, when unhappy with the edits automatically produced using the metadata, they found it a slow and frustrating itera-tive process to have to go back and tweak it. They described what can be considered "gaming" the system to generate the desired effect, using trial and error to amend the metadata. It was envisioned that the extra time and effort at this point to craft these "atoms" would theoretically save time in the future—as seen in the public framing of the approach. There is, however, a tension here, as the necessary new task of creating more detailed metadata requires time. This highlights a disconnect between the long-term aim of saving time and the short-term additional effort required by journalists to create metadata, with the burden in the short term falling on the journalist.

At the current stage of atomisation, the reason the journalists are codifying their craft into a machine-readable form is to enable automated recombination, adaptation, and future re-use. The hope is that this will make the creation of multiple versions of the same news story—currently a cumbersome, resource- and time-consuming pro-cess—efficient enough to be practicable and allow better engagement with audiences in all their diversity, thus meeting a core PSM goal of reaching all sections of society with information of importance to citizens. However, this "writing for machines" also has the secondary outcome of building databases/archives of BBC-vetted "journalistic knowledge" that could be mobilised by algorithmic systems for further use. As Caswell posits, structured knowledge such as this may, in the future, become "an emergent language—a pidgin resulting from the necessity of communication between human and machines" that provides not only the rich annotation needed to enhance the util-ity of existing forms of news but entirely new news artifacts that may transform the nature of journalism (Caswell 2018).

(In)Flexible Systems: Implications for Choice and Control

Flexibility through automated processes relies on the pre-existence of an encoded structure, which allows for a set of choices. The framing of atomisation as a process

that promises benefits of adaptation and personalisation through its provision of flexibility and choice omits one important aspect: the need for fixed structure and algorithmic rules as a pre-condition to functioning.

Newsbeat Explains and Squeezebox both afforded flexible composition—a
Newsbeat Explains story could be expanded and collapsed to varying degrees at the
will of the reader, whilst a Squeezebox video montage could be automatically short-
ened and lengthened to required time slots. What this meant in practice was the
requirement to inscribe a core structure of information to preserve the basis of narrative. These examples reveal how this flexibility of output is enabled and conditioned
through the act of inscribing inflexible structure in the form of templates or metadata.
This characteristic duality highlights a tension, the burden of which in these instances
fell on the journalist who must conform and adapt to new structured logics. As a lead
developer on Squeezebox said: "Can't break your thing into a structure? No objects,
no flexibility" (Interview 1). Gillespie has described this distinction in terms of competing "editorial" and "algorithmic" knowledge logics (2014: 192), the former emphasising
subjective actors' expertise gaining legitimacy through their institutionalisation and
the latter built on the concretisation of procedures of automation encoded by human
operators. The emerging narrative of personalisation and efficiency being used to
frame atomisation in the BBC avoids addressing the potential conflict between these
logics. Instead, it suggests an implicit assumption that when mobilised to achieve particular PSM goals such as reaching as many people as possible, these atomised
approaches will not simultaneously undermine other PSM editorial standards and commitments, such as balance, accountability, quality and shared experience.

However, we find that the new structural elements that enable recombination of
atoms have disrupted an established balance between choice and control. Previously,
the norm in a journalistic environment was focussed around the single, linear story,
whereby the journalist has complete control over final output, including the (single)
narrative and oversight of the way it looks, and audience members have little choice
regarding how to engage with it. To obtain the benefit of more choice, journalists had
to cede some control—in the case of Squeezebox to an automated system, and in
Newsbeat Explains to the audience. Journalists trialling Squeezebox felt that automating video creation for variable lengths could be useful in instances where they had to
reformat material for different platforms, e.g., creating short social media videos, but
also felt that this automation led to a loss of control. Some journalists liked identifying
and marking-up the story with metadata to rank shots in order of importance, noting
that this made them think differently about the narrative and how their metadata
could be useful beyond this activity. However, others expressed a concern over delegating decision-making to the algorithm and losing power to influence the quality of
the final output - as they did not have oversight of all re-combinations that could be
broadcast (Technical Document 4). Whilst editors are in control of marking up the content to create parameters within which the system can make automated cuts, they
expressed concern about losing control over sequencing—for example, shots being
ordered in undesirable ways that might be jarring, or appearing out of place, or incorrect shots being chosen. As multiple versions of output become possible, the nature
of editorial control and oversight over a story changes. The importance of precise

human control for the journalists was exemplified by their tendency to "reverse engineer" the Squeezebox algorithms (Interview 1). They reverted to a trial-and-error approach, where they would go back to stories to tweak the metadata mark-up in order to achieve the desired output (Technical Document 4). This suggests a lack of trust in algorithmic decision-making when editorial quality is at stake. It can also be seen as an interesting example of a breakdown in communication between journalist and machine that highlights how critical it is to ensure that the workings of algorithmic systems can be comprehended by journalists and any decisions can be subject to scrutiny and alteration.

Looking Ahead: Reusable Media

Atomisation is framed as a process that not only has immediate benefits but also promises efficiency benefits for the future, through enabling reuse of content and information from the database(s) of atoms. For example, Newsbeat Explains would create and store ready-made building blocks such as definitions or explainers, which would be available to pull into subsequent stories that refer to the same topic. Squeezebox content could be infinitely reversioned according to different mark-up and criteria. For journalists in particular, the potential here lies in re-using the material they spend time and effort researching, gathering, verifying and editing—often currently for single use. Newsbeat Explains and Squeezebox are experiments and thus have not been rolled out across the news departments; therefore, they do not begin to build this infrastructure and fulfil this perceived benefit of efficiency through re-use. However, if these types of approaches were applied at scale alongside other related forms of atomisation being researched at the BBC, they would begin to create an extensive, rich and valuable set of data, building on existing linked data infrastructure. The benefits of in-house stores of atomised but vetted information are particularly pertinent in the public service context, which relies on trusted information that can be traced and verified.

Journalists have always referred to, referenced and cribbed from previous coverage, but these new approaches aim to increasingly structure that information, making it machine-readable, and subsequently (human) traceable, searchable and primed for application to new scenarios. Over time, this could create an extensive database (or databases) of media with metadata that stores and makes readily available "queryable" and retrievable relevant information for future stories. It could become a "living archive," created to be in regular use and updating with metadata every time an atom is reused[6]. A lead developer pointed out that the BBC's object-based and atomised work currently involves "advanced branching playlists of content," where programmers "author paths through a graph of content explicitly in terms of sequencing media," rather than "a semantic structure in which content lives" (Interview 1). However, looking ahead, he said he expects ultimately that people trying to construct stories using these types of production tools will need to think of structure first—i.e., "think structure before/as you write/film" (Interview 1). Discussing future paths, he said "We've thought about adding semantic structure through tagging, but I think the structure itself representing the semantics is far more powerful … So, our structuring is too literal at the moment - but it's a starting point." In evaluation discussions, developers expressed hope that their findings will "pave the way to more radical propositions" (Technical Document 5).

Discussion–Implications for Public Service Journalism

Personalisation and efficiency were the two narratives being used to situate atomised news within the BBC's journalism. However, research into the functioning of the two prototypes indicates the limitations of such narratives for understanding the reality of the approaches—at least at the trial stage. Far from personalising, Newsbeat Explains enabled a limited degree of customisation by giving audience members more choice over the depth of a story and the route through it. And rather than save time and resources, Squeezebox necessitated increased effort and time for adding metadata, as well as checking, and sometimes tweaking, output. However, to understand the potential implications of such approaches writ large, it is necessary to take a step back from the detail of these trials and consider how the broader social and technical construction of atomisation can be understood in relation to public service obligations and aspirations.

The traditional singular, linear, and story-centric approach that has dominated public service broadcasting to date has fitted with the notion of journalism as a collective statement to a general public. Adapting, customising, and in future personalising the news, however, individualises information, which raises concerns for the established notion of shared and universal experience. Creating "flexible" news narratives to cater for audiences' preferences is intended to offer them greater choice in how they receive news in order to make it more inclusive. It could afford some unquestionable benefits, for instance enabling varying levels of depth and detail of news for audiences with differing levels of interest in, or knowledge of, a topic, or greater accessibility (see Leonard 2015). This ability to adapt news to serve differing levels of interest and knowledge could help PSM better accomplish a universal offering, enabling a wider public to access shared news stories and knowledge about current affairs. However, it could also result in over-catering to individual preferences and thus undermine PSM values around universality of information and diversity. As Bennet (2018) reminds us, choice has been a defining characteristic and "lynchpin" of the marketisation of the media. Choice, he argues, is attached to the ideology of empowering the audience to choose media and content to suit their own needs and desires. However, PSM exist to provide a universal offering and equality of access to information, which individualised approaches that cater to market dynamics could threaten. Furthermore, the legitimacy of BBC news has traditionally rested on the audience's trust that it is the output of a "professional" production process based around journalists' application of "expert" judgement informed by a web of commitments to values including impartiality, objectivity and accuracy. In these trials, this judgement was increasingly entangled with automated decisions as elements of content composition and sequencing were delegated to machines. One prevailing understanding of data-driven, automated and algorithmic technologies views them as more "objective" than humans and considers them as deriving from this a legitimacy in knowledge generation not available to journalists. From this perspective, the recording, recombining and reuse made possible by atomisation could bolster a key measure of public service news by feeding into mythologies of "algorithmic objectivity". However, this exists in tension with belief in the importance of "tacit elements of professional judgement" to journalistic authority (Carlson 2018, 1760), some of which may be sacrificed for the benefit of scaling the news into multiple versions. It is yet to be seen, however, if an increase in algorithmic judgement would correspond to a "decline in the authority of human judgement" (Carlson 2015, 429).

Atomisation is perceived primarily as a new way to respond to an old pressure, i.e., targeting individual preferences in order to appeal to a mass populace. This could develop in ways that have wider public appeal and help people access news but may simultaneously change important aspects of public service journalism that are valued as being its cornerstone. Atomisation has been shown to alter journalistic practice by requiring journalists to think beyond natural language and conceive of the news in ways that allow it to be encoded as machine-readable data. This suggests that if taken to grander scales and further extremes, atomising the news could, as Caswell argues (2018), result in an "emergent language" communicating and configuring the news.

Conclusion

In this study, we found that atomised news is a growing field of innovation at the BBC and makes up part of a broader research agenda around structured journalism and object-based approaches to media. We anticipate this will incrementally bring important changes to the socio-technical infrastructure underpinning BBC News that increase the amount and importance of structured data for journalism. In an increasingly data-centric information environment, understanding how influential organisations like the BBC are interpreting this challenge and building this capacity into the news production infrastructure is vital. The BBC is experimenting with atomised approaches to news production and delivery through journalist-facing production tools and audience-facing formats. These technologies of atomisation are being framed through narratives of personalisation and efficiency, driven by objectives of saving time and effort whilst increasing choice. These are all features common across the media industry, which suggests that the extent to which public service commitments have explicitly shaped the development of atomisation is limited. Through analysis of two examples, we identified three distinctive characteristics of atomised approaches that have implications for journalism—recording, recombining and re-use—drawing out some of the opportunities and challenges raised by the approach in a public service context. Newsbeat Explains and Squeezebox highlight the promise of news that is more scalable and flexible, achieved through new processes of recording, recombination and re-use. The implications for journalists' working practices and the nature of the news produced can be viewed through two emergent themes—writing for machines and (in)flexible systems at scale. The structured processes characteristic of atomised approaches to news can provide more choice for audiences but require journalists to "write for machines" by inscribing inflexible structure as well as delegate elements of control to computational processes.

One of the fundamental perceived benefits of atomisation and structured journalism is turning news work into a corpus of re-usable information or a "living archive," but this was not exemplified by the two cases studied. While the BBC's work in atomised news, and structured journalism more broadly, remains in an experimental phase, the growing portfolio of technologies and techniques for atomisation is building the organisation's capabilities and infrastructure for responding to datafication and the growing need for new forms of computational journalism. Beyond the cases studied, this can be seen in the BBC's first successful live trial of "semi-automated" news production from structured data in 2019. This trial reported that "it can be uncomfortable for journalists to see their craft deconstructed into algorithmically assembled blocks" (BBC News Labs 2019). Changes to technical artefacts, social arrangements, and the relationship between them have wide-reaching consequences for news production that can persist and shape journalism. This study's findings are of significance for what they indicate about how particular changes to a news organisation's socio-technical infrastructure—in this case the BBC—can contribute to shaping the nature of its journalism. We see atomised approaches building from, and simultaneously changing, journalistic practices, norms and values and challenging embedded notions of journalistic expertise and legitimacy. Similar themes have been found in socio-technical studies of changing contexts of journalism (Carlson 2015, 2018; Lewis and Usher 2014, 2016, Nielsen 2012) and are further confirmed here.

Atomised and structured approaches to journalism are becoming more central to, and have the disruptive ability to be transformative of, journalism at the BBC and beyond. However, the challenges for public service journalism go far beyond those of technical viability that are currently the priority for research and development. This paper has shown how employing a socio-technical approach to identify relevant human actors and technical actants in innovation activities (Lewis and Westlund 2015a) can help to explicate the implications of new ways of working and associated tensions that may arise. However, there is a need for deeper understanding of the interplay between editorial and technical logics when content creation is distributed between such data-driven, automated and algorithmic systems (actants) and journalists and technologists (actors). Further research is needed in this area, and we suggest it should specifically address: (a) mapping further examples of atomised and structured journalism to develop an understanding of the spectrum of applications, and theorising where the boundaries of these approaches lie—work already underway by Caswell (2018); (b) considering the politics of structured or atomised journalism in terms of how news is represented as atoms and metadata; and (c) the implications of this, including how power may be re-distributed between journalists and automated systems and the implications for PSM, specifically how they balance the different imperatives of these approaches, including "writing for machines," flexible composition and re-use, with their core values such as reach, universality, distinctiveness, diversity, independence, trust, transparency and accountability.

Notes

1. Where journalists, developers, data scientists and partners work together at the intersection of journalism, technology and data to explore opportunities for public service journalism.

2. IP Studio: Making programmes using Internet technology https://www.bbc.co.uk/rd/projects/ip-studio
3. BBC News still invests more than 50% of its budget in linear television, about 40% in radio, and 7% in online media, according to its former director of news and current affairs, James Harding, in January 2016 (Rigby 2016), whilst in 2015, 41% of UK respondents named television their main source of news, 10% radio, and 38% online media (Newman et al. 2015).
4. Author one is a Senior Researcher in BBC R&D and author two is a BBC Journalist.
5. R&D have just completed a project called "#newnews" which looked into how news stories might be reinvented through experimentation with adaptive and personalised prototypes. The project is not explicitly identified as part of the atomised strand of work but presents key characteristics of the atomised approach outlined in other BBC projects and prototypes.
6. It should be noted that the BBC does not view this as equating to a desire to create a sort of encyclopaedia of human knowledge; rather, its aim is to better input, organise, interrogate and showcase BBC content as well as support its public service editorial priorities.

Acknowledgements

We would like to acknowledge the help of the BBC, where both authors are employed and in particular the team at BBC News Labs.

The authors gratefully acknowledge comments on this paper from anonymous review and special issue editors Seth Lewis, Neil Thurman and Jessica Kunert.

Disclosure statement

In accordance with Taylor & Francis policy and our ethical obligation as researchers, we are reporting that we are both employed by the BBC, which may be affected by the research reported in the enclosed paper. I have disclosed those interests fully to Taylor & Francis, and I have in place an approved plan for managing any potential conflicts arising from this employment.

Funding

No grants were used to support this research.

ORCID

Rhianne Jones ⓘ https://orcid.org/0000-0002-8749-9953
Bronwyn Jones ⓘ http://orcid.org/0000-0003-2482-5181

References

Adair, Bill. 2014. "Creating new forms of journalism that put readers in charge." *Poynter*. https://www.poynter.org/news/creating-new-forms-journalism-put-readers-charge.
Anderson, C. W. 2015. "Between the Unique and the Pattern: Historical Tensions in our Understanding of Quantitative Journalism." *Digital Journalism* 3 (3): 349–363.
Anderson, C. W. 2018. *Apostles of Uncertainty. Data Journalism and the Politics of Doubt*. New York: Oxford University Press.

Anderson, C. W. and D. Caswell. 2018. Computational Journalism. In *The International Encyclopedia of Journalism Studies*, edited by T. Vos and F. Hanusch. Hoboken, NJ: Wiley-Blackwell.

Baym, N. K. 2013. "Data not seen, the uses and shortcomings of social media metrics." *First Monday* 18 (10).

BBC News Labs. n.d. "Atomised News Project." *BBC R&D*. Accessed July 26. http://bbcnewslabs.co.uk/projects/atomised-news/.

BBC News Labs. 2015. "A Manifesto for Structured Journalism". *BBC R&D*. Accessed April 24, 2019. http://bbcnewslabs.co.uk/2015/07/07/a-manifesto-for-structured-journalism.

BBC News Labs. 2019. "Stories by Numbers: Experimenting with Semi-automated Journalism". *BBC R&D*. Accessed March 22, 2019. http://bbcnewslabs.co.uk/2019/03/22/stories-by-numbers/.

BBC R&D. 2014a. "Elastic News. Exploring variable depth experiences on mobile to deepen users' understanding of a story". *BBC R&D*. Accessed April 24, 2019. https://www.bbc.co.uk/rd/projects/elastic-news

BBC R&D. 2014b. "Snackable News: Short-form video news stories". *BBC R&D*. Accessed April 24, 2019. https://www.bbc.co.uk/rd/projects/sna

Bennet, James. 2018. "Public Service Algorithms." In *A Future for Public Service Television*, edited by Des Freedman and Vana Goblot. London, UK: Goldsmiths Press.

Boczkowski, Pablo. 2004. "The Mutual Shaping of Technology and Society in Videotex Newspapers: Beyond the Diffusion and Social Shaping Perspectives." *The Information Society* 20: 255–267. https://doi.org/10.1080/01972240490480947

Brehmer, Matthew, Stephen Ingram, Jonathan Stray, and Tamara Munzner. 2014. Overview: The Design, Adoption, and Analysis of a Visual Document Mining Tool for Investigative Journalists. *IEEE Transactions on Visualization and Computer Graphics* 20 (12): 2271–2280.

Broussard, Meredith. 2014. "Artificial Intelligence for Investigative Reporting: Using an Expert System to Enhance Journalists' Ability to Discover Original Public Affairs Stories." *Digital Journalism* (online first).

Bucher, Taina. 2018. If … Then: Algorithmic Power and Politics. New York, NY: Oxford University Press.

Carlson, Matt. 2015. "The Robotic Reporter. Automated journalism and the redefinition of labor, compositional forms, and journalistic authority." *Digital Journalism* 3 (3): 416–431,

Carlson, Matt. 2018. "Automating Judgement? Algorithmic Judgement, News Knowledge and Journalistic Professionalism." *New Media and Society* 20 (5): 1755–1772. DOI: 10.1177/1461444817706684.

Caswell, David. 2015. "Structured Narratives as a Framework for Journalism: A Work in Progress." *Computational Models of Narrative* 2015, Atlanta, GA, USA.

Caswell, David. 2018. "Structured Journalism and the Semantic Units of News." Automation, Algorithms and News: An International Conference, Ludwig Maximilians Universität, Munich.

Caswell, David and Konstantin Dörr. 2017. "Automated Journalism 2.0: Event-driven narratives." *Journalism Practice* 12 (4): 477–496.

Chua, Reg. 2010. "So what is this Structured Journalism thing anyway? (Re)Structuring Journalism: Rethinking journalism and the business of journalism from the ground up. *Blog* https://structureofnews.wordpress.com/2010/08/12/structured-journalism/

Coddington, Mark. 2015. "Clarifying Journalism's Quantitative Turn." *Digital Journalism* 3 (3): 331–348,

de Vreese, Claes. 2005. "News framing: Theory and typology." *Information Design Journal + Document Design* 13 (1): 51–62. https://claesdevreese.files.wordpress.com/2015/09/devreese_2005_2.pdf

Diakopoulos, Nick. 2015. "Algorithmic Accountability." *Digital Journalism* 3 (3): 398–415.

Dörr, Konstantin. 2015. "Mapping the field of Algorithmic Journalism." *Digital Journalism* 700–722.

EBU. 2015. "Public Service Media Contribution to Society". *Media intelligence Service of the European Broadcasting Union*. https://www.ebu.ch/psm-contribution-society

Ekström, Mats. 2002. "Epistemologies of TV Journalism: A Theoretical Framework." *Journalism* 3 (3): 259–282.

Gillespie, Tarleton. 2014. "The Relevance of Algorithms." In *Media Technologies. Paths Forward in Social Research*, edited by Tarleton Gillespie, Pablo Boczkowski, and Kirsten Foot, 167–194. London, UK: MIT Press.

Gillespie, Tarleton, Pablo Boczkowski, and Kirsten Foot, eds. 2014. *Media Technologies. Paths Forward in Social Research*. London, UK: MIT Press.

Hall, Tony. 2017. "Tony Hall's speech at the launch of the Annual Plan for 2017/18." BBC website. Accessed April 24, 2019. http://www.bbc.co.uk/mediacentre/speeches/2017/tony-hall-annual-plan#heading-a-personalised-uniquely-tailored-bbc

Helberger, Natali. 2015. "Merely Facilitating or Actively Stimulating Diverse Media Choices? Public Service Media at the Crossroad." *International Journal of Communication* 9: 1324–1340.

Hendy, David. 2013. *Public Service Broadcasting*. Basingstoke: Palgrave Macmillan.

Holovaty, Adrian. 2006. "A fundamental way newspaper sites need to change." *Blog Post*. September. http://www.holovaty.com/writing/fundamental-change/

Kennedy, Helen. 2016. *Post, Mine Repeat. Social Media Mining Become Ordinary*. London, UK: Palgrave Macmillan.

Kennedy, Helen. 2018. "Living with Data: Aligning Data Studies and Data Activism Through a Focus on Everyday Experiences of Datafication." *Krisis* 1: 18–28.

Leonard, Max. 2015. Forecaster: Our Experimental Object-based weather forecast BBC R&D Blog. Accessed April 24, 2019. https://www.bbc.co.uk/rd/blog/2015-11-forecaster-our-experimental-object-based-weather-forecast.

Lewis, Seth C., Ed. 2015. "Journalism in an Era of Big Data: Cases, Concepts, and Critiques" [Special Issue]. Digital Journalism 3 (3).

Lewis, Seth C., Andrea Guzman, and Schmidt, Thomas. 2019. "Automation, Journalism, and Human-Machine Communication: Rethinking Roles and Relationships of Humans and Machines in News". *Digital Journalism* 1–19.

Lewis, Seth C., and Nikki Usher. 2013. "Open Source and Journalism: Toward New Frameworks for Imagining News Innovation." *Media, Culture & Society* 35 (5): 602–619.

Lewis, Seth C., and Nikki Usher. 2014. Code, Collaboration, and the Future of Journalism: A case study of the Hacks/Hackers global network." *Digital Journalism* 2 (3): 383–393. http://dx.doi.org/10.1080/21670811.2014.895504

Lewis, Seth C., and Nikki Usher. 2016. "Trading zones, boundary objects, and the pursuit of news innovation: A case study of journalists and programmers." *Convergence: The International Journal of Research into New Media Technologies* 22 (5): 543–560.

Lewis, Seth C., and Oscar Westlund. 2015a. "Actors, Actants, Audiences, and Activities in Cross-Media News Work." *Digital Journalism* 3 (1): 19–37.

Lewis, Seth C., and Oscar Westlund. 2015b. "Big Data and Journalism: Epistemology, expertise, economics, and ethics." *Digital Journalism 3* (3): 447–466.

Lievrouw, Leah, and Sonia Livingstone, eds. 2006. *Handbook of New Media: Social Shaping and Social Consequences – Fully Revised Student Edition*. London, UK: Sage.

McBride, Kelly, and B. Rosenstiel Thomas. 2013. *The New Ethics of Journalism: Principles for the 21st Century*. Los Angeles, CA: CQ Press.

Napoli, Philip. 2014. "Automated Media: An Institutional Theory Perspective on Algorithmic Media Production and Consumption." *Communication Theory* 24: 340–360

Neff, Gina. 2015. "Learning from documents: Applying new theories of materiality to journalism." *Journalism* 16 (1): 74–78. https://doi.org/10.1177/1464884914549294

Newman, Nic, David Levy, and Rasmus Kleis Nielsen. 2015. *Reuters Institute Digital News Report 2015: Tracking the Future of News*. Oxford, UK: Reuters Institute for the Study of Journalism.

Nielsen, Rasmus Kleis. 2012. "How Newspapers Began to Blog: Recognizing the role of technologists in old media organizations' development of new media technologies". *Information, Communication, and Society* 15 (6): 959–978.

Rigby, Elizabeth. 2016. "Head of BBC news signals big cuts ahead". *Times.co.uk* http://www.thetimes.co.uk/tto/news/medianews/article4660737.ece

Sehl, Annika, Alessio Cornia, and Rasmus Kleis Nielsen. 2018. Public Service News and Social Media. Digital News Report 2018. *Reuters institute for the Study of Journalism*. https://reutersin-stitute.politics.ox.ac.uk/sites/default/files/2018-03/sehl_et_al_1803_FINAL_0.pdf

Sehl, Annika, Alessio Cornia, and Rasmus Kleis Nielsen. 2017. Developing Digital News in Public Service Media. Digital News Project 2017." Reuters institute for the Study of Journalism. https://reutersinstitute.politics.ox.ac.uk/sites/default/files/2017-09/Sehl%2C%20Developing%20 Digital%20News%20in%20Public%20Service%20Media.pdf

Sehl, Annika, Alessio Cornia, and Rasmus Kleis Nielsen. 2016. "Public Service News and Digital Media. Digital News Project 2016." *Reuters Institute for the Study of Journalism*. https://reuter-sinstitute.politics.ox.ac.uk/sites/default/files/PublicServiceNewsandDigitalMedia.pdf.

Sørensen, Jannick and Hutchinson Jonathan. 2018. "Algorithms and Public Service Media". In *Public Service Media in the Networked Society*, edited by Gregory Ferrell Lowe, Hilde Van den Bulck, and Karen Donders. Göteborg: Nordicom.

Van Dijck, José, and Thomas Poell. 2015. "Making Public Television Social? Public Service Broadcasting and the Challenges of Social Media." *Television & New Media* 16 (2): 148–164.

Van den Bulck, Hilde and Hallvard Moe. 2017. "Public service media, universality and personalisa-tion through algorithms: mapping strategies and exploring dilemmas." *Media, Culture and Society* 1–18.

Van Es, Karen. 2017. "An Impending Crisis of Imagination Data-Driven Personalization in Public Service Broadcasters." *Media@LSE Working Papers* 43: 1–18. https://dspace.library.uu.nl/han-dle/1874/358206.

Young, Mary Lynn and Alfred Hermida. 2015. "From Mr. and Mrs. Outlier to Central Tendencies: Computational Journalism and Crime Reporting at the Los Angeles Times." *Digital Journalism* 3 (3): 381–397.

Westlund, Oscar, and Seth C. Lewis. 2014. "The Agents of Media Innovation Activities: Actors, Actants, and Audiences." *Journal of Media Innovations* 1 (2).

Zambrini, Barbara. 2017. 'Mobile-First News for Young People - Our Findings from Newsbeat Explains'. *BBC R&D Blog*. Accessed April 24, 2019. https://www.bbc.co.uk/rd/blog/2017-05-newsbeat-atomised-news-youth-research.

Towards a Design Orientation on Algorithms and Automation in News Production

Nicholas Diakopoulos (iD)

ABSTRACT
This essay responds to the articles in the special issue on "Algorithms, Automation, and News" by reflecting on two thematic threads apparent in the collection: (1) the role of journalistic values in technology, and (2) the hybridization of human and machine effort in news production workflows. I argue that to make further progress in these areas journalism studies should establish a design orientation towards journalistic technology, and seek to develop rigorous evaluation criteria and metrics that can help propel both scholarship and practice forward.

This past July the New York Times published an article about the future of autonomous vehicles entitled, "Despite High Hopes, Self-Driving Cars Are 'Way in the Future'" (Boudette 2019). Mainstream journalists were finally seriously reckoning with the reality that building self-driving cars was not going to be quite so easy after all. This type of cycle is common for technology: a new and shiny widget or advance in method is over-promised, it's hyped by the media, expectations go way up—and then, usually, the bubble pops and expectations come back to earth. Gartner (n.d.) calls the aftermath the "trough of disillusionment", which proceeds for some time before giving way to a "slope of enlightenment" as advances in efficiency are realized from the true capabilities of the technology in a final "plateau of productivity".

This special issue on "Algorithms, Automation, and News" comes at a time when we're in the process of transitioning through the "trough of disillusionment" period for these technologies in the domain of journalism. Several of the articles in this volume (Stray 2019; Ford and Hutchinson 2019; Jones and Jones, 2019a) deepen critiques of earlier technological exuberance by nuancing the capabilities and limitations of computational approaches for various journalistic use cases, from investigative journalism to chatbots. The articles here offer hints at why algorithmic news production is so hard, and ultimately how we can advance the field.

In this essay I hope to act as a sort of guide through this transition period, reflecting on some of the grand challenges to making algorithms, automation, and AI productive for journalism, as well as pointing out how the research endeavor might address these challenges by adopting a design orientation. I'll start by elaborating two major themes that appear throughout this edited collection, and which were (perhaps not coincidentally) important themes in my recent book, *Automating the News: How Algorithms are Rewriting the Media* (Diakopoulos 2019). These are (1) the role of journalistic values in technology, and (2) the hybridization of human and machine effort in news production workflows. Next I'll unpack these a bit further before offering some thoughts on where researchers can go from here to advance a design science of journalistic technology.

Journalistic Values

Journalism can be construed in a number of ways: as a practice, a profession, a business, an institution, a social field, an ideology, and probably some other ways too. Here I lean on the ideological view of journalism, which emphasizes shared beliefs in journalism about the importance of values like public service, objectivity, autonomy, immediacy, and ethics (Deuze 2005). Such commitments are reflected in the myriad aspirational codes of practice and ethics in the field. What is interesting about automation, algorithms, and AI is that they also serve to embed and encode the values of their designers and developers (Shilton 2018), and so offer a new medium for the expression of journalistic values, norms, and ethics. But this raises a crucial question: as these technologies are designed and developed, whose values come to be reflected in those designs? If journalists are not able to embed their own values, alternative values from stakeholders outside the field, such as non-journalistic media companies and platforms, may well fill the gap (Ananny and Crawford 2015).

Several of the articles in this collection explore the terrain of how journalistic values come to be embedded into algorithmic and automated approaches to news production. Milosavljević and Vobič (2019) outline the evolution of professional values in light of automation and consider tensions that arise with core values such as objectivity, autonomy, timeliness, ethics, and public service as automation technologies are implemented at news organizations. To take one example, the implementation of personalization may come into conflict with public service values by creating the conditions for a loss of shared context amongst news consumers. But negotiating such conflicts can lead to new logics of personalization that align the capabilities of the technology with the values and business models of a particular news organization (Bodó, 2019). Instead of adopting the version of an algorithm developed for use in another industry, news organizations may instead benefit by designing and building the technology themselves so that it better aligns their values with the implementation of the technology.

These values issues—including tensions and alignments—and how they are inscribed in technology are made salient in a variety of applications of automation explored in this collection, including in newsbots and their ability to operate in line with public service values (Ford and Hutchinson 2019; Jones and Jones, 2019a), investigative journalism and the importance of defining news values for identifying leads in data (Stray 2019), algorithmic curation systems and their alignment with democratic goals (Helberger 2019), and structured journalism and its potential to support

evidentiary value and boost trust (Caswell 2019). Professionally core ideas such as journalistic objectivity may indeed be furthered through the "mechanical objectivity" of
algorithms and automation (Carlson 2019). But just as with earlier appeals to such
objectivity around practices like photojournalism, we must recognize that the consist-
ency of an algorithmic process must not be confused with its inherently and deeply
sociotechnical nature. Engineers and designers of journalistic algorithms may well
need to don the mantle of professionalism, with commitments to steward the values
of journalism through the technologies they build. In other words, they too should be
professionalized into the field.

Hybrid Workflows and Practices

Human journalists still have some essential competitive advantages over algorithmic
and automated approaches to news production. They're more flexible and adaptable
to a rapidly changing world. They can exhibit creativity both in the types of stories
they find and in the expression of those stories as compelling narratives. And they can
gain access to important information that isn't digitized or otherwise accessible to
a machine. Some experts estimate that only about 15% of a reporter's job and about
9% of an editor's job could be automated using current levels of AI technology
(Manyika et al. 2017). Rather than substituting for journalists, these technologies are
more likely to *complement* human work by increasing its quality and efficiency
(Diakopoulos 2019). In the domain of journalism algorithms rarely operate at a level of
full autonomy; instead, they operate as mutually enhancing symbiotes with journalists.

As a result, algorithmic news production oftentimes creates new types of work for
people. For instance, human workers may need to populate data or knowledge sources, configure systems, or supervise and maintain the automation (Lindén et al. 2019).
In practice, what we see over and over again is a hybridization of algorithms with
human effort—people must do new types of work to fully realize the value of the
automation. For instance, Ford and Hutchinson (2019) examine how an automated
newsbot is really the result of careful human setup where a range of key editorial
decisions made at design time allow the bot to engage in interactions with end-users.
Monitoring and supervising bots to ensure high quality must also still be done by people, and can even lead to new roles such as the "Bot Development Producer" introduced at the BBC (Jones and Jones, 2019a). In the domain of structured journalism,
new tasks of "writing" for machines emerge as journalists datafy stories into units that
can be recomposed and re-used on the fly by the algorithm (Jones and Jones, 2019b).

As journalism and machines come to work together in hybrid workflows a central
concern is how people can continue to exert *control* over the algorithm. Oftentimes
with automated systems, control is limited and indirect—typically mediated through
metadata—which can frustrate people used to direct point-and-click styles of interaction where an action has an immediate and visible impact on an outcome. If direct
control is not offered, people may resort to "gaming" the algorithm to get it to do
what they want (Jones and Jones, 2019b; Diakopoulos 2019). Many of these challenges
boil down to questions of human–computer interaction, a field which journalism

studies scholars should engage and collaborate with further as they seek to under-stand how hybrid workflows impact journalistic practices (Aitamurto et al. 2019).

Looking Ahead: Design and Evaluation

Whether we're talking about values in technology or the evolution of hybrid work-flows the role of *design* is paramount. Journalism studies scholars who want to pursue questions of automation and algorithms with outcomes relevant to advancing the practice of journalism should strive to adopt a design orientation. How can news algo-rithms be designed to reflect particular journalistic values? How does the design of a news automation system impact the user experience of reporters or editors in a hybrid workflow? And how do various algorithmic news interface designs impact the recep-tion of information by the public? If we shift our perspective to consider how technol-ogies could be designed, we can envisage journalism as a field that has its values implemented in the technology, rather than a field simply subjected to the values implemented in technologies by others. Helberger (2019) perhaps comes closest in this collection with the idea of "diversity-sensitive design" which sets the stage for thinking about how algorithmic curators could be designed to support different visions of democracy. Of course there is still much work to do in reifying those ideas. A design orientation in journalism studies would mean an increased emphasis on studying how the artifacts of algorithms and automation can be created to support journalistic goals. Articles in this genre would strive to articulate *design guidelines* based on human-centered studies of technology in use. An industry still struggling to adapt might begin to look at scholarship with renewed interest as it strives for that "plateau of productivity" in employing algorithms and automation in news production.

A pragmatic envisioning of a design science for journalistic technology goes hand in hand with developing evaluation methods and metrics that are appropriate. How should we measure the alignment of technical implementations with organizational goals and values? How should we go about reliably and comparably measuring the cost-effectiveness of AI in investigative journalism? Do the more intimate conversa-tional styles expressed by chatbots truly induce trust in a quantifiably measurable way? Jones and Jones (2019a) in this collection clearly articulated the problem when, reflecting on their study of newsbots at the BBC, they wrote, "Across the case studies there was no systematic gathering of comparable statistics, comprehensive application of analytics or common instruments for measuring success, meaning evaluation lacked common criteria for deciding whether a bot experiment was successful and whether it had public value." Scholars that seek to support a design agenda for journalism tech-nology should seek to research, develop, and validate rigorous evaluation criteria that allow the field—both in scholarship and practice— to move past simplistic notions of clicks and engagement. If algorithms and automation are to be optimized for journal-istic purposes they must be fed the appropriate metrics. What then are the metrics which reflect a journalism built to support the public interest?

Disclosure statement

No potential conflict of interest was reported by the author.

ORCID

Nicholas Diakopoulos (iD) http://orcid.org/0000-0001-5005-6123

References

Aitamurto, T., M. Ananny, C. W. Anderson, L. Birnbaum, N. Diakopoulos, M. Hanson, J. Hullman, N. Ritchie. 2019. HCI for accurate, impartial and transparent journalism: Challenges and solutions. Workshop at the CHI Conference. https://dl.acm.org/citation.cfm?id=3299007

Ananny, M., and K. Crawford. 2015. "A Liminal Press: Situating News App Designers within a Field of Networked News Production." *Digital Journalism* 3 (2): 192–208.

Bodó, Balázs. 2019. "Selling News to Audiences – a Qualitative Inquiry into the Emerging Logics of Algorithmic News Personalization in European Quality News Media." *Digital Journalism*.

Boudette, Neal. 2019. *Despite High Hopes, Self-Driving Cars Are 'Way in the Future'*. New York Times, 17 July. https://www.nytimes.com/2019/07/17/business/self-driving-autonomous-cars.html

Carlson, Matt. 2019. "News Algorithms, Photojournalism and the Assumption of Mechanical Objectivity in Journalism." *Digital Journalism*.

Caswell, David. 2019. "Structured Journalism and the Semantic Units of News." *Digital Journalism*.

Deuze, M. 2005. "What Is Journalism?: Professional Identity and Ideology of Journalists Reconsidered." *Journalism* 6 (4): 442–64.

Diakopoulos, N. 2019. *Automating the News: How Algorithms Are Rewriting the Media*. Cambridge, MA: Harvard University Press.

Ford, Heather, and Jonathon Hutchinson. 2019. "Newsbots That Mediate Journalist and Audience Relationships." *Digital Journalism*.

Gartner, n.d. Hype Cycle. https://www.gartner.com/en/research/methodologies/gartner-hype-cycle

Helberger, Natali. 2019. "On the Democratic Role of News Recommenders." *Digital Journalism*.

Jones, Bronwyn, and Rhianne Jones. 2019a. "Public Service Chatbots: Automating Conversation with BBC News." *Digital Journalism*.

Jones, Rhianne, and Bronwyn Jones. 2019b. "Atomising the News: The (in)Flexibility of Structured Journalism." *Digital Journalism*.

Lindén, C.-G., H. Tuulonen, A. Bäck, N. Diakopoulos, M. Granroth-Wilding, L. Haapanen, et al. 2019. News automation: The rewards, risks and realities of 'machine journalism'. Retrieved from World Association of Newspapers and News Publishers website: http://anp.cl/wp-content/uploads/2019/03/WAN-IFRA_News_Automation.pdf.

Manyika, J., M. Chui, M. Miremadi, J. Bughin, K. George, P. Willmott, and M. Dewhurst. 2017. Harnessing automation for a future that works. Report from McKinsey Global Institute website: https://www.mckinsey.com/featured-insights/digital-disruption/harnessing-automation-for-a-future-that-works

Milosavljević, Marko, and Igor Vobič. 2019. "Human Still in the Loop: Editors Reconsider the Ideals of Professional Journalism Through Automation." *Digital Journalism*.

Shilton, K. 2018. "Values and Ethics in Human-Computer Interaction." *Foundations and Trends® in Human–Computer Interaction* 12 (2): 107–71.

Stray, Jonathan. 2019. "Making Artificial Intelligence Work for Investigative Journalism." *Digital Journalism*. doi:10.1080/21670811.2019.1630289.

Prioritizing the Audience's View of Automation in Journalism

Andrea L. Guzman

ABSTRACT
This commentary for the special issue on the automation of journalism highlights the progress made in this area of study before advocating for researchers to pay greater attention to the audience and its perceptions of the technologies of automation, including algorithms, artificial intelligence, chatbots, recommender and personalization systems, and automated news-writing software.

In reading through the articles for this special issue as well as surveying the growing number of books, journal articles, industry think pieces, and general news stories related to the automation of journalism, I am in awe of just how far this and related areas of study have progressed within less than a decade. When I first began teaching about algorithms and automated news-writing programs in my journalism and communication courses, I barely had enough material to cover one lesson, and most of that research came from outside of journalism studies and communication. Now, a growing number of communication and journalism scholars, myself included, teach entire courses in artificial intelligence and the automation of journalism that are built around emerging research from within the discipline.

Presentations regarding algorithms and the automation of journalism, and the integration of artificial intelligence into communication, also used to be few and far between at journalism and communication conferences; however, as this special issue demonstrates, the importance of and interest in these areas warrant stand-alone conferences. The study of algorithms and automation in journalism is no longer considered niche; within professional organizations in journalism and communication, this research is routinely included in conference sessions, and the study of people's communication with technology more broadly has been acknowledged through the recent formation of the Human-Machine Communication Interest Group as part of the International Communication Association (https://www.icahdq.org/group/hmc). The number of publications regarding the automation of journalism also has grown (Lewis, Guzman, and Schmidt 2019).

There is also a greater sense that the technologies automating aspects of journalism will have staying power, instead of being a technological fad. Five years ago, an editor at a large newspaper chain in the Chicago area chastised me for discussing automated news-writing software at a forum for journalists and journalism students. My transgression, according to them, was discussing a technology that was likely to have only limited use and the mention of which would only "scare" journalism students. It is true that the integration of artificial intelligence and automated technologies into journalism has sparked a range of reactions and reflections, not only in students, as I have observed in my own courses, but also in journalists (e.g., Carlson 2015; Thurman, Dörr, and Kunert 2017). However, the roles of both journalists and machines in the production and distribution of news have simultaneously evolved in a way that is more complex than the presumed displacement of human labor, as articles in this special issue demonstrate (particularly Milosavljević and Vobič 2019) and other scholars and practitioners have explained (e.g., Broussard 2018; Bucher 2017; Diakopoulos 2019; Marconi, Siegman, and Machine Journalist 2017; Wu, Tandoc, and Salmon 2019).

The study of the automation of journalism has continued to progress as the technologies in question and their integration into media industries have continued to evolve. Scholars and journalists have barely had time to make sense of one technological innovation before another has emerged. The articles in this special issue address news algorithms generally (e.g., Carlson 2019; Milosavljević and Vobič 2019) and within the context of recommender and personalization systems (e.g., Bodó 2019; Helberger 2019); software employed in structured journalism (e.g., Caswell 2019; Jones and Jones 2019b); chatbots, also referred to as "newsbots" (e.g., Ford and Hutchinson 2019; Jones and Jones 2019a); and AI programs that automate aspects of story-telling or sift through data (e.g., Stray 2019). There is no one way in which algorithms and automation affect journalism; there are many.

Within the span of a relatively few years, then, scholars and practitioners have made important advances in the study of the latest wave of technological innovation within journalism. The question that follows is how scholars can build upon this initial research to continue moving it forward toward an ever-more sophisticated understanding of the many facets of journalism in relation to algorithms, AI, and automation. Here I will briefly focus on one area of study regarding the automation of journalism that remains relatively less developed than other areas – the audience and consumers' views of technologies of automation within journalism.

My argument is not that the audience has been entirely overlooked within this emerging body of scholarship. As demonstrated by the articles in this special issue, scholars have taken the audience into consideration to varying degrees dependent upon the journalistic process being automated and the specific technology of automation being employed. For example, news recommendation and personalization software delivers news tailored to individuals. Research regarding these programs necessarily involves, or at least evokes, the audience, including how the audience is "configured" in algorithmic journalism (Anderson 2011) as newsrooms tailor technologies to a particular view of the audience (e.g., Bodó 2019) and how these technologies may impact audience members' engagement in society (e.g., Helberger 2019). Scholars have also studied consumers' perceptions of technology that selects news for them (e.g., Sundar and Nass 2001; Thurman et al. 2019). Similarly, some studies regarding the use of chatbots in journalism have directly focused on the audience and its assessment of these digital interlocutors designed to provide a more personalized and conversational experience (e.g., Ford and Hutchinson 2019), while other studies have more indirectly taken the audience into account (e.g., Jones and Jones 2019a). Within the literature regarding automated news-writing programs, scholars have focused on audience assessments of the quality of the content produced by automated programs (e.g., Clerwall 2014; Graefe et al. 2018; Jung et al. 2017; Van der Kaa and Krahmer 2014; Wölker and Powell 2018) as well as audience members' judgments of specific attributes of machine authors (e.g., Liu and Wei 2019; Waddell 2018).

In commenting on these studies within the context of the epistemic authority of algorithms, Carlson (2019) remarks that "few seem to question the underlying technology and its legitimacy as a creator of news content" (12). From Carlson's (2019) perspective, this research has not engaged enough with some of the more fundamental questions raised when machines step into roles previously associated with human journalists. Carlson's assessment reflects aspects of my own critique of this body of scholarship regarding the audience's view of automation in journalism.

Much of the initial scholarship regarding consumers' perceptions of automated journalism has examined their judgments of machine content, the product of the process of automated journalism, rather than the technology itself (cf., Lewis, Guzman, and Schmidt 2019). When research does directly study technology as message source, it focuses on the degree to which people associate desirable traits in human journalists, such as credibility, with machines. And so, research regarding the audience view of the automation of journalism, while important and useful, has often not directly engaged with the fundamental reason why such research is being undertaken in the first place – the fact that specific roles within the creation and distribution of news that once were associated with people are now being performed by software. In these instances, the very nature of the "communicator" has shifted from human to machine, but the larger ontological questions have not been addressed.

What is needed moving forward is a more thorough study of the various ways in which the audience may conceptualize and make sense of technologies stepping into a human role in the journalism process and what it means to the audience for machines to prioritize their news (recommender systems), to write aspects of their news (automated journalism), and to stand in for human reporters (chatbots). Fellow researchers and I have laid out what we refer to as a human-machine communication approach to the study of the automation of journalism (Lewis, Guzman, and Schmidt 2019), which has been extended to the study of AI technologies within communication more generally (Guzman and Lewis 2019). This approach provides specific theoretical and methodological guidance for future research regarding the audience's view of the automation of journalism. Because this approach is explained elsewhere, I do not discuss it in detail here except to expand upon one of its key elements critical to addressing what has been overlooked in this research thus far: better theoretical accounting for the nature of humans and machines and for the ontological shift in who or what is carrying out a specific journalistic process.

The human-machine communication approach ·to the automation of journalism breaks with long-held conceptualizations of technology as primarily a mediator of human interaction and instead theorizes specific technologies, such as automated news-writing programs and chatbots, as communicators (Lewis, Guzman, and Schmidt 2019; see Guzman 2018 for a general discussion.). The study of technology as a communicator within this approach requires consideration of the ontological nature of the software or device in question as a machine in relation to the human role it is now performing within journalism. Research has shown that people draw from their understanding of the characteristics and attributes they associate with the nature of machines in their judgment of particular technologies (e.g., Sundar 2008). People's conceptualizations of the differences and similarities between humans and machines can also inform their assessment of technology functioning as a communicator, including automated news-writing programs (Guzman In Press). Therefore, it is not theoretically adequate for scholars to extend frameworks developed around human journalists and journalism as a human process to the study of the automation of journalism without also taking into consideration the nature of the machine.

Carlson's (2019) essay within this issue provides an example of how to engage with the nature of the machine in research regarding the automation of journalism. Within the essay, Carlson draws upon the concept of "mechanical objectivity" to explore the perceived epistemic authority of algorithms within a journalism context. Carlson brings literature regarding an aspect of the nature of technology into dialogue with literature regarding aspects of the nature of journalism and of human journalists to make sense of technologies of journalism performing human-like roles. Similarly, scholars seeking to understand how the audience conceptualizes various technologies of automation and the reasoning behind these perceptions will need to pull from bodies of literature beyond journalism.

Journalism researchers have made meaningful progress in the study of algorithms and the automation of journalism, as demonstrated within the articles of this special issue. What cannot get lost in the efforts to further develop the design of these technologies and to trace their integration into and implications for the newsroom is consideration of the audience view of the automation of journalism: how audiences come to understand the programs that, increasingly, are determining what content they see, writing the stories they consume, and directly exchanging messages with them. These efforts must go beyond people's assessments of the quality of the product created during the automation process and directly examine how people understand technology within this particular communicative role, by wrestling with the nature of machines, of humans, and of journalism, even as they all continue to evolve.

References

Anderson, C. W. 2011. "Deliberative, Agonistic, and Algorithmic Audiences: Journalism's Vision of Its Public in an Age of Audience Transparency." *International Journal of Communication* 5 (11): 529–547.

Bodó, Balázs. 2019. "Selling News to Audiences – a Qualitative Inquiry into the Emerging Logics of Algorithmic News Personalization in European Quality News Media." *Digital Journalism*: 1–22. https://doi.org/10.1080/21670811.2019.1624185.

Broussard, Meredith. 2018. *Artificial Unintelligence: How Computers Misunderstand the World.* Cambridge, MA: The MIT Press.

Bucher, Taina. 2017. "Machines Don't Have Instincts': Articulating the Computational in Journalism." *New Media & Society* 19 (6): 918–933. https://doi.org/10.1177/1461444815624182.

Carlson, Matt. 2015. "The Robotic Reporter: Automated Journalism and the Redefinition of Labor." *Digital Journalism* 3 (3): 416–431. https://doi.org/10.1080/21670811.2014.976412.

Carlson, Matt. 2019. "News Algorithms, Photojournalism and the Assumption of Mechanical Objectivity in Journalism." *Digital Journalism*: 1–17. https://doi.org/10.1080/21670811.2019.1601577.

Caswell, David. 2019. "Structured Journalism and the Semantic Units of News." *Digital Journalism*: 1–23. https://doi.org/10.1080/21670811.2019.1651665.

Clerwall, Christer. 2014. "Enter the Robot Journalist: Users' Perceptions of Automated Content." *Journalism Practice* 8 (5): 519–531. https://doi.org/10.1080/17512786.2014.883116.

Diakopoulos, Nicholas. 2019. *Automating the News: How Algorithms Are Rewriting the Media.* Cambridge, MA: Harvard University Press.

Ford, Heather, and Jonathon Hutchinson. 2019. "Newsbots That Mediate Journalist and Audience Relationships." *Digital Journalism*: 1–19. https://doi.org/10.1080/21670811.2019.1626752.

Graefe, Andreas, Mario Haim, Bastian Haarmann, and Hans-Bernd Brosius. 2018. "Readers' Perception of Computer-Generated News: Credibility, Expertise, and Readability." *Journalism* 19 (5): 595–610. https://doi.org/10.1177/1464884916641269.

Guzman, Andrea L. 2018. "What Is Human-Machine Communication, Anyway?" In *Human-Machine Communication: Rethinking Communication, Technology, and Ourselves*, edited by Andrea L. Guzman, 1–28. New York: Peter Lang.

Guzman, Andrea L. In Press. "Ontological Boundaries between Humans and Computers and the Implications for Human-Machine Communication." *Human-Machine Communication* https://stars.library.ucf.edu/hmc/.

Guzman, Andrea L., and Seth C. Lewis. 2019. "Artificial Intelligence and Communication: A Human–Machine Communication Research Agenda." *New Media & Society* 20 (8): 1–18. https://doi.org/10.1177/1461444819858691.

Helberger, Natali. 2019. "On the Democratic Role of News Recommenders." *Digital Journalism* 19: 1–20. https://doi.org/10.1080/21670811.2019.1623700.

Jones, Bronwyn, and Rhianne Jones. 2019a. "Public Service Chatbots: Automating Conversation with BBC News." *Digital Journalism* 5: 1–22. https://doi.org/10.1080/21670811.2019.1609371.

Jones, Rhianne, and Bronwyn Jones. 2019b. "Atomising the News: The (in)Flexibility of Structured Journalism." *Digital Journalism*: 1–23. https://doi.org/10.1080/21670811.2019.1609372.

Jung, Jaemin, Haeyeop Song, Youngju Kim, Hyunsuk Im, and Sewook Oh. 2017. "Intrusion of Software Robots into Journalism: The Public's and Journalists' Perceptions of News Written by Algorithms and Human Journalists." *Computers in Human Behavior* 71: 291–298. https://doi.org/10.1016/j.chb.2017.02.022.

Lewis, Seth C., Andrea L. Guzman, and Thomas R. Schmidt. 2019. "Automation, Journalism, and Human–Machine Communication: Rethinking Roles and Relationships of Humans and Machines in News." *Digital Journalism* 7 (4): 409–427. https://doi.org/10.1080/21670811.2019.1577147.

Liu, Bingjie, and Lewen Wei. 2019. "Machine Authorship in Situ." *Digital Journalism* 7 (5): 635–657. https://doi.org/10.1080/21670811.2018.1510740.

Marconi, Francesco, Alex Siegma, and Machine Journalist. 2017. *The Future of Augmented Journalism: A Guide for Newsrooms in the Age of Smart Machines*. New York: Associated Press. https://insights.ap.org/uploads/images/the-future-of-augmented-journalism_ap-report.pdf.

Milosavljević, Marko, and Igor Vobič. 2019. "Human Still in the Loop: Editors Reconsider the Ideals of Professional Journalism through Automation." *Digital Journalism*: 1–19. https://doi.org/10.1080/21670811.2019.1601576.

Stray, Jonathan. 2019. "Making Artificial Intelligence Work for Investigative Journalism." *Digital Journalism*: 1–22. https://doi.org/10.1080/21670811.2019.1630289.

Sundar, S. Shyam. 2008. "The MAIN Model: A Heuristic Approach to Understanding Technology Effects on Credibility." In *Digital Media, Youth, and Credibility*, edited by Miriam J. Metzger and Andrew J. Flanagin, John D. & Catherine T. MacArthur, 73–100. *Foundation Series on Digital Media & Learning*. Cambridge, MA: MIT Press. https://doi.org/10.1162/dmal.9780262562324.073.

Sundar, S. Shyam, and Clifford Nass. 2001. "Conceptualizing Sources in Online News." *Journal of Communication* 51 (1): 52–72. https://doi.org/10.1111/j.1460-2466.2001.tb02872.x.

Thurman, Neil, Konstantin Dörr, and Jessica Kunert. 2017. "When Reporters Get Hands-on with Robo-Writing: Professionals Consider Automated Journalism's Capabilities and Consequences." *Digital Journalism* 5 (10): 1240–1259. https://doi.org/10.1080/21670811.2017.1289819.

Thurman, Neil, Judith Moeller, Natali Helberger, and Damian Trilling. 2019. "My Friends, Editors, Algorithms, and I: Examining Audience Attitudes to News Selection." *Digital Journalism* 7 (4): 447–469. https://doi.org/10.1080/21670811.2018.1493936.

Van der Kaa, Hill, and eEmiel Krahmer. 2014. "Journalist versus News Consumer: The Perceived Credibility of Machine Written News." In *Proceedings of the Computation + Journalism Conference*. https://pure.uvt.nl/portal/files/4314960/cj2014_session4_paper2.pdf.

Waddell, T. Franklin. 2018. "A Robot Wrote This?: How Perceived Machine Authorship Affects News Credibility." *Digital Journalism* 6 (2): 236–255. https://doi.org/10.1080/21670811.2017.1384319.

Wölker, Anja, and Thomas E. Powell. 2018. "Algorithms in the Newsroom? News Readers' Perceived Credibility and Selection of Automated Journalism." *Journalism: Theory, Practice & Criticism*. 1464884918757072.

Wu, Shangyuan, Edson C. Tandoc, and Charles T. Salmon. 2019. "Journalism Reconfigured: Assessing Human–Machine Relations and the Autonomous Power of Automation in News Production." *Journalism Studies* 20 (10): 1440–1457. https://doi.org/10.1080/1461670X.2018.1521299.

Index

Page numbers in **bold** refer to tables and those in *italic* refer to figures.